SUNSHINE

A CANCER JOURNEY

EMILY J JOHNSON

Dad,
I'm so sorry I never told you this before, or that we didn't get a chance to make things right.
I love you; I always have.
Thanks for the signs x

Trigger Warning: this publication contains references to subjects that some readers may find distressing including graphic details of cancer diagnosis, treatment, surgical procedures and parental death. Reader discretion is advised.

This is a work of creative nonfiction. The events are portrayed to the best of the author's memory. While all the stories in this book are true, some names and identifying details have been changed to protect the privacy of the people involved.

Cover design: Clare Baggaley

Edited and typeset by: Lisa Edwards

ISBN (ebook): 978-17398347-6-0

ISBN (paperback): 978-17398347-7-7

Created with Vellum

You have cancer.

Nothing prepares you to hear those three words.
And nothing prepares those who love you when you repeat them.

I have cancer.

HELLO, SUNSHINE
21 APRIL 2023

"WHERE ARE WE GOING?" I ASK BILLY, KNEELING IN FRONT of his bed. Billy lifts his head sleepily. His big brown eyes stare at me and his teddy-bear nose twitches ever so slightly, waiting to see if I'll repeat it. "*Do you want to go on ... an adventure?*" I whisper, grinning. Billy leaps from his bed, his eyes glistening with a puppyish exuberance, defying the white dusting that covers his chin.

Billy is more than a dog to me, he's my best friend. I love everything about him. His soft fawn fur, those little black ears, and his curly tail that swirls in circles every time he sees me. I love his smell and that wrinkly face only a mother could love. But more than that, I love his nature. He's a small bundle of joy, forever happy and ready for an adventure. His favourite place is right by my side. Me and Billy. He's been the only constant during years of great change.

I look up at the kitchen clock. It's 9.57am. Six hours until my doctor's appointment – plenty of time. I slip on his lead, grab my jacket and bag. There's not much we need, just some water and a little fresh milk. Everything else is there, waiting.

"Bye!"

I leave without waiting for a reply. I close the door and turn the key, leaving a different version of me behind: the mum, the carer, the worker, the cleaner, the cook, and every other role I've assumed over the years. I close my eyes and silently breathe.

Oh, how I love this feeling. *Freedom.* A temporary reprieve.

Billy is waiting on the sound of the lock turning and my command.

"Okay, let's go!"

He launches himself down the stairs to the front door and spins in circles, waiting for my descending arrival.

"I'm coming!" I giggle. His enthusiasm is infectious.

The world outside is so loud. A car speeds up the hill, foot to the floor, and someone shouts across the street. He doesn't care if his language offends.

Billy pulls me onto the pavement into a shaft of sunlight filtering between two buildings that sit unbearably close. There is no view from my windows, just these brick walls. The buildings look tired and grey despite the sunshine. Litter gathers in the gutters like ugly confetti and chewing gum sticks to the pavement in dot-to-dot patterns, weathered and worn. Billy doesn't notice, he's on a mission. He knows the route to the bus stop and drags me along.

"Spare us some change, miss?" a man slumped against the wall asks as we pass. The stench of stale urine from the alley behind him is nauseating.

"Here you go, Shaun." I slip him some coins from my purse. He looks up at me, surprised that I've remembered his name.

"Thank you, miss." He grins through missing teeth as Billy wags his tale at the friendly exchange.

Billy pulls me down the hill towards the bus stop, past the overflowing bins filled with rotting waste that spills and scatters across the pavement. We tiptoe around it. Tonight, it will be gone. The rats will devour whatever the seagulls leave behind.

We step onto the empty bus and head to the back seats. Billy curls up on the floor. He knows the drill. The bus pulls away, leaving behind the noise and chaos of the town centre. I lean back into the seat; my body relaxes as I push my hands into my coat pockets. Something collides with my fingers: it's a shell, with remnants of sand still clinging inside it. I run my thumb over it, remembering the day I collected the keepsake.

It had been a bitter January afternoon last year, and I needed to escape home. I stood on the empty beach in the rain, watching squalls whip up froth and dump mounds on the sand. The wind drove icy drops past my hood, stabbing my cheeks, losing themselves in salty tears. "*Please* help me," I begged of the sea. I left my heartache tumbling in its swell and picked up the shell before heading for home. My souvenir of sadness had stayed in my pocket, forgotten all this time.

But there is no need for tears now, not where I'm going. I slip the shell back into my pocket. I have the perfect place to keep it now.

Billy and I step off the bus, and he pulls me along the path with an excitement he can't seem to contain. We turn into a lane that leads to a private campsite. I wave at the warden as we pass him by and walk through into the small field. Sitting in the corner against a thick brambly hedge is a little white box on wheels.

"Hello, *Sunshine*." I always greet her like an old friend.

She's stored underneath an old oak tree, providing ample protection from all weathers and serving as the playground for much of the wildlife I share this little corner of the world with. The caravan overlooks an empty field owned by a local farmer. It's home to deer, foxes, pheasants, and many wild birds. This is my secret hideaway. I *never* tire of coming here.

I unlock the door and step inside. It's every bit as perfect as I remember. I've decorated my caravan with all my favourite things. The walls are cream, a couple of coats of fresh paint cover the dull beige vinyl underneath. A picture of the Taj Mahal hangs on the wall. It's the one I took at sunrise over a decade ago, moments before Paul proposed.

I unlock the side windows and push them outwards. The sound of a blackbird filters in and fills the small space with its cheerful song. Brightly coloured cushions rest on the faded sofa bed. A glass lantern hangs from the shelf above, it's the one I bought in Marrakech years ago. It's filled with battery-powered lights, and when it's raining, I turn them on and they cast diamonds of pink and turquoise all around the walls.

I take the shell out of my pocket and hold it momentarily. It's a reminder of how far I've come. I place it on the shelf gently, with my other treasures: dried flowers and seeds, an owl feather, a singing bowl from India, and candles I'm saving for a special occasion. I'm waiting for something to happen, something ... anything worthy of burning them.

In the middle of the shelf, draped in fairy lights, is a sign that serves as a reminder: '*All you need is love*'. A small string of colourful prayer flags hangs in front of the sign. They travelled to me from a friend in Nepal. It's a strange collection of oddities, they'd mean nothing to most people, but they mean everything to me. They are *my* wee treasures, in my special place. I've only owned this caravan a little while, but I fall in love with *Sunshine* a little bit more every time I return.

I unclip the skylight above me, pushing it wide open. The fresh spring air swirls around me, and I can smell a hint of cherry blossom from nearby trees. I fill a bowl of water for Billy, who guzzles it noisily while I light the camping stove and boil some water. I left coffee and honey in the cupboard last week.

"Come on, Billy," I call, stepping out onto the grass with my folding blue chair.

Billy follows me and lies down beside me as I settle back

with my coffee. It's in my favourite new mug. I slip off my shoes and savour the feeling of the damp grass under my feet. Long green blades push between my toes, tickling them. Billy sighs deeply and lays his head down. "You're the best puppy in the world," I remind him as I lean over and stroke his soft, warm head. He may be eight years old, but he will always be my puppy.

I look out across the field. This is *my* view. Small white daisies decorate the grass, and delicate pink blossom gathers at the edge of the field like pale confetti. Clumps of yellow dandelions make dot-to-dot patterns across a carpet of green. The trees are full of new life, budding with optimism for the spring season.

Everything is so vibrant. Everything is perfect.

Life is getting easier. I can't wait to spend time here this summer.

At last, I have my own sanctuary. I wish I could hold onto this feeling forever, bottle it in a jar and carry it home.

Two swallows dive in unison in front of me, swooping across the field just above the grass. "*Can I stay here forever?*" I whisper to them. I already know the answer. But I'm here now. I have the rest of my life to enjoy my caravan.

I close my eyes and bathe in the rays of the mild spring sun, listening to Billy's gentle snores. I feel so ... still. So peaceful.

Is this what life is meant to feel like?

I open my eyes and place my hand on my caravan. Its warmth is so comforting. I smile to myself.

Thank you, Sunshine.

DREAMS

2017–APRIL 2023

IN 2017, MY FAMILY LIFE HAD STARTED TO UNRAVEL. I HAD two teenage sons from my first marriage, and both had spiralled into mental illness. I blamed myself and became the classic enabler trying to make amends.

My second husband, Paul, whom I married in 2016, succumbed to the pressure of our complex blended family life, and slipped into depression and alcoholism to ease the fraying edges, underpinned by wounds from childhood trauma. I was propping up the whole family and hanging onto life by my fingernails. I told this story in my first book, *Pushing Through the Cracks*.

Looking back on that period now, I'm not sure how I survived it, but I found a damaging way to cope. Food was my drug. It eased my pain, and I spiralled into binge-eating to numb myself.

By 2018, things deteriorated further with my family's health, and Paul and I separated the following year. My eldest son, Thomas, had been sucked into online gambling – I had a teenage gambling addict. My life fell apart. I became an around-the-clock carer to my youngest son, Jack, who was struggling with untreated obsessive-compulsive disorder whilst he sat on a children's mental-health services list for almost three years waiting for help. It was an extremely challenging time in my life, and I had no respite other than sleep.

I set up a space in the attic to secretly eat in, and nap when I could, often in my coat and a woolly hat to keep out the damp drafts that whistled through gaps in the rafters. I desperately wanted a space of my own, somewhere just for me but I felt shackled to my town-centre flat. I owned a small share of my place through a housing association, and moving elsewhere wouldn't be easy. Selling my share would require a lengthy vetting process through the association.

But it wasn't just the flat, or area I longed to escape. I wanted to disappear from everyone, even myself. I was struggling with my own mental health and couldn't see a way out.

I sought refuge in my imagination. It felt like the only part of me that no one else could take. I stole moments to myself during a quick shower to close my eyes and dream of a different life. That dream morphed into a vision of a caravan. It was a dream that felt manageable ... achievable in some distant world. A little caravan in a field somewhere with no noise. Somewhere with no demands of me, no frightening drunken fights or remnants of drug use that often littered the alley I lived in.

I'd visualise my caravan surrounded by green trees and birdsong, with towering sunflowers and colourful butterflies and for those few precious minutes, I was somewhere else. It felt so real. I could feel the long damp grass under my bare feet, and the faint warmth of the spring sunshine on my face – and afterwards, I'd quietly weep because I desperately longed for that escape. My real world felt harsh, and the walls of my home closed back in on me. It felt dark and oppressive. There was no view to escape into, no sky or sunshine was visible, just brick walls from the building opposite only metres away. The energy in the flat hung heavy with years of progressively worsening mental illness, heartache, and desperate tears. My imagination became my sanctuary, and I'd escape into it as often as I could.

In 2019, I carefully cut out a picture of a caravan I'd found in a newspaper. I wrote '*My caravan*' on the top of the picture and pinned it on a board on my kitchen wall, where it sat for four long, difficult years, curling at the edges as it collected the dust of unfulfilled dreams.

Paul and I remained close friends after we separated, trying to navigate our friendship through extremely challenging times. The love between us never left, it just changed.

After the lockdowns of 2021 ended and things eased a little at home, Paul would sometimes invite me out for a couple of hours to escape the flat. I would always choose to visit a local second-hand caravan yard. I'd climb into the old caravans and imagine they were mine. Running my hands over the upholstery so I could bank away the sensation of the fabric in my mind to revisit in the next daydream.

In October 2022, I received a small amount of money from a family member. Perhaps I should have saved the nest egg, but for years I had lived a lonely miserable existence, in survival mode and saw the money as an opportunity to force the change I desperately needed. I began hunting selling sites and found a twenty-one-year-old caravan. The seller wanted a quick sale with everything thrown in. The ace card – it was in paid storage for three months in a local caravan park.

I've always acted from the heart, not the head and that was usually my downfall, especially financially. But my heart was pulling me to this caravan, it *felt* right.

I messaged the seller, having just enough to buy it, if I could find somewhere to keep it. We arranged to meet at the caravan park, and I dragged Paul along for the ride. It was early November, and the grass was frozen white with a hard frost.

The seller, a lady in her late thirties, arrived and smiled at me, but behind the smile, I sensed sadness. She unlocked the door, and we stepped inside out of the frigid temperatures. The caravan was small but in perfect condition, just a little dated.

"We had some wonderful holidays in here – the kids love it." The woman's face lit up. It was obvious she loved it too. "But ... I recently separated from my husband, and I just can't afford to keep it anymore..." she trailed off flatly.

Letting it go was difficult for her, I could tell. It was more than a caravan. It was a box full of her memories. She had poured herself into it and it was evident through her meticulous decoration. The cushions and curtains were colour-coordinated, and small cheerful signs hung on the walls with slogans confirming close-knit families spent time together.

I understood the reason for her sadness, I felt sad for her. I knew what may lie ahead of her. I'd been that woman too. She was in the grieving period for a relationship she thought would last forever. Even if she wanted her marriage to end, she would need time to mourn and heal the wounds she'd never shown anyone. Time to search for the missing parts of her she'd lost along the way. Maybe guilt would follow, especially when she looked at her children sleeping. I stood silent, momentarily revisiting that painful place.

Paul appeared at the caravan door interrupting the silence. He'd been checking the bodywork and assessing the practical things I might need. I only saw a perfectly preserved caravan that needed to be loved again, and I was already imagining myself in it.

"Can I just have a moment?" I asked.

"Of course," she agreed.

I squeezed past her and stepped outside. "*What do you think?*" I whispered to Paul.

"It's great, I've looked over it and the bodywork is immaculate. It's fully kitted out and even has a brand-new awning still in its bag! It's up to you ... but I think you should seriously consider it."

I walked around the perimeter of the caravan, pretending to inspect it but inside, I already knew it was mine.

"Can I give you a small deposit to hold it for me?" I asked stepping inside, keen to secure it but needing time to research where I could keep it.

"Yes, of course."

"Thank you." I curbed my enthusiasm as a pang of guilt swept over me. I didn't want to benefit from this woman's obvious heartache. We exchanged fifty pounds and agreed to speak in a few days.

Paul and I sat in the car in silence and watched her reverse out and drive away.

"I don't know why, but I think this is it. This is my caravan. I know it's old but it's perfect," I said, staring ahead at it.

"Have a think about it, but I agree, I don't think you will get much more for the money you have, and this is almost like new inside."

Paul started the car and slowly reversed away from the caravan.

"Now I just need to find somewhere to keep her," I muttered under my breath.

A few months earlier, I'd loosely shared my caravan dreams with a friend. She knew a local landowner with storage facilities and could get his number, should I need it. Within an hour of contacting her, I had it. Later that week we met at his yard, and he agreed to let me keep the caravan on his land nearby for a nominal fee.

After a short drive, I arrived, and my heart sank a little. It was a patch of unkempt grass at the back of some garages, overlooked by surrounding houses. Several empty vehicles were already parked there and judging by the number of dead leaves covering them, they'd been there for some time. It wasn't exactly the field of dreams I'd imagined, but at least it was a step on the path towards it.

"I've found a place to store the caravan! I'm going to do it!" I excitedly texted Paul, still sitting in my car watching the owner cycle away on his pushbike down the country lane.

The following weekend, I met the seller and completed the caravan sale. Once she left, I stepped back inside the caravan and closed the door. I sat on the sofa running my fingers over the aged blue cover. The familiar feeling of the tightly woven fabric – the one I had imagined a hundred times before, was now real. The caravan smelt of another family, and it needed a coat of paint inside, maybe new flooring to cover the stained carpet, but in time I would make it feel more like mine.

I stood up and went to the kitchen area to explore the layout properly. Like a child with a pile of Christmas presents before me, I opened each cupboard, excitedly searching for the treasure she'd left behind. Pots and pans hid in a secret flap under a gas oven and alongside was a miniature sink and microwave oven. Cupboards were squeezed in everywhere, housing everything I could possibly need – a toaster, camping kettle, crockery, a knife block and chopping boards. The drawers beneath held every kitchen utensil I'd ever imagined and more cutlery than my kitchen at home. Everything had its own allotted space. It was tiny living at its compact finest.

Two books were lying on a small shelf, one on top of the other. A crime thriller sat on top. I nudged it to the side and underneath sat a large hardback: *So Lucky* by Dawn Porter. I studied the cover. It had a large pink doughnut on the front, almost identical to the one I'd just chosen with my editor for the cover of my second book, *Belly,* the week before.

I opened an overhead cupboard and behind a rack of neatly stacked plates was a plastic bag, doubled over itself. I lifted it down and unravelled the bag. Inside was a metal mug stand with four mugs, still tagged and unused. I spun the mugs around and read each one:

Think happy thoughts

Be positive

Keep smiling

I turned the final one around:

Hello Sunshine

I gasped. *Sunshine.* That was me. It had been my nickname since childhood.

"Look, Paul, it's a sign!" I said, laughing as I held up my new mug. Paul looked up from the caravan manual he was studying.

"It sure is!" he said, grinning.

"That's it, I'm going to call her *Sunshine*. It's a hopeful name, isn't it? Hello, *Sunshine*," I said, running my hand across the kitchen bench.

The following January, *Sunshine* moved to the farmer's land where she stayed for a few weeks alongside the other old vehicles before being towed to her new home in a local campsite. I could visit her whenever I wanted. Finally, my dream had reached fruition. Whenever I could, I would catch a bus with Billy to *Sunshine* and we'd sit outside together, wrapped in a blanket, watching the squirrels and deer, and the birds in the trees. When spring came around, I'd walk barefoot on the cold, damp grass with Billy by my side, feeling the weak sunshine on my face.

SERENDIPITY

21 APRIL 2023

I OPENED THE FRONT DOOR AND THREW MY BAG DOWN ON the kitchen floor. "I'm sick of this heat!" I groaned, pulling at the collar of my jumper; it felt tight and suffocating. My skin was clammy, and a hot flush was rising through my chest.

I glanced up at the clock: 3.49pm. I had eleven minutes to get to my doctor's appointment. I shouldn't have stayed so long at *Sunshine*, but it was so hard to leave that place.

I pulled the jumper up over my head, catching my long hair clumsily. "Argh!" I cried out, flinging the jumper across the room angrily.

Tired and flustered, I searched for a thinner jumper in a pile of un-ironed clothes. A thin v-neck was the least crumpled. "That will have to do, Billy." I sighed, exhausted. Everything felt like hard work these days.

I pulled the jumper on, collected my keys, and headed out of the flat, grabbing the handrail to support my unsteady descent down the stairs. The occasional dizzy spell was one reason I wanted to see the doctor, that, and my itchy foot.

The doctor was running fifteen minutes behind, but I didn't

mind. The delay gave me time to waste on my phone with no cries of "*Mum!*" to interrupt me, no dinners to make, or laundry to put on, ample time to let another hot flush subside.

"*Bloody menopause!*" I sighed, fanning myself with one hand.

"Emily Johnson." The doctor called me from his office doorway. I looked up from my phone.

"Hello. Come in," he said, directing me into his office with his hand.

Dr Atkins knew my family history well. He was the same doctor I'd disclosed my disordered eating to four years earlier. He was one of the most popular doctors at the practice and for good reason. He listened, and there was always kindness in his eyes. I had been surprised to be offered a last-minute appointment with him a couple of days earlier. Someone had cancelled just before I called.

"What brings you in today?"

"A couple of things really, I've got a rash on my foot, and I had a virus about four weeks ago. I think it might have affected my ears; I keep feeling dizzy."

"Okay let's take a look," he said placing a blood-pressure cuff on my right arm. Satisfied with the reading, he gently palpated around my sinuses and checked my ears and throat before returning to his seat.

"It looks like it might be a bit of a viral hangover, I can't see anything, but you might have a little inflammation in your sinus or inner ear. I think it will settle down in a week or two on its own."

I felt instant relief – the dizziness was just the aftermath of a cold. It felt like I'd had one virus after another for almost two years.

"Now let's have a look at this foot," he said, putting on some gloves. I slipped off my left shoe and sock revealing a rash covering my toes.

"Oh yes, that's a rather nasty fungal infection," he said, examining the rash that had spread between my toes.

I grimaced in embarrassment. I swam twice a week at a local pool. It seemed I'd brought home an unsavoury souvenir.

"I will give you an anti-fungal cream and that should clear it up. You can pop your shoe and sock back on now." He turned back to his computer to prepare the prescription. "I've sent that downstairs to the pharmacy for you."

"How long do I need to use it?" I asked the doctor, who had turned back towards me when I began speaking and was now looking at me with a puzzled stare.

"Have you always had that asymmetrical shape to your neck?" he asked, his head slightly cocked to one side observing my throat.

Instinctively, I reached up and placed my hand over my neck. "Um... I don't know...?"

"Can you turn and face me and look up?"

I manoeuvred myself on the chair to face directly opposite him and glanced up to the ceiling.

"Hmm, can you swallow for me?"

I swallowed nothing, staring at the ceiling tiles.

"Okay, bring your head back down. Can you say your name and address?"

I recited my details for him as he watched my neck move whilst I spoke.

"I'm going to have a look at your neck now, is that ok?"

"Okay," I agreed as he stood up, put some gloves on and stepped behind me.

I moved my neck, following his movements left and right, as he gently felt the front area.

"There is a lump in the thyroid area," he said gently, pulling the plastic gloves off and throwing them in the bin by his desk.

"Is there?" I didn't know where the thyroid was, let alone notice a lump on it, but then I never looked at my neck, not really, just sometimes to criticise the wrinkles on it.

"Sometimes you can get nodules on the thyroid, or a swelling on the gland called a goitre. It's probably nothing to worry about but I'm going to refer you to the hospital for a thyroid ultrasound on what we call the Fast Track system. Now, don't be alarmed when you see the word 'cancer', all lumps must be investigated – it's just part of the Fast Track referral process."

Why would I be worried about this lump? It's hardly going to be cancer, is it?

"You should receive an appointment within two weeks. We need to run a blood test to check your thyroid levels too. If you take this form to the front desk, they will book you in."

"Okay... Can I ask... Did I cause this swelling through my binge-eating? You know, from all the sugar?" Blaming myself first for everything was my default setting.

The doctor stopped typing on his keyboard and turned to me. "No, Emily, you didn't cause it. It's nothing you did; it just happens sometimes."

"Okay." Satisfied I wasn't at fault this time, I got up and left, closing the door behind me.

I walked home thinking about the doctor's words. I'd had a lump in my breast in my early forties. A mammogram had revealed it was a benign cyst, and it went away of its own accord over time.

This one will be the same, I know it, I reassured myself.

The following week I had blood tests and a few days later, the results showed my thyroid levels were within normal range. That confirmed in my mind the benign nature of my lump.

By the following week, my dizziness disappeared, and my foot rash was gone. I returned to the summer plans I was making. I had tickets for two music gigs, a summer wedding to attend and a four-day work project with my employer at a big music festival. For the first time in years, I planned on *really* living.

Ten days later, a letter arrived from the hospital offering me an appointment the following week.

INCONCLUSIVE

4 MAY 2023

"EMILY JOHNSON?"

I looked up from my phone and saw a young doctor smiling at me. I gathered my belongings and followed him along a corridor into the ultrasound room.

"Hello, I'm Dr Thomas. If you slip your coat off and pop your belongings on the chair, then hop up on here." He gestured to an examination bed in the middle of the room.

The doctor adjusted the bed height before his assistant prepped my neck with a blue cover to protect my shirt from the cold gel. As he rolled the wand over my neck, it felt tender. Two weeks earlier, I hadn't even known there was a lump there, now there was no mistaking it.

The doctor periodically paused, capturing still images of the lump from different angles, and measuring it. "The average size for surgical removal is four centimetres. Yours looks like it's just under the threshold," he confirmed.

I felt relieved. It had only been nine months since the removal of a bunion under local anaesthetic. I'd been awake whilst a surgical saw was used to cut off the extra bone and still felt traumatised by the experience.

"I can't see anything of any immediate concern on the images, but due to the size of the mass, I'm going to take a biopsy using a fine needle. I will give you a little local anaesthetic around the area and get you nice and numb first." The doctor smiled but it did little to reassure me.

My heart began to race silently in my chest. I squeezed my hands into tight fists, the pain of my nails digging in, diverting my attention from my thoughts. I hadn't mentally prepared myself for a local anaesthetic in my neck and I underestimated the fear I still held about medical procedures, even minor ones.

"Right, small scratch now," he warned as he injected the anaesthetic into the front of my neck. I winced at the injection.

As he waited for my neck to numb, the doctor prepared the biopsy needle and made small talk about the unusually warm weather. I was grateful for the distraction.

Under the guidance of the ultrasound, he injected the needle into my neck, gently probing the mass to collect cells. I closed my eyes and hoped it would end soon. It was more uncomfortable than painful – like a strange dragging sensation inside my neck.

"All done."

I opened my eyes.

"It will take about two weeks to get the results back and you should receive a letter in the post."

"Okay, thank you." I climbed off the bed, gathered up my bag and coat, and left.

Later that evening, the anaesthesia had worn off and my neck was swollen and tender, and it was painful to swallow. The lump that had been silently growing in my neck was now visible and beginning to bruise.

After a long soak in a hot bath, I climbed into bed and lay in darkness, thinking about the day's events. The doctor hadn't seen anything of concern, my blood tests were normal.

It's nothing, just a stupid cyst. Why is my body doing this to me? I tutted to myself, irritated at my annoying body for giving me yet another inconvenient ailment as I drifted off to sleep.

Two weeks passed and I'd heard nothing from the hospital. I called and spoke to a nurse who confirmed my results were back, before being put on hold for what felt like ages. When she returned to the call, she apologised and advised the results were still being processed but I should hear something the following week. Something felt off about her tone and sudden change of information, but I dismissed it. Results were rarely given over the phone.

The following Wednesday a letter arrived from the hospital requesting I attend an appointment two days later with an endocrinologist.

DAD

SEPTEMBER 1995–MAY 2003

IN 1995, AT THE AGE OF TWENTY-THREE, I EMIGRATED TO Australia with my first husband, John. I began trying to rebuild my relationship with my dad, from whom I'd been estranged for many years. He'd moved to Australia when I was a teenager in the late 1980s after my parents' divorce. My dad had been absent for most of my childhood, both physically and emotionally. He frequently worked away, but even when he was at home, he was never a hands-on dad. Instead, he hovered on the edge of family life, observing awkwardly. It wasn't his fault; he just didn't know how to be a parent.

I was raised by my mother and never had that close connection with my dad that a daughter yearns for. I emigrated in my early twenties to be nearer him, hoping to reconnect, and to some degree, we did, but our relationship was far from a conventional father-daughter one. We were, in effect, strangers, learning to navigate our relationship, and it wasn't always easy.

After my parent's divorce, I'd stopped calling him Dad, and despite being a grown woman, I still couldn't address him as Dad when we reunited. It was as if the word was stuck in the back of my throat, and I couldn't understand why it was so difficult to say. My verbal block visibly upset him, yet we never spoke about it.

I'd been living in Australia for three years when my dad first began complaining of a dull ache on the side of his back. He dismissed the pain for over two years, believing it was muscular. So did his doctor on his annual health check-ups. When a couple of physio sessions intensified the pain, his doctor referred him for a routine ultrasound which revealed the cause of the ache – a suspicious mass on his right kidney. After some further tests he was scheduled to see a consultant urologist.

I took my dad to his first hospital appointment, armed with my usual optimism. He didn't want to face the results alone and was concerned he might not remember everything that was said. I'd never seen a consultant before or thought about cancer. I'd never had to. I sat beside my dad and two nurses, as a pleasant man in a sharp suit behind a desk told him he had kidney cancer. I remember the lump in my throat forming. I'd wanted to cry. The consultant told us it was treatable, and the prognosis was good, and Dad would have surgery to remove it.

Dad had given me the job of mentally recording the consultant's words so I could repeat them to him. I did as I was told, but my emotions were swirling. I was pregnant with my first child. I'd lost a baby months before this one and had been clinging to the hope of keeping this baby with every passing day of the pregnancy. I didn't need this stress. *Why is this happening now? It's not fair,* I thought, but I'd locked those thoughts away. How could I be so selfish? Guilt silenced me.

"That's it, then ... it's going to get me," Dad said as we walked back to the car following his appointment. My dad had only heard '*You have cancer*'. He'd plucked three words from a whole conversation and created a death sentence from them.

"You are not going to die!" I snapped back. I was angry at

everything, especially his willingness to give up on his life so easily. I was angry he was giving up on us ... on me.

"The doctor said it's treatable. Everything is going to be okay." I soothed him like a mother would her child.

Dad was scheduled for surgery within two weeks to remove his tumour along with his right kidney. I waited in a nearby cafeteria whilst he underwent his surgery, holding my bump and savouring my baby's faint kicks.

When he was back on the ward, I was allowed in to see him. I was taken aback by his appearance. I'd never visited anyone in hospital before. I was only twenty-eight and serious illness hadn't yet been a part of my life experience. Dad was connected to wires and drips, and a drain ran from his side, along with a bag collecting urine attached to a catheter. He looked pale and fragile, not like my dad. He was no longer the protector I'd yearned for – he was vulnerable, like a scared child. I didn't know how to feel, or act around him. The guilt resurfaced and I couldn't wait to leave and go back home and enjoy my pregnancy in my safe little world of denial.

The surgery was successful, his urologist believing the cancer was contained and fully removed. But a couple of months later, Dad noticed some tingling and unsteadiness in his legs. It was the first symptom of another small tumour pressing on his spine. Unfortunately, before his surgery, the cancer had already metastasised, and he needed further surgery.

I went with him to every appointment full of hope, but it wasn't a strong enough antidote for his pessimism.

"It's going to get me, honey. I know it will," he reminded me each time.

I was seven months pregnant when Dad was admitted to a different hospital for surgery to remove the tumour pressing on his spine. A couple of months later, whilst I was in hospital recovering from the birth of Thomas, he went to an oncology appointment with a friend instead of me, and was told his cancer was terminal.

I remember the moment he told me vividly, as if it were last week. I know where I was sitting, I can remember the shirt he was wearing and the look in his eyes. I had just come out of hospital that day with my newborn son. I was physically exhausted from the difficult birth and emotionally drained. I couldn't accept my dad's impending death, so instead, I went into a state of dissociative denial, pretending to myself, and him, that it wasn't happening. It was my only way to cope.

During the following sixteen months, Dad had several sessions of radiation treatment and further surgery to remove a second tumour that had wrapped around his spinal cord. The second operation was unsuccessful, and he became paralysed from the chest down.

From that point on, our roles reversed completely: I became his parent, and he became my child. The joy of parenting my young son was stolen by his cancer. I became my dad's full-time carer with the help of community nurses who came in once a day. I fed him and changed his bedding in between the nurses winching him up to change his adult nappies.

Dad resented his loss of dignity as much as he resented me caring for him, but he feared dying and was often both angry and depressed. He became almost childlike at times and clung to me emotionally for comfort. I held him and comforted him, but inside my head I was kicking and screaming, fighting against the inevitable.

This is not happening; this is NOT happening, I told myself.

I was faced with the difficult decision to place Dad in a

hospice against his wishes, but his care needs were greater than I could manage at home with a toddler to care for.

Eight weeks later, in May 2003, the cancer had spread to his brain, and Dad passed away one night, unexpectedly and alone in the hospice. I blamed myself. He'd begged me not to leave him that night, but I needed to feed my overtired toddler and put him to bed. It was my fault dad died alone. I should have been there, and that guilt remained buried within me, packaged neatly in a toxic parcel that I carried around.

I thought grieving for my dad would be a linear experience. People told me it would get easier with time and occasionally it did. Sometimes I could think of him and shake off the gentle sadness that remained, but I didn't just grieve him once. With every milestone my children reached, every passing birthday or special occasion, it would return and burn with the same searing pain as if he died yesterday, and I would have to begin grieving all over again.

WORLD THYROID DAY
25 MAY 2023

I ARRIVED EARLY FOR MY CONSULTANT APPOINTMENT. MY car engine had packed in a couple of months earlier, so I relied on the bus; a service conveniently stopped directly outside the hospital. Although on the second floor, there wasn't much of a view from the Endocrine Clinic waiting room. The expansive windows cast views across the side of the old hospital walls, with a large lone tree, the only greenery in sight.

I passed the time on my phone, revisiting an online search I began the night before for information on the thyroid gland. It seemed this small-but-mighty endocrine gland played a vital role in my body, affecting my metabolism as well as my heart, digestive system, muscles, bones and brain.

An unseen door opened in a corridor and the face of every patient waiting, looked up in hope of their name being called. A young woman with a warm smile called mine.

"My name is Katie. If you'd like to follow me, you'll be seeing Miss Jones today."

I followed the nurse along a windowless corridor until we reached the end. She opened a door and led me into a small, minimally decorated room with one window, opened just enough to allow the breeze a chance to filter in. Sitting behind the central desk was a consultant dressed in an impeccable two-piece suit.

"Good afternoon, Ms Johnson, please come in and take a seat," the consultant said.

Katie pulled up the chair beside me and sat down. I looked at her and she smiled again. Another nurse was sitting to the left of the consultant. Our eyes met and she smiled too.

What is this? A medical welcoming committee?

A slight panic arose in the pit of my stomach. In my experience with my dad's cancer journey, groups of medical staff often only meant one of two things: staff training or the delivery of difficult news. Neither of these nurses looked like they were in training.

"Do you have anyone with you today?" Miss Jones enquired.

"No ... I came on my own," I replied, puzzled.

"As you know we did an ultrasound and fine-needle aspiration from the mass on your thyroid and unfortunately the results were inconclusive. There is a small chance that the lesion could be cancerous and the only way to rule that out completely would be to remove it along with the right lobe of your thyroid and look at the pathology under a microscope."

My heart began thumping, and I squeezed the fingers of my right hand into a tight fist, welcoming the biting indent of my nails into the flesh of my palm to ground me.

The consultant loaded an animated video on a tablet, and I watched an AI demonstration of the surgical removal of a mass and right lobe of a thyroid – a partial thyroidectomy. I watched and nodded at appropriate bursts as she pointed out the anatomy of the thyroid area.

I watched but I couldn't see what was being shown. I

listened, but the words made no sense. I could only hear my own words hurtling around my mind.

I might have cancer.

My world was spinning, and my head and heart raced to catch up with the spin.

"But I don't understand ... my blood tests were all normal," I stuttered.

"This particular type of cancer cannot be detected in blood tests."

"If it is cancer, what will happen?" I hated anything being out of my control and needed to know every detail.

"Depending on the pathology results, we may recommend the removal of the rest of your thyroid, followed by radioactive iodine treatment to destroy any remaining cancerous thyroid cells – but we are jumping a little ahead of ourselves here. Let's get you booked in for surgery." Miss Jones picked up a large black diary and flipped through it. "How about in two weeks' time on the 15th of June?"

"Um. I think that will be okay – I just need to check with work and make some arrangements at home. I'm a full-time carer for my son. How long will I be in hospital for with the surgery?" I asked, frantically attempting to organise my life in my head.

Miss Jones looked up from her diary and over her glasses. "We will keep you in overnight. Is there anyone who can care for your son in your absence?"

"Yes, I will ask his older brother and father to help out."

I found it difficult to explain my home situation to anyone. To me it was normal, but to the outside world it was unimaginable.

"Very well, then. There is a small risk of a bleed from the surgical area after neck surgery as it is such a vascular area but if it occurs, its usually happens within the first six to twelve hours. The chances are minimal, but we keep all patients overnight as a precaution. You will be discharged the following morning all being well. Jane will take you to get some bloods taken now and run through your pre-op and I will see next week to run through the consent form. Do you have any questions?" the consultant asked.

My mind was blank and if I had any questions, they were stuck behind a mute wall of numb shock. "No ... not that I can think of."

"Katie will give you her contact details and some information on the surgery and aftercare." Katie turned towards me and handed me a collection of paperwork.

"I will see you next week – the reception will confirm an appointment now for you."

I nodded in acknowledgment as Jane led me out of the room. She steered me to the reception desk and arranged the appointment with the clerk whilst I stood there digesting what had just happened.

"That's next Friday at 11am." The clerk handed me a slip of confirmation.

"If you'd like to follow me this way," Jane interjected. She escorted me to the pre-op area.

As we neared it, she took my elbow in her hand. "Are you okay, love? Sounds like you already have so much to deal with at home and that was a lot to take in."

I felt genuine empathy through her touch and turned to her. "Oh, it's okay, I'm used to it." I sighed. "So just to recap, I've got a lump on my thyroid, and it may or may not be cancer but the only way to know is to remove it and half my thyroid?"

"Yes, that's right," she confirmed with an apologetic expression. "If you take this in with you, the nurses will run through your pre-op for you." She passed me a form. "You take care now, love." She squeezed my arm reassuringly, before turning around and heading back to the clinic.

I approached the desk. "I've been asked to come and see you for this," I said, passing the referral form to the nurse.

"If you could fill this out and bring it back to me when you've finished," the nurse recited with practiced ease, passing me a clipboard with several sheets of paper. I found an empty seat and filled them in before handing them back in.

Within a few minutes, I was called in and after a series of checks and questions, my pre-op was complete. I was diverted to a different clinic to have my blood taken. I took the deli-style ticket and sat down to wait my turn and used the opportunity to text work to let them know I might be back later than expected.

"Hi, I have to have a lump and part of my thyroid removed in two weeks. They are testing for cancer. I'm having some blood tests done now and might be another hour until I get back home."

Shortly after, my phone buzzed with a comforting text, suggesting I take the rest of my shift off.

I began to cry, oblivious to the people sat around me. I hadn't anticipated how formulating the text to my manager and saying *that* word, would factualise the events of the appointment into reality.

So that's why she asked me if I had anyone with me today.

After my blood was taken, I left the hospital and headed to the bus stop. I put my earplugs in, this time without music or videos and enforced a silent journey home. I wanted to block out other people's conversations about the weather or rising cost of electricity. I leant against the window, watching the pavements slip by.

I might have cancer. Why is this happening to me now? I'm just getting my life back together. It's not fair.

As I turned the corner of my block of flats and approached the front door, a butterfly caught my eye. It was resting on the brick wall, a beautiful orange and black Painted Lady with its white spotted wings spread wide, basking in the warm sunshine of the spring afternoon.

I stood still, observing. Its striking beauty seemed out of place against the harshness of the faded graffiti tag it rested beside. Within seconds, it flapped its wings a couple of times and flew directly towards my face. I jumped out of its way, startled, before turning to watch it fly into the sky above the tall buildings and their tired facades.

"Hi Jack, I'm home!" I called out, turning the key to the front door and stepping back into my busy life.

My surgery and the possibility of having cancer had already been put away in a mental box, compartmentalised until later that evening when I could let the news sink in, alone. A post popped up on my Facebook page that evening, a reminder to check my neck on World Thyroid Day. I spluttered, stunned at the accuracy – and cruel irony – of search algorithms.

That weekend, the weather promised to be warm and dry. I needed my view, my escape from the world, and my thoughts for a few hours. It had been over two weeks since I had made it to the caravan. I longed to walk barefoot on the grass and savour the faint fragrance of the honeysuckle bushes that were just beginning to bloom, to touch the daffodils that decorated the side of the lane like clumps of golden trumpets. It made me nostalgic for my mum, for the safety of our home and the innocence of my childhood, making perfume cocktails from fallen cherry-plum blossom.

Maybe in the field, all this would go away. I could go back to the life I was planning before all this began.

I didn't feel like taking the long trip to *Sunshine* by bus and arranged a lift from Paul, who happily obliged. Billy didn't care how he travelled, by car, or by bus, it was still an adventure that led him to our favourite place.

As Paul pulled in next to the caravan, I could breathe again, as if returning gifted air to my lungs. Every time I arrived; something had changed. The trees had filled out with dense new foliage that now formed an emerald canopy over the caravan. The iris bulbs I'd planted in March were blooming now. Their violet, pink, and blue flowers' rich perfume filled the air. Miniature daffodils I'd rescued from a supermarket sale added splashes of yellow amongst the pink and purple brigade. Blackbirds, blue tits and sparrows darted from branch to branch, chirping as squirrels hopped and chased one another from tree to tree. Bees and butterflies carried on about their business gathering pollen. Spring was in full swing, and the woodland was teaming with life.

Oh God, it feels so good to be back here. It feels like home.

I first fell in love with the idea of tiny living in my late twenties. My dad sold his home in 1998 and moved into a compact static home at a beachside park in Western Australia. I would sometimes stay overnight and lie on his sofa, listening to the waves lapping the shore as I fell asleep. It was a very special place. My dad always said out of all the homes he lived in; the tiny beachside home was his favourite place in the world. Now I had my own tiny home, surrounded by nature. It was *my* favourite place in the world.

The following week I met with the consultant again, and we discussed the risks of my surgery. Along with the regular complication of post-operative infection, she ran through the possible changes to my voice and risks of nerve damage to the laryngeal nerve which controls movement to the vocal cords. There was a minimal risk of bleeding beneath the wound, but I had undergone surgeries in the past with no complications. I'd been advised that my surgeon was the best in the country, and I didn't doubt it. Her calm, authoritative manner instilled trust in me. But that night I lay awake until the early hours, my mind racing over the appointment.

What if I die under anaesthetic?

What if it is cancer?

My poor kids. Paul... My mum. How would they cope?

My life is such a tangled mess.

Oh God, I don't have a will...

My clothes are lying on the floor...

Who will feed the dog?

What about the ironing?

I don't have life insurance.

It will take them forever to sort the junk in the loft...

Oh ... oh. Shut up, mind! I need to sleep!

BROKEN BUTTERFLY

15 JUNE 2023

A FEW DAYS LATER, I WOKE AND GLANCED AT THE CLOCK: 4.23am. It was the day of my surgery, and my empty stomach churned as I reached for my phone. I'd set the alarm for 5.30am but my mind was too alert to return to sleep.

I slowly scrolled through social media, skipping posts that showed hospital patients or cancer stories. I'd avoided internet searches on thyroid cancer for two weeks. It was a rabbit hole I didn't want to dive into before my surgery.

I got up and snuck downstairs past Billy, who glanced up at me sleepily before burying his head once again in the soft billows of blankets he slept in.

I liked the hush just before dawn when the rest of the town centre was still sleeping. The quiet stillness belonged to me, and I kept it all to myself. I ran a bath and watched as the mounds of white bubbles piled up upon themselves.

Pulling my t-shirt over my head, I caught my reflection in the bathroom mirror. I stared at my bare shoulders and the lump on my neck, cupping it gently under my right hand. I could feel the lump, it was still agitated from the biopsy and had remained swollen ever since.

I can't wait to get this thing out of me.

I stepped into the bath and lay back, sinking under clouds of lavender-scented bubbles as I washed the water over my body, soaking away a night of sweat and anticipation. The thoughts began.

How painful will this be? What if ... it's cancer?

I took a deep breath and slipped under the warm water, drowning the thoughts and bathed my hair and body for the last time for a couple of days.

I got dressed and silently slipped outside to wait for Paul. I didn't want my sons to wake. I'd said goodbye the night before and left instructions in my absence. I couldn't bring their anticipatory anxiety with me; I had packed enough of my own.

Paul arrived shortly after, and I climbed in the car with the dog. The journey was silent. I didn't dare dip into my fears with Paul. I didn't want to begin the day in tears.

Paul pulled up in the bus stop outside the hospital just before a bus pulled in behind him, forcing a swift goodbye. It was easier that way for us both.

I arrived on the day-surgery ward and was herded into a room with eight other women, mostly older than me. There was one young girl, no more than twenty, with pink hair and a nervous twitch of her right foot. Her purple headphones and loud music blocked out the rest of the world.

The television had an '*out of order*' sign stuck to the front. Its faded paper and curling edges suggested it had been there for a while. A fan idled noisily from side to side making little difference to the heavy air. Despite being just after 7am, it was forecast to be the warmest June day yet and the waiting room was already uncomfortably hot.

Everyone sat quietly waiting to be called, the anxiety was palpable. All but one woman was silent. Margaret, a lady in her sixties, introduced herself and began to ask each patient what they were in for, unfiltered and unable to read the discomfort she was causing.

I looked at my feet.

Don't ask me please. I'm not here to get a pin put in my broken arm. I'm here because I might have cancer and I'm not ready to tell a room of strangers.

I bent down and began a fake search in my bag for something I didn't need.

Margaret turned to an elderly lady in the corner. "What's your name? What are you are you in for then?" she asked, in a way the woman found difficult to ignore.

"Edna... I've got a lump on my thyroid and it needs to come out. Just hope it's not cancer." She trailed off and leant down to her bag on the floor terminating the conversation.

I looked up. *We are the same. I hope it's not cancer too.*

A nurse arrived and called a patient, interrupting Margaret's line of questioning before she reached me. One by one, the women were called, each by a different nurse, and led away to begin their preparations for surgery.

"Edna Barton. Emily Johnson?"

My stomach somersaulted. Butterflies danced in the empty space.

"If you'd both like to follow me."

A nurse ushered us into a long corridor. Edna was slow on her feet. I followed behind at her pace.

We entered a dark empty room with four beds. The blinds were drawn against the early morning sun, cooling it down comfortably. The nurse directed us to a bed, pulling a blue curtain between us. It was all that separated us and offered little privacy from the conversation she began with Edna.

"Hello Edna. You've not had anything to eat since 10pm last night?"

"Yes, I had a cup of tea and a biscuit," Edna replied.

"And what time was that?" the nurse asked.

"After dinner."

"Yes, but what time did you eat your biscuit, Edna?"

"Um ... um, about seven I think." Edna stumbled through the admissions questions and could sense the nurse's mild irritation masked by a practiced patience.

Finally, Edna was helped into her gown and surgical socks before heading to the toilet one last time. The nurse appeared around the curtain and ran through the same obligatory details with me, before leaving me alone to wrestle with a pair of impossibly tight surgical socks.

Shortly after Edna's return, Miss Jones arrived. I shuffled uncomfortably listening to Edna's persistent questioning. Then Miss Jones appeared around the curtain to me, her silent surgical assistant in tow.

"Good morning, Ms Johnson. How are you today?" She glanced through my notes.

Miss Jones carried herself with a confident authority. I had been told twice by staff she was a remarkable surgeon. Her reputation amongst the hospital staff made me feel safe.

"Today I will be performing a partial lobectomy, right lobe," she confirmed before drawing a large vertical arrow on the right side of my neck with a marker pen. "We will see you around mid-morning." She smiled reassuringly before turning and leaving the room.

Within minutes, an anaesthetist arrived to speak with Edna. I pushed in my earbuds and silenced another awkward conversation I didn't want to hear.

Moments later, I heard Edna crying and pulled out one ear bud.

"I'm not going to die under anaesthetic, am I?" She was weeping gently.

"No, we will take great care of you, don't you worry now. We will be up to collect you soon, okay?" a voice reassured Edna.

The old lady was only saying what I'd lain awake thinking a few nights before.

I heard the anaesthetist's footsteps approaching me, another confident woman whose energy I could sense before she appeared. She was dressed in blue scrubs, but beneath her cap I could see her caramel-blonde hair. A gold chain hung around her neck with a '*Mum*' pendant in the middle of a heart and it captured my gaze.

She is not just a doctor; she is someone's mum.

The anaesthetist picked up my folder of notes, glanced through the tick list and ran through the questions. "Excellent!" she declared, placing my notes on the side table. "You are second on the list today, so I imagine you will be collected around 10.30. I will see you in theatre." She smiled and left.

I had almost two hours to sit and wait for my turn. I pushed my earbuds back in and watched some videos, thirty-second bursts of mindless action to momentarily distract my brain.

Twenty minutes later, a nurse in scrubs appeared and took Edna away.

"I will be okay, won't I?" Edna's words faded as she was led away down the corridor towards theatre.

The room fell silent. The only sounds were the whirring of the fans and a rhythmic sound of a wall clock that dragged its thin metal arms lazily behind its gentle ticks.

I stood up and walked to the large window and pulled the fabric blind to one side. The world outside was bustling into life. I looked down on the cars moving in short bursts towards traffic light standstills and school children eagerly skipping along, holding onto pushchairs and mothers' hands. The sky was filled with misty clouds that would soon burn away to reveal the blue haze of a hot Thursday in June.

I sat back down and put on a show I'd downloaded to watch. It passed the time.

I glanced back up at the clock. 10.04. *Not long now.*

The realisation turned my empty stomach over, and nauseous nerves filled my body as my heart accelerated. I scrolled through my music, finding something calming I could close my eyes too. I needed to escape.

Breathe in, breathe out, breathe in, breathe out... I recited inwardly, in time to the rhythm of my breath. Each time the fearful thoughts crept in, I repeated the words, pushing them away.

I'd struggled in the past with guided meditation. I'd close my eyes and attempt to slow down my thoughts, but a hundred more would rush in and crowd my mind. But this simple breathing technique had helped me overcome my anxious mind years before.

I am safe. I am safe, I repeated silently over and over, a comforting mantra. I could feel my heart slowing and nervous system settling with the rhythmic breathing. The nauseous feeling subsided, replaced with a subtle calm.

The sound of approaching footsteps pulled me back into the room. A nurse in scrubs appeared from behind the blue curtain.

"Hello, I'm here to collect you for surgery. Can you bring all your belongings with you?"

I grabbed my bag and followed the nurse out of the room and down to the corridor towards the storage locker. She locked my bag away before steering me towards theatre as we chatted about the new state-of-the-art surgical wing.

I'd never walked to a theatre before. It felt strange to be walking along in a hospital gown, as if I were strolling to the shops and casually chatting to a passer-by. It helped minimise the fear a little.

I was led into a small room with two surgical nurses and

instructed to lie on the bed in preparation for the anaesthetist. My hair was rolled up and tucked into a paper hat whilst the staff chatted about the upcoming strikes.

The anaesthetist appeared through the door and came around to my right side. "Hello again."

"What do you like to do in your spare time then, Emily?" a nurse asked.

"Um... I like to write."

"Oh, what do you write? Poetry?" the anaesthetist asked.

"No, I've written two books, both about mental illness."

"Oh, how interesting. Are they published?"

Whilst I explained the self-publication route I'd chosen, I was aware of my hand being swabbed with something cold. I knew what she was doing with the questioning and was grateful for the distraction.

"That's fantastic. Small scratch now."

I winced. I hated the strange pull the cannula had when first put in.

"Will you write any more books? I'm just putting in your anaesthetic now."

I felt a little strange. "Yes, I plan to, I'd love to write a—"

Beep... Beep... Beep...

"Hello Emily. You are in hospital in recovery, your surgery is over."

A man's voice pulls me back from soaring on a cocktail of drugs over an imaginary mountain range. *"I'm flying over the Mountains of Mourne,"* I whisper.

"'Course you are," the voice responded flatly. *"You are in the surgical recovery unit in Poole hospital."*

Behind his words a symphony of beeps and footsteps faded

in, and I became aware it was all over. I opened my eyes to see a man standing next to me.

"My name is Simon, and I am going to be looking after you today. How are you feeling? Are you in any pain?" he asked.

I swallowed, searching for some relief against the dryness in my mouth. *"I can't feel any pain, I just feel woozy,"* I whispered.

"That's okay, just rest for now." He'd barely finished the sentence before my eyes closed letting me slip back into a half-conscious state.

"How are you feeling now?" Simon roused me from my doze again.

I searched my body for signs of pain. I felt strange, as if my neck were dislodged. It wasn't painful, but I knew it had been operated on. "I just feel ... uncomfortable," I mumbled, glancing up at the clock. It was 1.31pm. I'd lost three hours.

"It's time for your pain medication." He lifted my hand and syringed something directly into my cannula. I lay still, watching patients in various states of recovery, blissfully unaware of their surroundings.

I closed my eyes and drifted off to sleep. The sounds of the recovery room merged into my strange dreams.

"Emily..."

I opened my eyes. Simon was sitting next to me, leaning back casually into a chair smiling, holding a pen and my notes, his left leg crossed over his right. Simon was perhaps forty. His sweeping fringe cut across his forehead and his thick, black-rimmed glasses enhanced his cool, edgy look. He looked like a musician, not a nurse.

"I'm going on my break now. Paulina will be looking after you."

Paulina appeared by my bedside. She was my age, a mop of blonde curls pinned upon her head. She had the busy energy of woman who worked too hard.

"Hello," she said, relieving Simon, who collected his coffee mug from the nurses' station and left the ward. "How are you feeling?" Paulina tidied the cup and straw beside my bed, before smoothing my bed covers with a motherly touch.

"I'm okay, thank you," I croaked, forcing a smile.

Pretend. Smiling solves everything.

"Good, I'm here if you needed anything," she said and left, swiftly pulling half the blue curtain back around me with her departure. I heard her gently sigh. I could sense her exhaustion.

Before Simon returned, I was transferred to the Head and Neck ward, accompanied by an opaque plastic box, sealed shut with black cable ties. I watched a nurse tuck it at the end of the bed on top of my notes, but I couldn't read the label on top. Its contents were a mystery.

My bed was parked in a bay with a sunny window overlooking the harbour with three other women. It was late afternoon and a muggy thirty-three degrees outside. With one wall made up entirely of windows and no air conditioning, it felt more like forty-three degrees on the ward. The other three patients were all considerably older than me and each had substantial facial surgical wounds.

"What are you in for, love?" a woman opposite asked as our eyes met.

"I had part of my thyroid removed for cancer screening," I said croakily. My wound seemed insignificant to that of the woman whose face had stitches from her neck, under her jaw and up to her ear.

"Ahh. Did you hear that, Doris? She had thyroid surgery," she relayed loudly to the lady next to her.

"Mmm," Doris agreed, nodding as she sipped from a plastic cup of water. She was stitched from neck to temple and her papery-thin skin was heavily bruised. Her hands trembled around the cup.

"I'm Jean, I had tongue cancer and Doris here – she's eighty-four, can you believe it?! She's had throat cancer and Maureen over there, she's had cancer in the roof of her mouth, isn't that right, Maureen?" Jean explained. It was obvious these women had united in friendship whilst staying on the ward.

I nodded at them all in acknowledgment. *"I'm so sorry,"* I whispered.

I felt fraudulent. I had just come in for a partial thyroidectomy. These patients had significant wounds that would leave them with permanent facial disfigurement. But being placed with three cancer patients was unnerving. Did my doctor already know something I didn't?

As the pain relief wore off and the afternoon heat intensified, I baked in the sweltering room. I was exhausted, hot, and sore and a vice-like headache was now gripping my head in painful waves. I slowly climbed out of bed and leant over the chair, attempting to lift my bag but dropped it. The contents tumbled out onto the floor noisily, disturbing Jean who looked up at me.

"Come here, love. Let me help you."

Jean, well into her seventies, walked over and began picking up my things that had scattered across the floor. I felt useless. Jean must have caught the expression on my face.

"It's okay love, you'll be back on your feet in no time," she reassured, patting my forearm.

"Thank you," I whispered.

I slowly walked to the bathroom with a facecloth, pulling my gown closed from behind. It felt good to be standing upright and moving slowly.

Turning on the tap, I soaked the cloth in cold water and wiped it around the nape of my neck before holding it over my face; the cooling relief was instantaneous.

Doris smiled as I passed her walking back to my bed. "You alright, love?"

I smiled and nodded, lying. I wasn't okay at all. Once behind the curtain, I sat on the bed and pulled the wet cloth into a ball over my face and silently cried into it.

I feel weak. And scared. But I can't tell anyone. I have to be strong.

I glanced around my cubicle. Behind my bed was a small poster taped to the wall. Its macabre images immediately captured my attention.

Management of acute haematoma following thyroid surgery.

SCOOP

S – SKIN EXPOSURE

C – CUT SUTURES

O – OPEN SKIN

O – OPEN MUSCLES

P – PACK WOUND

Each line was accompanied by a gruesome real-life image of action required in case of a post-surgical bleed. I looked at the opaque plastic box on the shelf, labelled '*SCOOP KIT*' and shuddered. I eased myself back into bed slowly.

As the sun set, the ward cooled down and one by one the fans were turned off. I managed a little soup and ice-cream for dinner and settled into bed exhausted. My head continued to pound long after the other patients were asleep.

Just after 3am a nurse popped her head around the corner of the curtain. "*You are still not asleep?*" she whispered.

"I can't shift this headache," I replied, twitching my foot anxiously on the bed.

"I will get you some morphine. That will help you sleep." She disappeared into the corridor, returning at 4am and watching me swallow the thick liquid medicine.

"Now, get some rest," she whispered, removing the empty pot from the side table, and leaving me.

I closed my eyes, longing for sleep and must have drifted off around 5am.

Just before seven, the ward lights came on and startled me from my sleep. The headache, although dulled, greeted me almost immediately and the sound of the clattering trolleys and nurses' conversations jarred my exhausted mind.

Shortly after breakfast, Katie appeared and sat down beside me. "Hello, I've got your discharge information here. You can get dressed and leave when you're ready." She smiled, assuming I would welcome the news. But it had been less than twenty-four hours since my operation and the two hours' sleep, along with the surgical aftermath and headache, had caught up with me.

"But... I..." I trailed off, holding back tears, feeling foolish. I felt like I'd been sawn in two and was being discharged back to life as if nothing had happened. The thought completely overwhelmed me.

"I know it's difficult. I am sorry but there is no clinical reason to keep you in hospital."

I felt her kindness. It wasn't her fault.

"You should hear from the hospital within two to three weeks by letter or phone with the pathology results. Don't worry if you don't hear from us in that time. We've scheduled an appointment on the 7th of July with Miss Jones and she will go through them then."

Katie stood up. "Take care and I will see you in clinic in three weeks."

"Okay, thank you," I whispered.

"Hi, I've been discharged. Can you pick me up?" I texted Paul.

He replied instantly: *"Of course I can. I will be there in twenty minutes. I will text you when I park up in the entrance x"*

I slowly got dressed and gathered my belongings and lifted my bag onto my back, wincing at the pain of its weight pulling at my neck. I shuffled out to the door, waving goodbye to Jean, Doris and Maureen.

A nurse who had been engrossed in paperwork at the desk, looked up. "You off now, then?"

"Yes, I am," I croaked.

"Is someone meeting you?"

"Yes."

"Ok, good. Take care of yourself." She returned her gaze to her desk.

I turned away, fighting back tears, and carefully made my way down the corridors to the lifts.

Pull yourself together. Stop being so weak.

My inner troll had awoken from the anaesthetic too and was beginning to chastise me.

My phone buzzed in my pocket. Paul had arrived.

"There is no space in the entrance, I'm just outside in the bus stop. I'll be waiting for you x"

I made my way to the exit and outside. The bright sunshine hit my face, and I screwed up my eyes. Paul spotted me and his expression dropped.

"Wait... Wait there. Don't walk any further, I'm coming!" he called out, walking towards me.

I dropped my bag, grabbing the hospital railing for support and began to sob, ignoring the stares of passers-by. Seeing Paul's familiar face had dissolved my resolve to be strong and hold it together. I needed someone to hold me up, to hug me and care for me. Just this once.

"Come here," he soothed, pulling me into his arms. "Let's get you back now so you can rest."

Paul dropped me home. As he lifted my bag out of the car and took me to the front door, he paused. "Let me come in to help you, please." His eyes were pleading with concern.

"No. I'm okay, I don't need any help." I blocked any further discussion, or entrance to the flat.

It had been four years since Paul had moved out and although we'd remained separated, we'd clung to each other through extraordinarily difficult circumstances with an unbreakable friendship. I had been in a relationship since the age of fifteen and never really experienced being single or alone until he moved out. Since the day Paul left, he had not returned, and I had never invited him back in. I put up protective barriers around my life and my sons and no one came in other than the mental-health workers. I met my friends in coffee shops or on a park bench and greeted neighbours at the door. Mental illness backed me into a dark corner of shame and isolation, and I had still not opened my home to rid it from that energy. Not even a cancer scare had coaxed me from that place.

Jack heard me arrive home. "Mum... How are you?" he asked sheepishly, his eyes scanning me anxiously.

"I'm okay, son, just sore and tired. I need to lie down," I croaked.

"Come in, Mum, you don't have to do anything," Jack reassured, leading me to the sofa to lie down. "Tell me if you need anything, okay?"

"Thanks." I didn't protest this time. My head was still pounding, and my throat was full of a thick mucus I couldn't cough up. Although the headache and surgical pain was manageable with pain killers, my emotions couldn't be so easily soothed.

"Can you get my laptop from the kitchen, please?" There was something I needed to do.

Jack left, before reappearing moments later with it. Once

he'd gone back upstairs, I opened the laptop and created a new document.

And so, this book began. Just for a few minutes each day, I needed to record how I was feeling. I couldn't speak about it to my family, but I could speak to the keyboard and leave my feelings there.

I slept deeply that night, despite being propped upright on several cushions. A mixture of codeine and exhaustion ensured it.

The following few days passed slowly. The headache, a probable result of my neck being placed in an extended position during surgery, slowly eased.

I knew so little of the thyroid's function prior to surgery, and I was in for a rude awakening. The butterfly-shaped gland at the front of my neck had been cut in half and was in shock from such a brutal interruption to its usual functioning. I was bloated, constipated, and exhausted to a degree I had never experienced before. No one warned me about those side effects, or the many others that came afterwards from my body not being able to produce enough thyroxine – a hormone produced by the thyroid gland which affects many of the body's systems.

After a week or so, when the stitches had been removed, I was able to bathe carefully, although I was unable to get my wound wet for a further few days when the dressing finally came off. My neck had a small incision – just a 2.5-inch line – in a natural fold of the neck. The spot was chosen for minimal scarring, and it was healing well.

A text from Paul interrupted my doze on a Sunday morning: *"Do you feel up to a visit to the caravan today? I've got a little surprise for you. I can pick you up and drop you back later X*"

It had been eight days since the surgery, and I felt exhausted. I didn't want to play mum. I wanted to curl up in a ball and wake up when all this was over. But I could curl up at *Sunshine* and do nothing for a little while at least.

"*Okay, let's say 11. What kind of surprise?*" I didn't like surprises.

"*Wait and see! See you outside at 11.*"

I leant over to Billy, who was still snoring beside me. "*Where are we going?*" I whispered by his ear. He lifted his head and stared at me intently, waiting.

"*We're going to...*" Billy cocked his head to one side.

"The Adventure Caravan!"

Billy leapt up without bothering to stretch and launched himself off the bed, ready for action. Telling him where we were going never lost its magic and it gave me the push I needed to get up out of bed.

Paul arrived to collect us. As we neared *Sunshine*, I could see my surprise waiting. Paul had set up the awning alongside it. As he pulled the car in, that's when I could see the real surprise. Paul had levelled the small patch of gravel in front of the caravan and covered it with a ground sheet. Around the edges sat a collection of pots with summer flowers, and mismatched shrubs that formed a square border of sorts. In the middle, was a new sun lounger with a blanket and cushion. He'd made me a garden.

"Oh Paul!" I gasped, tears filling my eyes.

I climbed out of the car eager to see it. Pots of bright pansies, marigolds and blue trailing lobelia decorated the corners with shrubs I didn't recognise. Some looked a little tired.

"Do you like it?" Paul grinned, like an enthusiastic child.

I beamed. "I love it! Where did you get all these plants?"

"They were throwing some away at the nursery down the road. I thought you could bring them back to life here."

"I bought these ones," Paul said, pointing to the pansies and marigolds. "Oh, and I made you this." He disappeared into the awning and returned with a terracotta plant base glued to a small block of wood. "It's to feed your birds. I can fix it on here." He walked towards the fence and rested the makeshift bird feeder on the flat top of a wooden pole.

"Oh... I love it... Thank you." I stepped forward into his arms and buried my face in his chest so he couldn't see my tears as I clung to his waist.

Just before my dad became paralysed, he'd bought me a terracotta bird feeder for my birthday and fixed it on the pergola pole outside my kitchen window. He'd seen how much I loved feeding the wild birds in Australia. Each day, I would stand at the sink washing the dishes as I watched colourful parakeets feast on sunflower seeds. It was the last gift my dad gave me before he died.

"I knew this would make you smile," Paul said, gently pushing my hair away from my eyes.

I curled up on the lounger in the shade of the trees and watched the birds cautiously discovering the new feeder filled with sunflower seeds. I stayed for hours. It made me forget everything, just for a while. Nature – this place – was soothing me.

About ten days after the surgery, I awoke with a strange and uncomfortable pressure in my throat, as if I were squeezing my neck. The scar was swollen with a large spongy lump surrounding it, the size of a small egg. I knew it wasn't normal, and the strangling feeling was both uncomfortable and frightening.

I called the ward contact who arranged for me to see another doctor in the Outpatients department to rule out infection. I had developed a seroma – a common post-operative complication that could form in any surgical wound where tissue was removed, creating an empty cavity. A collection of clear fluid had filled up the space left by the removal of part of my thyroid.

I was already scheduled to see my surgeon the following week and she would assess the seroma and decide on treatment. Reassured by the upcoming appointment, the A&E doctor sent me home and advised me to rest more and refrain from lifting or straining my neck.

As the week wore on, I had an increasingly sinking feeling about the pathology results. I'd been distracted by my surgical recovery and the added discomfort of the seroma. But behind the scenes, despite my sunny optimism, something was gnawing in my gut, especially at night when the world around me fell silent.

I lay awake unable to sleep. My instinct was telling me I had cancer. I didn't want to let my mind wander to that outcome in any detail, yet I struggled not to. I couldn't tell anyone close to me how strong that fear was. I didn't want to verbalise *that* word to anyone for maybe that would mean solidifying it into reality.

By day eighteen, I still hadn't received a call from the hospital telling me the mass was benign. I waited for the postman every single day hoping for the letter giving me the all-clear, but it never arrived.

I HAVE CANCER
7 JULY 2023

After a restless night's sleep, I awoke late, stretched, yawned loudly and for a moment or two, forgot the enormity of the day ahead. The realisation quickly slapped my senses awake and a nauseous feeling filled my throat.

What if it is cancer? Then what?

I didn't want to think beyond that day and into the future 'what-ifs.'

I climbed out of bed and passed Billy who was already up and out of his bed, stirred by my movement. I leant over the sink to the kitchen window and peeled the blinds open between my fingers to catch a glimpse of the sky. Outside awaited the perfect English summer's day. Hazy sunshine filled the patch of blue sky I could see. A handful of wispy clouds were daubed across it. I could hear people laughing out in the busy road. I envied their carefree oblivion.

I couldn't stomach breakfast, not even a coffee. Mixed in with the anxious knots were waves of relief that the waiting was finally over. I wanted to get on with my life, no matter what that entailed, rather than continue residing in a tormenting no-man's-land of the unknown.

After a quick shower, I rifled through my summer clothes for something bright and cheerful: a turquoise t-shirt, and a beautiful silk kimono jacket with shades of green, turquoise, blue and pink. I put on my best jeans and a pair of bright-pink shoes. Colour always cheered me up and I needed to face the appointment armed as optimistically as my clothes would allow.

I walked to the bus stop at the end of the road and waited in the warm sunshine, before hopping on the first bus that arrived moments later. The appointment was one I *should* have taken someone with me, but unlike my dad, I didn't want anyone with me and had rejected any offers of lifts or moral support. If it was the news I was expecting, I wanted to receive it myself, alone, so that I could process it without anyone else's emotions to contend with.

What if it's cancer?

No, I would have seen the signs...

But what if it is cancer?

I couldn't prevent the thoughts sneaking into my mind during the bus journey.

Sure, you'll deal with it no matter what.

I could hear the words in my mind as if my mother were beside me speaking them in her Belfast accent, with a matter-of-fact resignation to the blows life had dealt me. And she was right. I *would* deal with whatever the appointment brought me. The thought momentarily soothed the knots in my stomach.

The bus pulled up outside the hospital and I stepped off, my stomach lurched at what was coming. I closed my eyes and turned my head towards the warm July sunshine. I took a deep breath in.

This is it.

The last ten weeks had been building to this moment. I went into the now-familiar Endocrine Clinic and checked myself in for my 11am appointment before finding a seat away from everyone else. Voices approaching the clinic temporarily distracted me, stalling the incessant twitching of my right foot.

"You sit there, I will check in."

Two men and a woman entered the clinic. It was Edna with her husband and son. The men sat on the other side of the clinic whilst Edna confirmed her arrival before sitting down next to them. I looked at their anxious faces. We'd all shared the same tense three-week wait.

My surgeon was running behind schedule, the longest wait I'd encountered so far in the clinic.

Why today of all days?

It was torturous. Every moment felt like an hour dragging itself by.

I glanced at my phone for the thirtieth time in ten minutes. 11.20am. I'd muted it, turning on aeroplane mode when I'd arrived. I couldn't read messages or reply. I couldn't face anything and nothing could distract me.

Is this how dad felt?

I checked again: 11.21am. My heart raced.

And again 11.22... 11.23... 11.24... 11.25... 11.26am.

My foot tapped up and down rapidly. I closed my eyes and took a deep breath in.

I am safe. I am safe, I repeated over and over, my soothing mantra.

If you are here, please help me. Please ... Dad.

As I opened my eyes, I caught sight of a butterfly fluttering outside the window right in front of me. There it was, delicately dancing by. A dance just for me. I pulled my head back to stop the tears running down my face. "*Thanks, Dad,*" I whispered.

I looked at my phone again: 11.28am.

The surgeon's door opened. A woman came out with a man. I read their pained expressions. Maybe it was bad news. I watched for movement near the door, fighting back the urge to throw up through nerves.

One more glance: 11.31am.

The door opened, and a nurse entered the waiting room. "Emily Johnson."

My stomach momentarily somersaulted and my heart pumped loudly in my chest, echoing in my ears.

"Sorry about the wait, we are running a bit behind today," the nurse said apologetically as she ushered me towards the surgeon's office.

"Good morning, Ms Johnson, I'm sorry to have kept you waiting today," Miss Jones greeted me as the nurse took her seat beside her. Katie was sitting to my right. The familiar panel of three staff were waiting for me. My heart was racing faster. I knew it didn't take three staff to deliver good news. After some formalities about my post-operative wound care, it was down to business.

"As you are aware, we removed your right thyroid lobe along with the mass and sent it to pathology for testing. The nodule was a little larger than we originally thought and measured 4.5cm. It has shown a single focus of capsular invasion. This means it was classified as malignant, although minimally invasive at this stage. This type of cancer is called Follicular Thyroid Cancer and it's..."

The next few sentences were simply noise echoing around a room. All I heard was one sentence repeating and it was my own, silent one.

I have cancer. I have CANCER!

"In light of the fact that the tumour was over 4cm we would recommend removing the rest of your thyroid for two main reasons. Firstly, to facilitate radioactive iodine treatment and for this to be effective we need to remove all residual thyroid tissue. Essentially this is the same surgery you have already had. You will also be required to take replacement thyroxine daily after your surgery," she continued.

"Secondly, if you have no thyroid tissue remaining, we can periodically test your blood for thyroglobulin and if this is indicated it can be a sign of tumour regrowth. Have you noticed any changes in your voice since your surgery?"

"No, not now. I was a bit husky to begin with but it's ... it's ok ... now. I just feel like I'm being ... strangled most of the time," I stuttered.

"Yes, I can see you have some swelling. It's what we call a seroma, fluid has collected in the thyroid bed. I will drain it when I do your next surgery," she reassured. "I will refer you to the ENT department who will perform a vocal-cord check to ensure there is no damage to your vocal cords prior to your next surgery. You won't be required to come back in for another pre-op assessment, but we will need to check your thyroid function pre-operatively so you will have some blood tests two days before surgery. Now let's get a date booked in the diary for your surgery." She picked up her diary, flicking forward through the pages. "How's the 21st of July?"

Two weeks? I wasn't prepared to go through all this again in just two weeks. I had a summer wedding to attend, tickets to a music festival. I had planned to live my life that summer for the first time in six years.

Why is this happening now? Am I being punished?

I bit my lip, fighting back fearful tears.

Oh my god, I have cancer.

She must have seen the expression on my face. "Or we can wait a month or so? I have an opening on the 24th of August," she offered gently.

"Is it okay to delay until then? I have a wedding to attend, work and other commitments I'd planned to go to." Putting off cancer treatments for a wedding and festival seemed absurd but I had longed for some joy after years of hiding away from life.

"I am more than happy to postpone your surgery until then. After which you will be referred to Dr Singh in the Oncology department who will see you after your surgery and explain the radioactive iodine treatment and what that involves."

"Okay, thank you." I nodded as she pencilled my name into her diary.

"Katie will take you through to her office and give you some information to take home. Do you have any questions for me?" She removed her glasses.

"Could you tell me long has the cancer been there?"

"It's hard to say. Follicular cancer is very slow-growing, so I suspect, years. It was minimally invasive, so it looks like the timing of it being found now was excellent."

"Has it ... all gone?" I asked tentatively.

"I am confident that I have removed it all, however we will remove the remaining thyroid lobe and send that to pathology for further testing. The radioactive iodine will destroy any remaining tissue left in the thyroid bed and any thyroid cancer cells that may be elsewhere in the body."

"Okay, thank you." I had nothing else to ask. I was numb.

"I will see you in August." Miss Jones smiled and Katie stood up, signalling the end of my appointment.

"If you'd like to follow me," Katie said, opening the office door.

"Thank you... Bye." I looked back at the consultant and nurse sat beside her and followed Katie out and into the corridor to another office.

"Take a seat here." Katie gestured whilst placing some cancer information leaflets on the table. "Are you okay? I know that was a bit of a shock for you, wasn't it?"

"I'm okay ... I think. It is okay to delay this surgery and treatment, isn't it?" I asked, feeling foolish now I'd left the specialist's office.

What if it spreads?

"Miss Jones is an extremely well-respected, knowledgeable surgeon and she wouldn't have agreed to you delaying treatment unless it was safe to. Anyway, I think a little bit of joy over summer will be good for you, don't you? Here is my email and telephone number. If you have any questions in the meantime, please get in touch. You should hear from the ENT department in about three weeks for your vocal cord check and I will be in touch with you before your surgery to arrange the consent and blood tests." Katie smiled warmly.

I stood up, collecting my pile of cancer leaflets and walked towards the door. "Thank you."

I left, closing the door quietly behind me. I moved quickly, hoping Edna wouldn't recognise me and spark up a conversation. I was over an hour late and I knew that when I turned my phone on, I had several people anxiously awaiting contact from me. They needed to know my news before Edna or anyone else.

I left the hospital on autopilot, detached from my body. My mind was somewhere completely different attempting to process every emotion, all at once. Shock, fear, relief, guilt, anger. Over and over, the emotions tumbled around together.

I have cancer. It has been found by accident. I am so lucky it was caught.

I had been walking through life with cancer, maybe for years, but it had been found and could be treated. I had a cancer with an excellent prognosis. Maybe I *should* feel lucky. But I still had to go through more surgery and radiation, and I was scared.

You have a treatable cancer, Emily. Be grateful.

My mind was in overdrive. I stepped into the sunshine and found a grassy spot in front of the hospital and sat down, leaning up against the wall. I needed to sit down, to ground and breathe and try to put my mind back into my body and stop a thousand thoughts spinning me around.

Closing my eyes, I tilted my face up toward the sunshine and took some deep breaths to settle the nerves from what was about to come. It was time to tell everyone else. I turned my phone back on and pushed my ear buds in. I video called Paul. I needed to see his face as I told him the news. He answered almost immediately.

"Hi, how did you get on?" he asked, his eyes searching for clues.

"I'm fine, well I... um... I... I have cancer—"

"Oh Emily, *no!*"

"No, listen, it's okay, I promise. It's called follicular cancer, it's probably been there for years, but she thinks she got it all out. Paul, I... I feel so lucky it was found."

Despite the brightness of the sunshine, I could still see his face on the video call clearly enough to see he was crying. "Please don't get upset. You'll start me off. I am absolutely fine, I promise," I lied.

"So, what happens now? Do you have to have treatment? Chemo or something?" he asked, wiping his tears away with the back of his hand.

"I have to come in for another operation to remove the other side of my thyroid, then I will come back in to have a special type of radioactive pill. Look, let me explain it all when I see you tomorrow. I need to get home and have a coffee and tell the boys and Mum."

"Okay, listen you get yourself home safely. I wish you'd let me come today, Emily. I wish I could be there for you."

"No, no honestly, I'm fine. I will text you later. Bye." I blew him a kiss with my hand, before ending the call.

I sat there for a moment thinking about Paul's reaction. *That wasn't too bad. See, as long as I'm okay, they will all be okay,* I reassured myself.

My stomach was growling noisily for something to line it. I collected up the leaflets and walked the short distance to the bus stop opposite the hospital, managing to catch one that was offloading passengers.

I found an empty seat at the back of the bus. I didn't want to converse with anyone, not today, not after that bombshell. I texted some of my friends who I knew would be waiting on an update. I kept it objective and simple:

"I've just seen the specialist. I have follicular thyroid cancer, luckily caught in the early stages but I will need to go back into hospital and have another operation and then have radiation treatment. It's a bit of a shock so I'm just going to take some time to digest it all. Thank you for all your love and well wishes, it means a lot to me. Love you xx"

I turned my phone to silent and glanced down at the leaflets given to me. My cancer had been found early. I was one of the lucky ones. I felt momentarily elated, stunned by the serendipitous events that had led to its chance discovery. That elation was soon replaced by guilt.

What about all the people who can't be treated. What about Dad? Why do I get to live?

I arrived home and opened the front door. Jack had been anxiously awaiting my return. As he left his room and appeared at the top of the stairs, I went to the bottom of the staircase and our eyes met.

"How did you get on, Mum?" he asked cautiously, his tone loaded with apprehension.

"Well Jack, I have cancer but it's treatable, but I'm going to need more surgery and radiation," I blurted out.

"What...? Mum, no... *NO!*" he cried out before running downstairs towards me.

"Hey, I'm going to be okay. I'm not going anywhere! Your mum plans on sticking around." I reassured, laughing. The words came out without any thought or planning and my nervous attempt to lighten the situation failed miserably.

"How can you laugh, Mum? It's not funny. You have cancer. Mum, what if you die?" He turned away from me holding a door to steady himself. I was taken aback by his reaction.

"Oh love, it's okay." I rubbed his back soothingly.

"No, it's not okay, Mum. You have cancer!" he cried as his body convulsed in painful sobs.

"Jack, please don't cry, I'm okay, love. I'll have the treatment and everything's going to be okay, I promise."

Jack had only heard the word cancer, and he created my death sentence from it. He couldn't hear my reassurances. But Jack didn't know I was reassuring myself too. His crying pulled at my heart painfully, and I began to cry with him. My son was nineteen years old but still my child, one who had fought for so long against his own demons – the anxiety, the crippling OCD – and now I had *that* disease, the one that kills people. The one that stole my dad from me, and Jack knew that story too, inside out.

I should have sat quietly, listened to his concerns and not tried to invalidate his feelings and understandable response to such shocking news, yet logic and reason left when the words first tumbled out of my mouth. I had no idea how to cope with his reaction, or no immediate empathy for his feelings because I was still trying to process my own.

Jack opened the lounge door, leaving me in the hallway as the door closed behind him. I could hear his gentle sobs but stood anchored to the spot. I took a sharp breath in and swallowed hard against the lump of shock and sadness stuck in my throat.

He needs me to be strong, not crying.

I tilted my head back and fought hard against the deluge of tears. Tears for him, for Thomas, Paul, my mum. Tears for me, too.

I pushed the door open. Jack was sitting with his back to me. He rarely cried; he hated anyone seeing him cry. Men aren't meant to cry, right? Society wrongly taught him that one, not me.

"Jack, please, love. It's going to be okay, please trust me. It's been caught in the early stages. I'm very lucky."

"You're not lucky, Mum, how can you be lucky? It's cancer!"

"It's been contained."

"You don't know that! That's what they told your dad. He died, Mum."

Jack was right, I didn't know anything for certain. "I know, but that was a long time ago and he didn't get it checked for two years."

"You didn't even know you had it, Mum! What if it's already spread and they don't know?"

"Jack, please. I'm going to be okay; I promise."

Jack stood up, wiping his face with his sleeve, then came towards me, pulling me into a hug. He needed to feel his mum was okay, he needed to hold onto her. "If anything happens to you, Mum, I just couldn't..." He trailed off, unable to verbalise the unthinkable.

"Shh, I'm not going anywhere, I promise." I squeezed him tightly, savouring the hug I needed from him, as much as he wanted one from me.

"I'm going back to my room; I need to be alone for a bit."

As I watched him leave, I felt relief it was over. I had to face Thomas now and tell him. What if he reacted in the same way?

I followed Jack up the stairs a second or two later and just caught him disappearing into his room before I moved across the landing towards Thomas's room. I took a deep breath and tapped on his door. "Hi Thomas, are you okay?"

Thomas pulled his headphones off his head and rested them behind his ears. "How did you get on, Mum?" he asked, quietly.

"Well, um ... it was cancer, Thomas. I need to have surgery and then radiation treatment, but it was caught early and I'm very lucky. I'm going to be okay; I promise." I delivered the news gently as I could.

Thomas was still, his eyes filled with fear. He looked up at me and nodded, before standing and hugging me. "*It's okay*," he whispered into my shoulder.

I felt a wave of relief fill my body. Thomas was quiet, he'd barely uttered a word. In some ways that was easier, yet I knew Thomas bottled things. He kept his cards close to his chest but that inability to express his emotions usually resulted in periodic eruptions of anger or tears.

"Are you okay?" I asked hesitantly.

"Yep, are you sure everything's going to be okay, Mum?"

"Yes, Thomas, I'm just going to pop outside for a bit. Listen, I'm going to be fine, I promise." I wanted to protect my sons from my fear.

"Okay." Thomas pulled his headphones back up onto his head and spun around to his computer monitor, signalling the end of the conversation.

I left his room and paused on the landing. Telling my sons was harder than I thought it would be.

Why did they both look so scared? Did they not believe me?

I went downstairs and grabbed my keys off the hook, before heading out into the narrow lane outside. I sat on the pavement and leant against the brick wall, closing my eyes and turning my face towards the shaft of sunlight filtering through. I'd sat in the lane a hundred times over the last few years. I'd cried there. I'd escaped there. Although it was a thoroughfare for many people, and often littered with rubbish, it was my little space away from the rest of the world.

After a few minutes, I texted Mum: "*Are you free for a call?*"

I may have been fifty-one, but I would always be her little girl. A little girl in a woman's body who still needed her mum but wanted to spare her the upset of my cancer diagnosis. She lived in Ireland, and it had been a long time since I'd made it back home to her. Too long.

Within a moment or two of sending the text, my phone rang. My stomach instantly turned over with nerves. Mum had been waiting too.

"Well, how did you get on?" There was no time for the usual pleasantries.

"Yes it was fine, Mum. It had some suspect cells, but I was very lucky. It's been removed, but I do need to go back in a few weeks for the other side to be removed." It was a diluted account of the truth, and I avoided *that* word.

"Jesus, Mary and Joseph, Emily, not more surgery? You've been through the wars enough already, love. Isn't it just as well that doctor found it?"

"I'm fine, Mum, I'm going in at the end of August so I've got some time yet. Anyway, it's nothing to worry about, I promise," I reassured. "Can you let Uncle Gus know?" My dad's brother would be waiting for news too.

"Yes of course I will. As long as you are okay, that's all I worry about. You're still my wee girl, you know."

"Mum, I'm *fine,*" I lied.

I'm not really fine, I've got cancer and I'm scared.

"Right, I'd better go. Speak soon. Bye, Mum."

"Bye, love, you take care now."

"I will." I ended the call, relieved. I hated lying.

I texted my brother next, this time giving the objective

details. Two years older than me, Ryan was a practical man, preferring facts without the sugar coating.

My phone rang instantly. It had been months since our last conversation. Life had got in the way.

"Have you told Mum?" he asked, concerned. We both recognised Mum's age, along with the distance from us both, left her vulnerable.

"Yes, but I wasn't completely honest. I don't want her to worry. I didn't even tell her it was cancer. I just said it was some cells that were suspect and removed. Don't tell her, will you?"

"No, I won't, I promise. Are you okay?" His tone was serious. We'd both lost our father to cancer. We'd experienced a different version of this disease. We knew it was deadly, and I could hear his fear.

"Ryan, I'm fine! It's been found early and I'm going to be okay. Right, I've got to go, speak soon. Bye."

Now everyone closest to me had been told and it was time for me to digest the details alone.

That night, I lay in bed unable to sleep and did the inevitable online searching I'd tried so hard to avoid until almost 4am. In some ways, it helped to read more about the type of cancer I had – it was reassuring – but as with any online search, I wandered into worst-case scenarios I immediately wished I could unread. And, for the first time, I allowed myself to explore my biggest fear: dying.

It was the first time in my life I had actually considered it. I'd only seen death once before. The morning Dad died, I'd stayed in the family room at the hospice for several hours, mustering the courage to see him before his body was taken away. When I eventually went in to view his body, I remember staring at him, not knowing how to feel or what to say to him. Would he hear me? How could he? He was gone. I remember that pain flooding my body physically, like a beast in my belly, rising and strangling my throat.

At fifty-nine, my dad was still young and handsome, with just a few salt-and-pepper greys dusting the curls on his temples. He looked peaceful, younger in death somehow. I remember touching his hand and quickly pulling away. It was cold and lifeless. I wanted to say so many things. I wanted to call him Dad, and tell him I loved him, but instead I left without saying a word, or looking back.

Death was so final. If I died now, I'd feel ripped off by life. I'd spent years not living, not really, not appreciating my life or body. There were so many things I still wanted to do. Regret and guilt began rising in my throat and I began to cry.

Is this how dad felt?

The following day, I met with Paul in a local coffee shop and claimed the hug I'd needed for hours. He held my hand across the table as I went over the details of my conversation with the consultant and every so often, I stopped to let the tears fall. "I just can't believe it, Paul. What if ... I hadn't been to the doctor. What if it hadn't changed my jumper that day and it hadn't been found?"

"I know." Paul squeezed my hand, his eyes filled with tears. It was harder to witness his emotions than I expected. "How about I drive you out to the caravan and you can rest in the chair outside for a couple of hours? I will drop you back whenever you are ready. Would you like that?"

"Mm hmm." I nodded. I couldn't think of anywhere else I'd rather be. It was the place I felt most free from the entanglement of my busy life.

After a quick stop at a local supermarket, Paul returned to

the car and popped a bag behind the seat before driving me to *Sunshine*. "Stay there and rest for me. I will be back in a minute."

Once I was settled in the lounger, Paul disappeared around the side of the caravan, then inside, and reappeared with a tray a few minutes later. "Here we are," he said, passing me a tray with a glass of water and cinnamon bun. On the side was an old jar containing a handful of bright-yellow dandelions.

I looked up at his face. "Thank you." I smiled, swallowing against the emotions that were surfacing. I found it hard letting people love me. I cared for everyone willingly but struggled with accepting that care back.

We sat in silence, Billy between us, oblivious to the news that had just devastated our lives.

It was approaching dinnertime and as much as I wanted to stay, I needed to get home. I had delivered the news of my diagnosis to my sons the day before and not spent any significant time with them since then. We all needed to process the news in our own way.

I spent another evening searching the internet for facts about cancer, the treatments, the risk of surgery and risk of recurrence. The information was endless and some of it very frightening. Behind this quest was a longing to know why I had cancer. How long had it been there? What caused it? I had so many questions, all of which were impossible to answer.

I eventually fell asleep and awoke early the next morning to Jack quietly calling me.

"Mum... Mum, are you awake? I think Thomas had a bit of a meltdown before bed. He tried to cut his hair off last night."

"What... *What?*" I questioned sleepily, pulling myself up and out of bed and rubbing my eyes. "What do you mean he cut his hair. With what?"

Thomas *never* cut his own hair. He had shoulder-length wavy curls and beard.

"He used some clippers. I think he was crying, Mum."

My heart dropped. Thomas had been so quiet when I told him about the cancer. Maybe this was my fault somehow?

"Can you feed the dog for me, Jack? I'll be back in a minute."

I left the dog hungrily running in circles with Jack and headed upstairs to Thomas's room. Sleeping in his bed was a man I didn't recognise. A man with a half hacked-at beard and shaved patches on his skull with long strands of hair. I gasped, holding back tears at the state of his head. There were scratches where the blunt hair clippers had tugged at his skin, cutting it.

I ran my hands through his remaining hair gently, waking him. He looked up at me and without saying anything, held out his hand out towards mine. I sat down next to him on his bed and placed my hand over his. "What happened. What made you cut your hair?

Thomas shrugged. "I just got upset about it everything and angry at myself last night, I guess. I've made a mess of it, Mum. I can't go out to the barbers like this. Can you help fix it?"

I ran my fingers over the spiky bald skin and the hair that remained. "I will give it a go. Get up and come downstairs and I'll see what I can do."

I left his room, filled with misplaced guilt. I didn't ask for cancer but somehow, I felt responsible for his reaction.

A few minutes later, Thomas appeared sheepishly. Now standing up, I could see the full extent of his butchered hair. "Come here, sit down."

I smiled at Thomas, patting the stool. "It's going to be okay, Thomas. I promise," I said, lifting up the strands of hair on his scratched scalp.

I shaped his hair, returning some resemblance of a normal haircut in silence. Neither of us knew what to say.

SUMMER OF JOY

JULY–AUG 2023

I'D POSTPONED MY TREATMENT UNTIL THE END OF SUMMER to try and grab some pleasure out of life before the next round of surgery and treatment. It was that determination that got me through weeks living with symptoms I wasn't prepared for. Aside from the seroma that continued to press on my windpipe leaving me with a sensation of being strangled, there were both physical and mental affects from the first surgery.

The surgeon couldn't prescribe any replacement thyroid hormones between surgeries as there was a risk that the higher levels in my body could encourage more rapid cancer-cell growth. My thyroid had been halved and it was evidentially spluttering along, unable to produce enough of the hormones for my body to function properly.

I had no appetite, yet my stomach was bloated, and constipation became my new normal. I was gaining weight, and all my clothes felt tight. My hair, usually curly and shiny, became dry and brittle and my scalp and face, itchy with flaky skin. The fatigue was overwhelming at times, the worst lethargy I have ever experienced. I would get up late every day and within an hour or two feel like I needed to lie down once again. By the afternoons, I *had* to sleep. The simplest of tasks exhausted me and the fatigue made me miserable. As the weeks wore on, I felt much more than just miserable at times. I felt extremely low, and some days, overwhelmed with a sense of hopelessness that I just couldn't shake.

Cancer isolated me. I couldn't sit this one out and no one could take it for me. I understood why my dad was scared. But unlike him, I hid my true feelings along with my fears. It was such a dark and lonely place because I didn't feel I could burden anyone close to me with how I was really feeling. On the days the hopeless heaviness hung over me, I would sit alone in the kitchen and cry. Not just because I had cancer. Honestly, I don't even know why.

I couldn't think straight, and often found myself stood in the supermarket in a foggy state, wondering why I was even there, or walk into a room and be dumbfounded as to what had sent me in there. I was also of menopausal age, and I couldn't differentiate between the thyroid fatigue and menopause symptoms. It was incredibly frustrating and at times, I turned that frustration inward. I didn't feel like myself anymore.

At night, my hands would tingle with pins and needles, and I began to experience unexpected cramps in my calves, or sudden shooting pains in my chest and head. Those were the most terrifying because they would send in me into mild panic, especially if they happened in the early hours. It would awaken the beast in my mind that would creep forward and whisper they hadn't *really* got all the cancer, and just like dad, it had already spread around my body. The unfamiliar symptoms would only affirm it for me. I let the beast in my mind attack me, chastising me for delaying my own surgery. Sleep was hard to find on those nights.

I tried to continue with life as normal, but nothing felt normal anymore. My body certainly didn't. I joined a few online thyroid groups, and these became a valuable source of information and support during this time. I found other people all over the world who were experiencing everything I was and for the first time since my surgery, I didn't feel like I was imagining the symptoms.

In late July, I returned to work on reduced hours and managed for a few weeks. The hardest part were the video calls with my management team, for every time they asked me if I was doing okay, I would burst into tears. I wasn't coping with trying to fulfil all my roles as a mother, carer, and worker with cancer. Yet I was my own harshest critic. *I should be able to manage,* I'd remind myself regularly.

The hospital was there for my physical treatment, and ensured I was supported by a cancer support worker who connected me with charities who could help with the emotional fallout of a diagnosis. I didn't know how to navigate my feelings, or the emotional reactions of my loved ones. A couple of times, I called a cancer-charity helpline and just sat and cried down the phone, unable to formulate my words. They let me cry and that anonymous place to let go was what I most needed at times.

I kept an outward smile painted on, mostly for the benefit of others. I wanted Jack, Thomas, Mum and Paul to think I was coping, but behind the cheerful facade, doubts gnawed away. Would it get me too? I brushed them away as best I could but like sweeping up leaves in a storm, no matter how much I tried, the doubts kept returning.

There were moments of happiness in my summer of joy. I was able to cut short my planned work project at the music festival. My employer was very understanding and allowed me to work shorter shifts and rest at the accommodation in-between. I needed it, with my body still struggling on half a thyroid, it was absolutely exhausting. But in all honesty, standing in a state-of-the-art pop-up shop helping customers choose hair products, and watching whilst they styled their festival hair was the perfect antidote for a cancer diagnosis. The sun was shining, the music was thumping, and colourful festival flags flapped high in the blue skies above. People were happy and they gifted glimmers of their happiness to me. I could forget the cancer narrative for a few hours.

In mid-August, I was invited back into hospital for a vocal cord check-up. A rare complication of thyroid surgery is injury to the laryngeal nerve which can cause vocal-cord palsy, making the voice weak, as well as causing difficulties with breathing and swallowing. After some local anaesthetic spray, a tiny camera would be placed up my nose and down the back of my throat, giving the doctor a view of the vocal cord's movement. I'd read online it wasn't painful, just uncomfortable, but I was still dreading the test.

I was met by a cheerful young doctor who led me into an exam room and ushered me to sit in a chair in the centre of the room. After running through the procedure with me, the doctor prepared the equipment as I stared out of the window across the bay. It was a hot August day, and the large hospital windows drew in the baking sunlight.

"I'm going to give a couple of sprays in your nose. I'm afraid it doesn't taste nice," he warned before pushing a long white nozzle into my nostril and spraying the innocuous-looking liquid from a small bottle.

Instantly an acrid taste trickled down and filled my mouth, and I swallowed hard against it. "You weren't wrong. That's awful!" I said, pulling a face at the vile taste.

"Yes, so I've heard. Sorry about that." Clearly, I wasn't the first patient to react the same way.

After a few minutes, the bitter taste had diminished, and my throat was numb.

"Now if you can sit very still, I'm going to pop the camera up the right nostril. You might be able to feel this but there should be no pain."

I closed my eyes. I didn't want to see the camera going in. It was uncomfortable, like a nasal swab that kept on going, tickling the back of my nose. The sensation made my eyes water, but I couldn't move.

"Right, the camera is in place. Can you say 'eeee' for me," the doctor instructed.

"Eeee."

"And once again, please."

"Eeee."

"All done. The vocal cords look good and there is no sign of any damage from your previous surgery so you can proceed with the next one. I'm just going to remove the camera."

Within a moment the camera was gently pulled back out.

"All the best with your surgery," the doctor said warmly as he opened the door to let me out.

"Thank you."

Hospital visit number nine was complete.

Despite my body struggling with debilitating symptoms, I searched for moments of joy in the simplest of things. I took bus trips to *Sunshine* with Billy and would take my time wandering the winding country lane that led to the caravan. Time hadn't changed, but my value of every passing moment, had.

Summer was in full swing and the bushes that lined the path were teaming with life. Birds, butterflies, and bees all feasted on a buffet from the unruly summer hedgerows, heavy with blackberries and wild blooms. Sometimes a week or more would pass in between visits, but each time I would see further evidence of nature's abundance. I had been hiding myself away for nearly a decade and had almost forgotten how beautiful the natural world was.

I'd pull up a chair outside the caravan and laze for a couple of hours, basking in the glorious late-afternoon warmth. My little patch of wilderness was filled with an unseen magic that soothed me. I named it '*Healing Corner*'. Often the bus trips would take all the energy I had, and I would feel physically drained, but there were days I could summon a little more energy to kick off my shoes and walk around on the long grass, dodging the daisies and buttercups that decorated the field.

On the days when it all felt too much, I'd lie on my back on the grass observing the sky. I'd watch the clouds changing shape as they gently rolled by, and the birds swooping high above me. I'd follow tiny aeroplanes higher still, flying in straight lines, leaving faint trails behind them and think of their passengers sitting in rows and wonder where they were going.

Billy was always lying right beside me. I'd watch him observing his world quietly. He instinctively knew the art of 'being' and he was teaching me without knowing. His stillness reminded me of when I had a regular meditation practice in my late thirties. A different life took over by my forties with the arrival of chronic mental illness and I abandoned the practice. Mindfulness was replaced by survival. Life had given me no choice to be mindful now; I had to stop and make time for myself. My body needed me too.

I had delayed my surgery for my commitment to working at the music festival, but I also had tickets to another one. This festival was a wash out, with heavy summer rain turning the fields into rivers of thick mud. It wasn't uncommon with the unpredictable British summer weather and often considered part of the festival experience, but with so little energy, it was one I could have done without.

As I waded through the ankle-deep mud, I questioned my choice to delay the surgery, but it was already too late by then. I settled in a chair in a plastic coat with an umbrella and made the best of it for a few hours, determined to enjoy myself. My diagnosis had shown me life could change in the blink of an eye, and I was learning to savour the best moments, despite the challenges.

A beautiful English summer's day was the perfect backdrop for my friend's wedding. I'd had an accidental part to play in the couple's meeting many years beforehand and they'd insisted on my attendance when the invitations went out the year before. During the speeches, I understood why, as they thanked me for helping their paths cross all those years ago.

It was the most wonderful outdoor celebration in glorious August sunshine. I spent much of the day sitting down to conserve my energy for the twelve hours of festival-themed fun. I was exhausted, having gone through almost nine weeks without any medication to support the remaining thyroid lobe. My weight had ballooned, and I felt heavy and miserable in my oversized dress, but I clung to the beacon of happiness the wedding had promised during my recovery, and nothing would have stopped me being a part of their special day. Not even cancer.

As the sun set over the flags that fluttered in the evening sky, a bittersweet sadness fell over me. It was the last event from my 'summer of joy' and now it was ending. I had less than a week to my surgery and I knew life would be a little different again, and probably harder.

A couple of days after the wedding, the surgeon's secretary called. My operation had been cancelled due to staff strikes. Without full theatre staff, the surgeon had no choice but to cancel her lists. I would have to wait for a new date.

Why didn't I just take the date I was offered in July?! If I had it would all be over now.

The delay meant my radiation treatment might also be pushed back into the following year. I wanted it to be over in 2023. I wanted to draw a line under it all and now through my own choice to put fun in front of cancer treatment, things had been delayed. I was frustrated with myself and a little scared. If any cancer remained, it was still there and the delay in surgery was granting it more time to grow ... and maybe spread.

Thankfully, my operation was rescheduled for three weeks later. It was disappointing but with a date fixed, I resigned myself to the inevitable delay. It felt reassuring to have an anchor point for the next stage of the journey.

LIFE-CHANGING
14 SEPTEMBER 2023

I AWOKE EARLY AND IN GOOD SPIRITS ON THE DAY OF MY surgery. I knew what to expect this time. After a quick shower, I quietly dressed, trying not to wake the dog or my sons. The silence gave me time to run over in my mind the days ahead and capture any last-minute things I needed to prepare. As a carer, leaving for short breaks was like planning a military operation. Both my sons were young men but they both required additional support, especially Jack. I knew he would miss me enormously.

I arranged for Paul to give me a lift to the hospital and take the dog for a few days. A text alerted me to his arrival outside the flat.

I slipped the dog's lead over his head as he lay curled up in his bed still. "*Where are we going?*" I whispered, grinning. Billy looked up at me confused at the early morning awakening, then jumped up, ready.

I scanned the kitchen plugs one last time, before stepping out of the front door, Billy pulling me behind him. I turned around to lock the door and stopped.

"No." I sighed under my breath. I knew what was coming and couldn't prevent it.

I dropped my bag and Billy's lead, pushed the door open and went straight to the kitchen. *Off, off, off,* I repeated silently, scanning the kettle, toaster, and air-fryer switches on the wall sockets.

I moved to the oven. *Off, off, off.*

Then the hob.

I pushed hard on the freezer and fridge doors to close them, even more tightly closed than they already were. "That's closed... That's closed... That's closed," I repeated aloud as if verbalising would ensure the doors really were closed.

I knew logically they were closed; I knew the switches were off, I could see them, but *I couldn't* accept it. Saying it aloud marked the beginning of rounding up the process in my mind.

"Oh, come on, Emily. They're *off!!*" I shouted at myself, frustrated knowing Paul was sitting outside waiting and I had to get to the hospital. Pressure always made it worse. I took a deep breath in.

"Off off off ... off off off off... That's closed... That's closed!" I repeated at an increasingly angry volume, touching the switches to confirm it.

I turned away and went to the front door and pushed it open without looking back. I needed to walk away and sit with the anxiety I was feeling. Sometimes, no matter how many times I repeated the checking, it was never enough.

I'd experienced brief bouts of depression and obsessive-compulsive disorder following my dad's death. Usually, the episodes were exaggerated by high-stress situations, including his death, and the aftermath of my divorce from John. I had never been formally diagnosed; I'd never thought to seek help, I just accepted the behaviour was a part of me, a quirky need to check and triple-check things. It wasn't until Jack was diagnosed with chronic OCD and I'd parented him through some extremely difficult years, that I understood it better and recognised I had experienced a much milder version of this debilitating anxiety disorder myself.

I locked the door and picked up my bag and Billy's lead. "Let's go!" I exclaimed and Billy bounded down the stairs in the excitement of an unknown adventure. Billy's joy distracted me, preventing me from running back up the stairs to check, again.

"Everything okay?" Paul was waiting at the flat entrance.

"Yes. Sorry, I'm running a few minutes late." I kept my compulsive rituals to myself.

The journey to the hospital was easy – with little traffic and the conversation, lighter this time. We chatted about the dog and his food, his favourite walks, and the logistics of picking me up the following day after my discharge.

Paul pulled into the bus stop, and I unclicked my belt, leaning across for a final hug.

"Bye, Emily. Take care and message me as soon as you are out, okay?" Paul called through the open door after me.

"Will do. Bye, Billy," I called back, closing the car door and waiting to wave, as Paul's car disappeared into the distance.

I turned to the hospital and made me way into the familiar day ward, back to the waiting room of women waiting for various surgeries. The television was still broken and the fans were still the only sound in the uncomfortably silent room.

Within ten minutes, a nurse called two ladies' names, along with mine, and she led us to the same ward at the end of the corridor, directing us to three adjacent beds.

"Ms Johnson, you are the first on the list today. Miss Jones and the anaesthetist will be here to see you shortly. Now if you can slip out of your clothes and pop on this gown, I will measure you for your socks," the nurse instructed.

Within ten minutes we were all in our hospital gowns and surgical socks, waiting.

"I'm Amy, and this is Suzanne." The woman in the bed next to me gave the introduction. They had made acquaintance whilst I was with the nurse.

"Hi." I nodded, acknowledging them both. We were three women united in pre-surgical nerves.

"Are you having your thyroid removed today too?" Amy asked. She'd overheard my check-in conversation with the nurse.

"Yes, I'm having the second lobe removed, I already had the first one and a lump removed in June," I confirmed.

"I have a lump too; they are taking out half today ... to test it for cancer. The needle biopsy was inconclusive," Amy said, nervously.

A wave of empathy swept over me. I was a few weeks ahead of her on the same journey and didn't want to burden her with how my story was unfolding.

"Do you mind me asking why you are having the other side removed?"

"Um... I had cancer in the lobe, so they are removing the other for testing and radioactive iodine treatment," I explained, almost apologetically.

I could see Amy's expression. She was clearly nervous of what lay ahead.

"What was recovery like after your operation? I'm worried about looking after my teenagers after this. They throw you out the next morning."

"It's okay, you'll be fine, I promise. You just need to rest and be kind to yourself." I stopped, interrupted by the surgeon and her assistant who had arrived.

"Good morning. We are performing the completion lobectomy left lobe today." Miss Jones pulled the lid off her marker and drew a thick arrow on my neck. "I shall be going in through the same scar and all being well, you should be going home tomorrow morning. Any questions?"

I shook my head. "No, thank you."

"Good. I will see you in theatre shortly." She smiled before turning and disappearing with her assistant following her behind the curtain that she pulled to separate me from Amy.

A few minutes later, an anaesthetist arrived and went through the formalities.

Just after 8.45am, a nurse arrived to take me down to theatre.

"Bye, ladies, all the best with your surgery."

"Bye. Good luck!" they chorused together.

"Thanks. I will see you on the ward after, we can catch up properly then." I turned back to the nurse waiting to take me down.

After locking my bag in the patient lockers, we walked towards theatre. The anaesthetist reappeared through double doors as I climbed onto the bed. He was a cheerful doctor with a warm smile.

"Right, let's get a hat on to cover up all that hair, nurse," he said to one of the staff who was busy prepping something behind me. She scooped my long hair up and tucked it inside a blue cap and placed my head back down.

"Now, just a small scratch." He wiped a cold swab across my right hand. I barely felt the cannula needle go in this time. I glanced up at the clock on the wall above: 8.53 am.

"Okay. I'm going to send you off to a nice little sleep now." He smiled, looking down at me as he pumped something into the cannula. "You might feel a cold sensation going up your arm." The cool feeling chased his words up to my elbow and I felt the inevitable slip into comfortable oblivion.

"Emily, your operation is over, you are in recovery."

I am aware of a woman's voice calling my name and slowly open my eyes to the familiar surrounds of recovery. The clock on the wall has moved to 11.36am. My mouth feels dry, and my throat is constricted. The oxygen mask over my mouth and nose whistles quietly.

"We can take this off now." A nurse smiles as she removes my mask. "My name is Amara and I'm going to be looking after you today in recovery."

She has long, black, braided hair with streaks of vibrant red ribbon woven through it and the most beautiful smile.

"Are you in any pain?"

I shake my head, still not fully awake or even aware of my body lying on this bed. My system is full of anaesthesia and pleasantly numb. I close my eyes and drift in and out of a drug-induced doze.

"How are you feeling?"

I open my eyes to Amara's smile. The room is filled with footsteps and mechanical beeps. I glance at the clock behind her: 12.16pm. I am through the second operation and feel no pain. I feel much more alert and aware of my surroundings, and that awareness brings a familiar recognition: my bladder is full.

"I'm okay, though ... I will need the toilet soon. I'm so sorry."

"You need to urinate now? "

"*I think I'd better,*" I whisper sheepishly.

Within moments, Amara and a colleague return and pull the blue curtain around in one well-rehearsed movement. "Can you lift your body up?" Amara asks.

I stretch my left arm gingerly across my body and grab the right arm rail as they lift me onto the bedpan. As I manoeuvre my body into place, I feel a tightness pull painfully across the right side of my neck. "*Ftttt*" I suck in air. The sharp pain fades almost immediately but the tightness remains.

"I will be back soon," Amara says, leaving me alone.

She appears moments later and despite being under these covers, I feel exposed. She slides the bedpan from under me and passes it to her colleague who disappears with it.

After she leaves, I lean over the bed and reach for my water cup. I have been in recovery for over an hour and my stomach is rumbling emptily. *I'm starving.*

As it approaches 1pm, a nurse greets Amara next to me. "Great news, Head and Neck have a bed ready for Emily, so she will be going up to the ward shortly." She smiles enthusiastically.

I am relieved to be leaving. Someone nearby is vomiting behind a curtain, and the noise is making me queasy.

Within twenty minutes she returns. "Unfortunately, the ward had to give your bed to an emergency case, so you are going to be staying down here with us until another one becomes available. Can you move Emily to the end of the paediatric recovery room until her bed is ready, please?"

Within a few moments, Amara, and another nurse wheel me and shortly after, another patient, to an empty paediatric bay at the end of the ward. It is quiet, away from the machines and monitors and vomiting patients. The walls are decorated cheerfully with cartoon murals.

"You both might be here for a while so can I get you a drink and maybe an ice cream or something to eat?" a different nurse asks.

Anything to soothe my parched throat sounds appealing. "*Yes please,*" I whisper, accepting the invitation willingly.

"Not yet, thanks," I hear the other patient decline weakly.

Amara passes me my bag and I unzip it, taking out my phone. I turn it on and text Paul, Mum, Ryan and Thomas and a handful of friends who have all been eagerly awaiting an update.

"*Surgery over, all went well, just sitting in recovery waiting for a bed. Will message later when settled xx*" I put my phone back in my bag and laid it across the bed.

"Let's sit you up there a bit." Amara adjusts my bed, propping me up so I am side by side to the other patient. I can't twist my body to see her, but her voice is familiar. It's Amy. She went in after me.

"How are you feeling?" I ask her.

"*Rough, but glad it's over,*" she whispers back.

"Here we are."

A nurse comes through the main door with a small cheese sandwich, pot of apple juice and tub of vanilla ice cream. I peel the lid from the juice and sip, wincing as I swallow. It feels sharp against my irritated throat. I take a second sip and swallow, this time with greater difficulty. I set it down and pull the lid from the ice cream, already melting and malleable. I suck a teaspoon of the cold ice cream and swallow past the strange tightness in my throat. It's so sweet and delicious, but I need to eat something more substantial. I tear a small piece of the soft sandwich and put it in my mouth, sucking it to soften it further. The sharpness of the cheese momentarily delights my palette, but it's too painful to swallow. I resign myself to the ice cream, it seems the easiest option.

"Hopefully you will feel better when you get up to the ward," I reassure Amy as I swallow another mouthful of ice cream with increasing difficulty.

Amara returns to the end of my bed just in time to catch me wincing as I force it down. "Is everything okay?" she asks.

"It just hurts to swallow," I croak, holding my neck.

Amara looks at my neck and I catch a look of concern as she

manoeuvres around to my right-hand side. "I'm just going to lay you down a moment."

She takes the ice cream from my hand, drops the bed, and removes the pillow from behind my head. "Can I get a hand in here?" she calls out.

Another nurse appears and her expression changes. Amara gently feels the right side of my neck and they glance at each other.

"Shall I press it?" the nurse on my left-hand side asks Amara.

"Yes."

The nurse reaches behind my head to the wall and presses something and suddenly a shrill alarm rings out. Within seconds the blue curtains are pulled around me separating me from Amy and face after face appears at the end of the bed, and each one has the same concerned look.

Panic sets in – my heart begins beating loudly in my chest.

What's happening?

I scream without uttering a word. I am too terrified to move.

"Can you call theatre and let Miss Jones know, please?" Amara instructs someone.

I'm flanked by three staff and four more are at the end of my bed watching me.

Amara places an oxygen mask over my face. "It's okay, Emily," she soothes, stroking my forehead for a second.

What's going on?

"Ok," Amara responds to someone calling from the main recovery room, then turns back to me. "Emily, your surgeon is still in theatre, we are going to get Miss Jones' registrar to look at your surgical wound."

The surgeon's registrar appeared from behind the blue curtain. "Hi there, I'm just going to have a feel of your neck, Emily... Sorry," she apologises as she leans over me and presses around my dressing. A strange feeling pulls from the right side of my neck.

"Can we open the SCOOP kit please?" she instructs within seconds. I hear a snipping sound. Someone cuts the black cable ties of the opaque plastic box next to me.

"I need a theatre prepped now please!" she calls to the staff at the end of the bed.

One nurse leaves. The anaesthetist appears around the curtain; his expression is serious. He leaves immediately.

Mum... Mum, I'm so scared. I want my mum.

Thump. Thump. Thump.

My heart is pumping faster and faster.

Two staff stand either side of me. One removes the dressing as the other is prepping something next to me.

Paper is ripping. The sounds of metal touching clinks by my left ear.

Someone else is on my right is holding something to my neck. I don't know what it is, but it feels soft.

I feel the scissors snip and something is pulled out from my neck.

I can feel them opening my neck and pushing something in.

A nurse is holding a wad of sterile dressings in my open wound. The kind blonde one who brought me my ice cream.

I feel pressure inside my throat, but there is no pain.

I cannot move. I am frozen in fear.

Am I going to die? My eyes search the staff's faces for answers.

Moments later, maybe more or less, I don't know, I've no sense of time, my surgeon appears by my bed and puts her hand on my leg. "There seems to be a bit of a bleed, so we are going to take you back to theatre and sort this out, okay?" She says it so calmly as she pats my leg.

Thank God you are here.

The blonde angel to my left holds onto my neck to stem the oozing blood flow. Amara is standing beside her.

"You are doing so well, Emily. Are you okay?" She is stroking my left hand.

"I'm scared." I feel a single tear run down my left cheek.

I can't cry now. I don't want it to hurt.

"I know, it's okay, we will look after you." Amara is rubbing my hand gently. "Is there anyone you would like us to contact?"

Someone is at the end of my bed is holding up my bag. She has my phone in her hand.

"*Paul*," I whisper, pulling the oxygen mask off. "The number's in my phone. Please don't tell my mum or children!" I cry out, weakly.

I can't speak. Why can't I speak? Oh God, I can't bear them to know this is happening. What if ... I die?

My phone is put by my hand and my thumb placed over it to unlock it. "Look for Paul on WhatsApp... Please ... don't tell ... my mum or sons..." I trail off as the oxygen mask is placed back over my face.

People surround me and the bed begins to move quickly, out of the room and into a corridor. The angel in blue scrubs is still by my side walking sideways, holding my neck together, gently pressing down.

I'm pushed through some double doors, then two more, into a bright white room. The lights feel blinding. People in blue scrubs are gathered around me watching me intently me as others quickly scramble a theatre bed to move me onto. They're talking about things I don't understand.

"We are going to move you to this bed now," someone tells me. There are eight or so staff surrounding me, holding a piece of the sheet underneath me.

"Everyone ready. One, two, three and ... lift."

My body is lifted to the left and placed on a theatre bed. I can see the bloodied bed I've left behind in my peripheral vision.

People are talking, giving instructions. I can hear metal instruments and plastic rustling.

My angel in blue scrubs is still by my side. She leans over me, putting something new, something softer into my open neck. She hasn't left my side.

I feel something unfamiliar around my neck. A warm trail is running down my chest, a strange cool streak is chasing after it. It's running under my left breast and down my side. It's settling under my back, it's like a warm bath beneath me.

What is this strange feeling? Oh God, it's my blood.

My blood is leaving my body in a steady flow. People are moving around me in the white room. Machines are beeping, and I'm suspended in stillness. I can't move my body. I'm too terrified to. I'm staring at the doctors' and nurses' faces.

Why are they looking at me like that? Am I going to die? Is my life over ... like this? I want my mum.

Someone else has arrived. They're standing at the edge of the room staring. He is not wearing blue like the others. He is wearing a black t-shirt. I can't turn my body to look at him, but he is there. I feel him. Now he is joined by another man who's wearing a suit. They're not moving.

Why can't the staff see them?

Who are you? Why are you standing there?

The answer is instant.

"It's Dad, honey."

Oh Dad... Dad... Granda...? What are you doing here? I see you; I feel you, Dad.

I can feel their immense love, radiating over me, they are wrapping me in it, with safety and comfort.

I'm not scared anymore.

They step back.

Why is it so bright in here? That overhead light is getting brighter. I think it's getting ... whiter. I feel ... so peaceful.

I'm lying on this bed; I know I am ... but ... but ... I can't feel my body. I'm not scared now. What is this feeling, it's so pure and loving ... it's so comforting.

I feel as if I'm being held above my body by love itself and it is filling this entire room.

Why can't the staff feel it too?

I feel invisibly suspended in a state of bliss, an overwhelming state of love and I know I am surrounded by *something.*

I sense a crowd gathering near the ceiling. I can't make them out, they're like shadows.

Who are all these people?

I stare at the ceiling tiles. *Why is the ceiling so white?*

From the left-hand corner of the ceiling, something speaks to me without the need for words. I hear the voice so clearly, but it is not my dad's, nor Granda's, and it is not from any of the staff. They are oblivious.

"It doesn't hurt here, Emily."

I know. I reply without speaking.

"There is no pain, only love."

I ... feel it. It's so ... beautiful.

"It only hurts for those you leave behind."

Thomas... Jack... Mum... Paul. My awareness immediately comes back to my two beautiful sons, my mum. And Paul.

It speaks again. *"Nothing else matters here. Only love."*

I want to stay here in the company of this loving presence forever. Nothing else matters now. Only this love.

Time has ceased to exist.

This feeling of love and serenity is so overwhelmingly beautiful yet somehow familiar.

I've known this before.

"Emily, are you okay?"

I look up at the angel who is still holding dressings in my neck, stemming the blood flow.

"*It's so ... beautiful isn't it? I feel so peaceful,*" I whisper, smiling at her.

She stares at the clinician opposite her who is doing something to the cannula in my right hand. "That's not what your vitals are telling us," she says with a concerned tone, without breaking her gaze from him.

This emergency is unfolding around me, but I am perfectly still. Just a person lying on a theatre bed in a white room. It isn't me, just my body. My soul is effortlessly peaceful and bathing in this beautiful love.

Something inside me speaks to the ceiling. *My boys. I can't leave them.*

The anaesthetist's face appears over the top of my head, gently moving my hair away from my forehead as he adjusts something on the mask over my face. I look up into his brown eyes. He's not *just* a doctor, he's human. I feel his compassion.

You make me feel safe.

"It's okay now, Emily. We might have to put you into a special sleep in Critical Care whilst these tissues heal. We are going to look after you now," he soothes me.

I believe you... Your eyes ... they're so kind.

"Take a nice deep breath in for me."

I can feel my body again. I gasp and struggle in the plastic mask with the strong chemical smell. I can't catch my breath.

I can't breathe properly. Why can't I breathe?

My cheeks puff out against the mask frantically.

I ...can't... bre...

Beep... Beep... Beep.

CRITICAL CARE

14 SEPTEMBER 2023

"*Emily, you are in recovery; the surgery is over.*"

I heard someone's faint words and familiar machine sounds in some distant part of my consciousness. I slipped back into my dreams in a faraway place.

Sometime later, I was transferred to the Critical Care unit. I had no recollection of arriving.

A hissing sound and a jolt around both my legs roused me around 5pm. Two plastic cuffs were wrapped around my calves, hugging them tightly as they expanded and squeezed mechanically every thirty seconds, before deflating rapidly with a sharp burst of air. I was unable to have a blood-thinning injection having already experienced one bleed. The cuffs would minimise the risk of blood clots as I lay in Critical Care.

I wiggled my toes, and my left foot caught painfully on something under the cover. I winced, freeing it. On the top of my foot, already bruised heavily, was another cannula taped down. I didn't know when it was put in, or why. My arms and wrists had several bits of sticking tape over cotton-wool pads like a human pin cushion. Each one with dark, purple bruises already forming where they had tried to take blood.

What happened to me down there?

I was attached to machines on my right-hand side, a fabric cuff wrapped around my right arm, automatically checking my blood pressure every thirty minutes. There were tubes and wires attached to my cannula and chest, and something clipped onto my finger. I felt high and disorientated on a cocktail of surgical drugs and strong painkillers, but a strange euphoria swept over me. I was higher still on the life-affirming experience in the theatre.

It doesn't matter what happened. I'm alive!

I felt momentarily giddy with the excitement at the realisation.

"Hello Emily, welcome to Critical Care. My name is Sarah and I'm going to be looking after you for a while. Are you in any pain?" a nurse said, moving to my left side, and placing her hand on mine. I shook my head. "I have a visitor to see you. Is it okay to bring them in?" she asked.

"*Yes please*," I whispered. My throat felt dry and scratched and my voice was barely audible.

I glimpsed Paul's face, following behind the nurse. He looked terrified, his face ashen.

"Oh, Emily," he exclaimed, his face crumpling with relief. He pulled up a chair beside me and gently picked up my left hand, placing it in his. His warmth, instantly comforting. "I've been so worried, Emily. I missed a call from the hospital, and I didn't know what happened ... and they couldn't tell me when I called back..." He trailed off.

He was staring at my neck and his eyes scanned over all the machines and wires. "Oh, my darling, you poor thing, I'm so sorry you went through this." Paul's eyes filled with tears and his hand trembled over mine. His familiar face grounded me to the reality of what had happened, and the euphoria was beginning to dissipate with an earthly bump.

The curtain swished back revealing my surgeon, still in her operating scrubs. "Hello."

"This is my ... er... This is Paul," I said introducing him. My husband ... separated husband ... friend. It was too complex to explain.

Miss Jones smiled at Paul in acknowledgement. "Hello. How are you feeling?" she asked, turning to me, gently examining around my dressing.

"I'm okay, a bit bruised and sore."

"Yes, that's to be expected. You had a bleed from a vein in your neck on the right side. There was some scar tissue from the previous surgery and as that area of the neck is very vascular, these things can happen. The bruising might track down here a little further," she said, pointing to my chest.

"Was this because I tried to eat something?"

Was all this my fault?

"No, it was nothing you did, I assure you." She patted my leg through the covers. It was a subtle gesture of kindness that spoke volumes."You may find your voice a little hoarse over the next few days. There was some bruising of the left vocal cord, but it should settle down."

"Okay."

"Right. I will leave you to rest now. Good evening." She left, pulling the curtain back behind her.

"*Can you get my bag for me, please? I need to text the boys and Mum.*"

Paul picked up my bag from under the chair and passed me my phone. I turned the camera on and flipped it around. It was the first time I'd seen the extent of my emergency surgery. My neck had a ring of swelling all around it, bloated with fluid and blood, and already heavily bruised in places. My face was ghostly grey. I felt a wave of emotion rising. It was shock.

"Can you take a picture of me please to send to the kids? I don't want them or Mum to know I'm in Critical Care."

I faked a smile, holding my thumbs up. Paul took the picture and passed the phone back. I looked grey and shattered but my false smile hid my location or the extent of the day's events. I sent a simple text: "*Shattered and off to sleep but all okay,*" and closed my phone.

We both glanced at the clock. It was almost 7pm and my hand to hold had to leave. Visiting in Critical Care was restricted. Seeing me was both distressing and comforting for Paul. I was inside the experience and seemed calmer than him. He, on the other hand, had to see someone he loved, bruised, and bloodied, in Critical Care and hooked up to machines.

Paul stood up and leaned over the bed, gently kissing my forehead. "I will come back tomorrow evening. I will leave my phone on all night. Please call me if you need to talk, okay?"

"I'm okay, promise. It's over now, I'm safe." I squeezed his hand, smiling weakly. Paul left and I closed my eyes, exhausted.

Moments later, I heard a familiar voice approaching and my name mentioned. A nurse pulled back the curtain for another doctor, still in scrubs.

"Ah, here she is, the cheese-sandwich girl!" My anaesthetist chuckled.

"I didn't even get to eat the sandwich, honest!" I croaked, trying to convince him I hadn't caused the bleed.

"I know. How are you feeling now?" he asked, with a more serious tone.

"Glad to be here! Bit tired and sore."

"That's understandable. Thankfully, the bleed wasn't in your thyroid bed, so we didn't have to put you into an induced sleep."

"Thank you for looking after me today, doctor. I remember

your face and words just before I went to sleep." The painkillers were lowering my inhibitions, but I meant it.

"That's okay. Good, good, right, get some rest now." He left, pulling the curtain across.

As it approached 7.20pm, a group of different nurses appeared for the shift change. The handover meeting place was near the end of my bed at an impromptu nurses' station with a computer next to the windowsill seat. I could hear the various patient details being discussed. It was one nurse to one patient in Critical Care.

"In bed eleven, we have Emily Johnson. She is a critical bleed, post-completion thyroidectomy. She had 10mg of..."

My brain didn't grasp anymore. *Critical bleed. It was critical?* It was the first time I had heard those words, and it shook me.

A little while later a nurse pulled back my curtain. "Hello, I'm Seema. I will be taking care of you tonight." She approached my bed smiling, before resting her hand on my left arm. I was grateful for her touch.

"Would you like an ice lolly, or maybe some ice cream?"

"I'll try an ice lolly."

As the numbing anaesthesia wore off, I felt like I'd been hit by a truck. My chest felt painful and bruised and my neck felt sawn in two. The lolly's icy texture readily melted on my tongue and with each successful swallow, my confidence grew. I reached for a cup of water beside the bed and eagerly sipped it.

Seema returned. "Have you used the toilet since you arrived here?

"No, no I haven't."

"Do you want a catheter tonight?"

"Um ... no. I'm okay." I couldn't face any more prodding and poking.

"Let's get you a bedpan, or we can try to get you up onto a commode."

"I'll try the commode." It seemed a more dignified option.

Seema reappeared with a commode chair and disconnected my calf cuffs and monitors before swinging my legs to the edge of the bed. I was too weak to dwell on the loss of dignity as she removed my underwear. Seema lifted me under my arms and manoeuvred me onto the commode before leaving me alone. My body felt heavy and cumbersome. Even urinating required energy I didn't have.

"Are you finished?" Seema slipped in behind the curtain.

"Yes, thank you."

She steadied me to my feet and cleaned me, before pulling up my underwear and returning me to my bed. Once reconnected to the monitors, wires, and cuffs, I watched her wheel the commode away. There was nothing I could do but surrender to the experience of being cared for, even with the most intimate tasks.

Sleep eluded me, the scenes from recovery and theatre, vividly replaying over and over. The noise of the medical machines around me merged in my mind, becoming part of the story. I remembered the feeling of the blood running down my body.

I thought I was going to die.

The comforting feeling that my dad and Granda were there with me and something else that brought with it that feeling of immense love and peace.

What happened in that room? How critical was I?

The questions tumbled over and over. It was too much to process and despite feeling exhausted, my mind was on high alert and racing.

Critical Care was a noisy environment. I was in a bay with three other patients, all with their own medical monitoring equipment. Our machines ticked along like medical metronomes, just a little out of sync, leaving a continuous soundtrack of beeps and puffs of discharging air. Occasionally the patient diagonally across from me would rouse from his semi-conscious state and mutter incoherently.

Aside from the noise, I couldn't settle. It was as if my surgeries had sent every atom in my body into a spin. My skin felt itchy, my insides restless with adrenaline. I pushed my earbuds in and turned on a sleep meditation. The melodic piped music and hushed waterfall sounds worked, momentarily soothing me into sleep until the cuffs around my calves discharged, startling me once again.

I was dwelling on the edge of exhaustion. I glanced at the time: 1.36am. *Please let me sleep*, I pleaded with my overactive brain, closing my eyes, and settling back into the meditation music and a welcome doze.

Something pulls me back from my sleep. A fluttering sensation in my chest, the flutter becomes a pump, gathering pace, faster and faster and I realise it's my heart – pumping furiously.

I don't feel right. Oh God ... am I bleeding out?

My heartbeat is quickening to a strange and uncomfortable pace as if preparing to burst through my chest. I feel around my dressing searching for blood. There is none. Panic sets in. "Can somebody help me, please?" I call, croakily.

I pull the monitor from my finger, knowing it will trigger an alarm. Within seconds the monitor alarm beeps, and a different nurse appears from behind my blue curtain. "I don't feel right... My heart is racing."

"Can I get some help in here please?" she calls.

An alarm rings – a different one this time. Within moments

another nurse and two doctors arrive. The bright lights go on. They are talking about my racing heart in phrases I don't understand.

"183 bpm resting, supraventricular tachycardia."

A doctor begins to draw blood from my arm, it's painful. No blood will come, he moves down to my wrist. "I'm just going test your magnesium and calcium levels."

My arms and legs begin to shake uncontrollably. I'm terrified. "*What's happening to me?*" I whisper.

"Your heart is beating a little fast, but we are not sure why. Sometimes this can happen after a thyroidectomy if the body releases a surge of hormones."

The doctors begin to discuss the blood results they've evaluated at the end of the bed. In surgery they knew I was bleeding; they could see it and knew how to fix it. No one knows why my heartbeat is reaching dangerous levels and it is frightening me.

"Right let's pump through magnesium, stat."

The staff are surrounding me again, concerned looks upon their faces. The doctor hooks a bag of liquid magnesium to my cannula after flushing it with saline. It feels strangely cold pushing against the warmth of the blood in my veins. The tremors ease and my heart settles down to a more normal rhythm, though elevated still.

"*Could this be from all the anaesthetic drugs? I had two today. Or stress? I was pretty scared,*" I whisper.

"It's unlikely it was stress as you were sleeping. We've given hundreds of anaesthetics, and it doesn't normally cause this kind of reaction. We will monitor you closely. Try to get some rest now." He smiles, patting my forearm.

The two doctors and nurses leave and pull my curtain across, and the lights go off once again, but I can't sleep. I feel alone. Scared and childlike.

Is this how you felt, Dad? I'm so sorry I wasn't there for you.

I place my right hand in my left and close my eyes and pretend someone is sitting next to me, holding my hand.

Just after 2am, Seema appears and pulls the curtain back. "What happened?! I leave you to go on my break and all this excitement happens!" she says, grinning as she holds my left hand.

I squeeze her hand, grabbing it tightly for comfort. *Please don't leave me.* I plead silently.

Does she know how comforting it feels to hold her hand?

"You must rest now, okay? Here is your call button – push this if you need me."

"Okay."

I close my eyes and drift in and out of light dreams, still aware of an orchestra of mechanical sounds in the background. I am exhausted and not even the cuffs discharging stir me this time.

Boom.

Without warning, the fluttering is back.

Pump, pump, pump – my heart is racing again.

I don't like this feeling. What is happening?

I look at the monitor: 181 bpm. It is 4.06am... It's been over three hours since the first episode.

I push the call button and Seema appears within seconds. Within moments, two doctors and a nurse arrive. The bright lights come back on. The same doctor begins trying to pull blood from my fragile veins. He moves to my left wrist this time. There are no more places on my arm left to try. The needle stings and pulls painfully but he draws enough to test it at the end of my bed. My arms and legs begin twitching uncontrollably.

I'm scared, I don't like this feeling, please make it stop.

"Your calcium and magnesium levels are within normal range. I'm going to give you some beta blockers through your IV line, and this should settle your heart down into a normal rhythm. We might have to refer you to cardiologist if these episodes continue."

The young doctor smiles at me reassuringly as he slowly syringes the medication into my cannula. His blond, textured hair hangs over his forehead. The streaks in it appear naturally sun-kissed, as if between shifts, he is running into the surf with a board under his arm. Only in a wetsuit – this is England, not the Australian coast I once lived beside.

My heart settles and I relax, reassured by the doctor's obvious relief.

"That's better. We'll pop on some heart sensors for an ECG and do some periodical tests. Seema will be with you shortly to set it up."

Seema appears moments later and pulls my covers down to my waist. She lowers my gown, exposing my chest. She lifts my breasts, attaching the sticky pads underneath in various places.

Despite my exhaustion, my cheeks burn with humiliation. There is something so disarming about laying under sterile white light and the most intimate parts of your body laid bare and being handled. There is nothing extraordinary about my breasts, but I've endured a love/hate relationship with them most of my adult life. It is worse now my half century milestone is sending them on an inevitable journey towards my armpits.

I pull the gown up covering my chest and seconds later Seema pulls it back down for another tape position.

"Sorry," she murmurs under her breath, aware of my discomfort.

After the ECG, my heart rate remains higher than normal,

but the beta blockers settle it down to the top end of normal range. Seema leaves me to rest just after 5.00am.

Exhausted, I finally close my eyes and drifted in and out of a light sleep, periodically disturbed by the discharge of the cuffs around my calves.

Someone returns to my bedside and stands beside me, lightly holding my right hand. I stir from my sleep, without opening my eyes. It feels so safe, so familiar and warm. I lie there for a moment savouring the comforting feel of their touch.

I open my eyes expecting Seema there, ready to adjust my drip, but I am alone. It spooks me a little. I haven't imagined it; I know I haven't... Someone was here holding my hand.

Apart from the machine noises, the ward is still in low-lit semi-darkness and hushed. I may be exhausted, but I am lucid and am not mistaken. Someone has been with me.

"*Was that you, Dad?*" I whisper into the darkness.

It was impossible to return to sleep and just after 6.30am I gave up trying. The blinds were already open, and the sky was brushed with cerise, pink, and orange streaks that faded into the bright morning sunlight bouncing off the bay. The sun felt like my anchor point, the only familiar thing about Critical Care. It was a strange and frightening world of its own. In there the outside world ceased to exist.

Seema appeared at 7am with a small white pot containing my thyroid medication. It was the first day of the rest of my life on medication, but I didn't care. It was a small price to pay to remove the cancer. I took my tablets and lay back once again, shifting uncomfortably on the upright bed, strapped to the monitors and cuffs expanding monotonously.

I could hear the faint voices of the nurses gathering for the handover before starting their shifts. I strained to hear my name and caught some words ... *thyroid ... critical bleed ... heart episodes ... ECG.*

Just after 7.35am a nurse popped her head around the side of the curtain. "Hi, I'm Moe, I'm going to be looking after you today. Breakfast is coming soon!" she said cheerfully.

I could hear the clatter of the breakfast trolley approaching the ward entrance.

"Have you been able to use the bathroom yet?"

"No, just the commode but I would like to go to the bathroom today," I asked, hoping to avoid any further assisted toilet episodes.

"I can get you a walking frame and you can try after breakfast. Is that okay?"

"Yes, thank you."

"Here is your breakfast!" a cheery voice called to me from behind the curtain before an orderly came around and placed a tray on my table. "Orange juice and porridge, with a sachet of honey," she announced enthusiastically.

I'd not eaten since arriving at Critical Care, only ice lollies, and suddenly the grey-looking porridge seemed inviting, despite its watery appearance. I slowly ate it all, scraping clean the dark blue plastic bowl. I sipped at the orange juice; its citrus tang tasting sharper than usual after the sweetness of the honey.

Moe returned to check on me a few minutes later. "Oh, you ate it all. Well done! Right, shall we get you up and over to the bathroom?"

They were as keen to get me moving as I was. "Okay, let's give it try."

Moe disconnected the monitors and cuffs, unwrapping them from my calves. The relief was instant. She carefully pulled my legs to the edge of the bed and steadied me to standing, then guided my hands forward to grasp the walking frame.

I slowly nudged it forward shuffling behind, bracing my shoulders stiffly to support my neck. I moved past the other two patients, one conscious, one not, finally able to put faces to the voice and moans I had been listening to for hours. I saw the Critical Care unit for the first time in its entirety, as Moe led me to the bathroom.

"Would you like me to come in with you?"

"No... I will be okay I think," I declined, ignoring the dizzy weakness in my body.

"Okay, I'll wait outside. Leave it unlocked and call me if you need me."

She opened the bathroom door wide enough to allow me to enter on the walking frame. I shuffled in and closed the door behind me. I parked the walking frame and gently lowered myself onto the toilet. Just the simple act of going to the toilet unaided felt triumphant.

Above the basin was a mirror, capturing my reflection. My curly hair was already knotted and piled up on my head and my billowing white hospital gown barely fixed at the back, the ties coming undone. I had several balls of cotton wool taped in various places on my limbs and two cannulas still taped in place.

I flushed the toilet and moved carefully to the sink. I could see myself properly now. I gasped and felt tears rising. My face was flushed bright red and my neck, swollen and spongy with dark purple bruises running around my neck. It snaked behind my right ear and down to my breasts then mingled with a putrid yellow and green tinge across my entire chest. I looked like I had been in a dreadful accident, and I felt it.

I ran my fingers under the warm water. It was somehow reviving. Perhaps it was a reminder of normality outside this place. I washed my hands slowly, rubbing foamy bubbles gently around the cannula. I pulled the flannel out of my bag and soaked it in warm water, before holding it up to my face. It smelt of home, its warmth and familiar scent momentarily comforting. I dabbed it around my face, and around the nape of my neck ignoring the uncomfortable pull of the cannula on my hand. Resting the cloth on the side of the sink, I pulled out my brush and toothpaste and slowly cleaned my teeth, a simple act which felt like the first ownership of my own body since leaving home.

I didn't have the energy or pain tolerance to wash the rest of my body, but I needed to get out of the gown. I pulled at the ties of the already loose gown and let it fall to the floor, kicking it aside with my foot. I glanced up and saw my body in its entirety, naked apart from pants and the dot-to-dot ECG stickers and taped-down cotton-wool balls, disguising bruises forming underneath them. I saw the reflection of a battered body I hadn't been able to look at in a mirror for years; the body I loathed because in my eyes, it wasn't slim or toned enough. A body I resented and verbally abused.

"I'm so ... sorry," I cried out, running my hands over the bruises, tears now running down my cheeks. "I'm so, so sorry." I was exhausted and in pain and my emotions were on the same unpredictable ride as my heart rhythm.

"Everything okay in there?" Moe called through the door.

"Yes ... yes I'm fine, just ... getting dressed."

"Oh, well done."

I reached over and pulled my leggings and a red t-shirt – the same clothes I'd worn into the hospital – off the walking frame and through my tears, slowly got dressed. I dragged the discarded gown across the floor with my toe and slowly squatted to pick it up, before turning to the door and opening it.

Moe led me back to my bed and re-attached the monitors. My heart was racing a little from the exertion of my bathroom trip. I sank back into the pillows, still propped up and closed my eyes.

Later that morning, the doctors decided I would need to

remain in Critical Care until the following day. My heart rhythms had been a cause for concern.

Lunch arrived and it was another liquid one – soup – which I devoured, much to the delight of Moe. They weren't used to patients eating. Moe periodically topped up the painkillers and delivered ice lollies to keep my swelling down. They were fast becoming the highlight of my stay in Critical Care.

Shortly after lunch, the now-familiar strange feeling began in my chest. My monitor alarm sounded to alert Moe to my heart rate rising. From nowhere, it had jumped to 152 bpm resting. Not as fast as the night before, but still uncomfortably fast.

Moe appeared within seconds. "Everything okay, Emily?"

"My heart just started again. I was lying here not doing anything."

She stood watching the machine, waiting to see if it would settle. Within a minute or so it slowly returned to 92 – still high, but better."I'm going to chat with the doctor, I will be back in a moment."

I nodded. It seemed less frightening in daylight. I lay back on the pillows, closing my eyes, awaiting her return. I needed to stay calm. I put my hand over my heart. I could feel it pumping under my palm. "*It's okay. It's all going to be okay,*" I whispered to my heart, soothing my body gently as I followed my breath slowing down.

Moe returned. "We are going to do another ECG now." She began re-connecting the wires between my body and the ECG equipment. The test lasted a minute or two and appeared normal, although a little faster than it should be.

"I'm sure this is all the stress of yesterday you know. I think this is my body reacting," I said, watching Moe as she detached the electrodes.

"Maybe, but we need to keep an eye on it. Right, get some rest now." She pulled the curtain back across.

My mind and body were craving sleep, but I was too tense. I watched the clock above the window slowly tick around to visiting time.

"Unfortunately, we cannot allow flowers in this ward, but I will pop these in some water in the staff room until you leave," a nurse holding a bunch of sunflowers informed a visitor near the entrance.

"*Oh, okay no worries, thank you.*"

It was my brother's voice. A wave of nerves and excitement swept over me. It had been four years since I had seen him. We periodically spoke on the phone, but I'd distanced myself from everyone when my family's mental health declined in 2018.

By 2020, my weight had ballooned, and I was deeply ashamed of myself and struggling with binge-eating disorder. I knew my family loved me, but I still couldn't face them seeing me that way, so I stopped contacting them. When they reached out to me, I faked happiness. I was a good actor.

My apprehension dissolved when Ryan and April, his wife, arrived and hugged me warmly. We chatted enthusiastically for half an hour as if the last four years had evaporated. I'd missed them both.

"Mum doesn't know I'm in here, does she? You didn't tell her, did you?" Mum was staying with Ryan for a couple of weeks.

"No, I haven't said anything, but I will now. I wanted to see you for myself and make sure you were okay first."

Now she would know everything. I could no longer hide it was cancer,

Moe came in mid-chat with more painkillers, and it seemed a natural way to end their visit. We hugged and vowed to get together again soon.

As I waved them goodbye, regret washed over me. So many

years had slipped by without being in each other's lives. It had been such a waste of love.

Paul arrived later that afternoon. He'd left Billy with a friend of mine, Lexi, who'd baked a cake earlier that day and sent in a piece for me. I eagerly sucked on the soft, warm cake; it was the tastiest thing I had eaten in days. I closed my eyes savouring the sweet strawberry jam filling, crunching every little seed between my teeth as if it were the first time I had tasted strawberries.

Paul seemed calmer. Seeing me dressed and sitting up in bed reassured him. I didn't want visiting time to end – Paul was a tangible link to normal life outside Critical Care and when he left, I returned to the world of medical monitors and my thoughts.

As the clock approached 7.25pm, the nurses gathered at the station near the end of my bed for the shift handover. Seema appeared from behind the curtain, smiling.

"Ah, here's my favourite patient," she said, taking my hands in hers and holding them tightly.

I beamed, relieved to see her familiar face. "Hello. Can you do me a favour? I have something for you and the other staff in that bag. Could you pass it to me please?" I pointed at a cloth bag on the chair behind my bed.

I worked for a large company that sold luxury body and bath products. When this journey began, I asked my work colleagues to save some stock for me when it became available. By the time I had my second operation, I had quite a collection and brought a large bag in with me. Due to the turn of events, I had not yet been able to hand them out to everyone who'd cared for me. Seema placed the bag at the end of the bed.

"Thank you for being so kind to me and looking after me. Please take something for yourself. These are from my team at work." I gestured, leaning forward, pulling the bag open.

"For me? Oh no ... it's okay, it's my job to look after you." Seema shook her head.

"Please, I want you to."

She hesitated momentarily, then reached into the bag and chose one product, unscrewing the lid to smell its lavender scent. "Mmm, it smells lovely, thank you. I will give this to my son."

The night before, Seema had told me about the son she cared for in between her nursing shifts.

"Please, take another for yourself then," I encouraged.

"No ... no it's fine."

"Please, there's plenty."

Seema's eyes lit up and she dived into the bag and pulled out another body cream. "Thank you so much!" She reached forward to hug me gently.

"Can you tell the other staff when you finish your handover to come and take something for themselves too?

"Yes, I will." She disappeared behind the curtain.

I could hear the nurses' excited chatter as they settled down to handover. Shortly after, Moe returned with a handful of other staff.

"Oh, what's all this?" Moe asked, looking at the bag of goodies at the end of the bed.

"Thank you all for being so kind and for looking after me. Please help yourself to something."

"Are you sure?" Moe questioned.

"Yes, please help yourself."

"Okay!" Moe pulled out a pot of body cream. "Thank you so much." she beamed, turning to her colleagues who were watching.

"Please, choose something."

The nurses turned and grinned at each other and helped themselves, before thanking me and returning to work. Bringing a little joy to the staff gifted me a glimmer of normality and uplifted me.

The following morning there was no glorious sunrise to watch. Stormy clouds brought heavy rains that drove against the large windows all morning, between loud claps of thunder. The oppressive grey light amplified the sterility of the fluorescent ward lighting.

After breakfast, I eased myself out of bed and walked to the bathroom on the walking frame. It felt a little easier to move and seemed like enormous progress from my position just twenty-four hours earlier.

Alison, my nurse for the day, smiled at me as I approached the toilet. "Look at you go. Well done. I'm right here if you need anything."

"Thank you, will do." I felt steadier on my feet, yet still grateful for the walking frame.

I parked the frame by the sink and looked up at my reflection. My hair was dishevelled and piled on my head in a crude bun. The curls were beginning to mat in knots from lying in bed for three days. I glanced down at my bruised chest, raising my neck a little to examine the swelling which had created purple rolls running around my neck. I looked grey and washed out and the lack of sleep was amplifying my sickly pallor.

I still had no change of clothes and the effort of washing from the small sink didn't feel like a valuable use of the little energy I had left. I manoeuvred the walker around and edged my way to the door and shuffled back to my bed.

The surfing doctor appeared at the end of my bed ten minutes later. "Good morning. How are you feeling today?"

"I'm okay, tired. Still not slept really."

"Yes, Critical Care is not the quietest place," he said, shaking his head empathetically. "I'm happy for you to be discharged from here today. You'll be moved up to the Head and Neck ward shortly, once a bed is ready for you."

"I can't go home yet?" I asked, deflated. I desperately wanted to wash and get some sleep.

"No, I'm afraid not. Hopefully, you can go home tomorrow but we need to keep you in tonight for observation on the ward."

"Okay, thank you for everything."

"That's okay. You take care." He stepped away, behind the curtain to the patient in the bay next door.

I climbed off the bed and slowly gathered my belongings together before getting back in. I pushed my earbuds in and lay back, closing my eyes. The gentle relaxation music blocked out the ward sounds.

Breathe in... Breathe out.

Breathe in... Breathe out.

I could feel my heart rate slowing down. I felt as if I were sinking into the bed with a comfortable heaviness. The words in my mind traced the movement of my breath, sending me somewhere far away from the hospital and into a doze.

"*Hello Emily, your bed is ready on the ward.*"

A voice pulled me back from the peaceful place I'd finally found.

Alison had arrived with a wheelchair. "Let's get you into this."

Still dazed, I climbed up and into the wheelchair as she took my bag and hung it over the handle, placing my notes across my knees.

"I'm just going to see who can take you upstairs. Won't be long."

"No problem, thank you."

The wheelchair was facing the bed, looking across the back of the hospital towards the bay behind it. The rain had stopped but the sky was still heavy with thundery purple clouds.

I looked at my bed. It was the first time I had properly observed my space in Critical Care. A total of eight machines were stacked on top of one another, all linked to a monitor. Each one had been responsible for measuring a different function of my body. There was a tangle of wires and disconnected drips with empty bags hanging from a stand. A SCOOP kit, still sealed, sat on the unit behind the bed in front of a window with a view of nowhere, just a brick wall opposite.

I looked up at the clock, anchoring myself back into time and stared out of the large window across the dark sky threatening to rain again. Something caught my eye across the back of the building amongst the aluminium ducts and brickwork. A lone butterfly fluttered in front of the building. It seemed so out of place. There were no trees, no greenery to entice it. I had just been put in a wheelchair facing that way for the first time in three days and there it was – a butterfly.

Thanks, Dad.

I sat watching its delicate movement for a moment or two until footsteps approached from behind me.

"Right then, let's get you up to the ward." Alison had returned to take me herself. She spun the wheelchair around and pushed me towards the exit.

I felt a little lost. Critical Care, though uncomfortable and frightening at times, had been my safe space for three days. The staff had become familiar and there was comfort in that familiarity. Alison wheeled me through a door and corridors I didn't recall coming through and it provoked feelings I couldn't label. I was taken back to the ward I'd been on after my first surgery and through a stroke of good luck, the only space left for me was a private side room near the nurse's station.

Once settled in and the routine observations done, I was left alone, and the door closed behind me. I sat on the edge of the bed facing the window. The wall opposite housed another wing of the hospital. A flash of lightning lit up the hospital walls and a loud clap of thunder heralded the start of more heavy autumn rain. I returned to my bed and watched the rain hitting the window, silently crying.

Opposite my bed was a large wall clock. The room was blissfully quiet, the only sounds were the rain and the mechanical clicking of time ticking by, occasionally accompanied by the muffled voices of the nurses outside my door. I had discouraged visitors that day thinking I would be going home and was too exhausted to entertain any conversation.

Just after five, dinner arrived and I sat on my bed, facing the rainy window eating the feast before me: a jacket potato with cheese and boiled vegetables. I scooped a mouthful of the potato into my mouth. The buttery cheesy flavour melted on my tongue. I closed my eyes and savoured the texture. Food had never tasted so good.

After dinner, I climbed back into bed, my hair still piled on my head, wearing the same clothes I'd worn into hospital three days earlier. I had delayed speaking to my sons in Critical Care but now settled on the ward, I could no longer avoid calling Thomas and Jack.

"Hi Mum, how are you?" Jack answered and swapped the call to a video chat. I had avoided any visual contact since my surgery, not wanting them to see me in the state I was in, or the attached to so many wires.

"I'm good, how are you both?"

"Mum ... your neck!" Jack was visibly taken back by my appearance.

"I know, it's a bit bruised," I replied, minimising my appearance.

Thomas appeared behind Jack. "How come you are still in hospital?"

"Okay, listen... I've got something to tell you both. I'm fine now I promise, but ... I had a bit of a bleed in my neck after the surgery, after I texted you Thomas, and I had to go back into surgery. I've been in Critical Care since then. I didn't tell you because I didn't want you to worry. Honestly, I'm fine now, it's okay."

"Mum!" Jack exclaimed before disappearing from view.

He passed the phone to Thomas and stood up; the angle of the phone changed towards the ceiling. "Why didn't you tell us? Are you okay?" I could hear the panic in Jack's voice.

Thomas was stunned into silence. Their reactions were exactly the reason why I hadn't told them and now it seemed it was the right decision.

"I didn't want to worry either of you. I'm fine I promise, I will tell you more about it when I'm home."

"When are you coming home, Mum?" Jack asked.

"In the next couple of days, I think. I will stay in touch now."

Jack returned into view. "Take care, Mum. Love you."

"I love you too." I smiled, waving at them before ending the call. I didn't want them to see me crying.

I lay back on the pillows. I felt breathless as if I couldn't hold onto the air. My voice seemed hoarser than usual when talking to my sons. Exhaustion took over, overriding the insomnia and I finally fell asleep.

A pain in my neck stirred me from my sleep and I shifted on the pillows which had slid down the bed. I glanced up at the clock: 5.17am. The staff had left me to sleep, and I was relieved for I felt the most refreshed I had in days.

I lay in bed going over the events of the previous few days: the terrifying bleed, hearing my dad's voice in the theatre ... and the voice of something else. The heart episodes. It was all too much to take in, and process. But I was going home today. It was finally over.

The ward was still hushed, but in the privacy of the room I quietly packed up my things. Someone had been through my bag and labelled everything: my glasses, phone charger, tablets – everything had a white hospital label identifying them as mine. For a moment, I was back in the hospice after Dad's death with the small box of his belongings, labelled just like mine. Only he was dead, and I had survived.

Just after 7am, a nurse arrived with my medication and painkillers.

"Morning, here we are. You're going home today, I hear."

"Yes ... that's right," I croaked.

She was the first person I'd spoken to since the night before. It seemed harder to talk.

The sound of the breakfast trolley rumbled up the corridor – food delivery had become the highlight of the long days spent watching clocks.

I sat on the bed, facing the window eating my porridge slowly, savouring the sweetness of the honey before eating my toast. It didn't matter that it was cold by then. I took my time, enjoying the sensation of the crunchy, dry bread. Everything, even cold toast, held a new, childlike magic as if I was tasting everything for the first time, all over again. I'd been forced to slow down and with hours to idle away, prolonging mealtimes was an effective way to pass time. Dad had stayed in hospital three times after his surgeries, and I remember his complaints of boredom, and how much his eyes would light up when I came to see him. Now I understood why.

Just after 10am, a nurse arrived. "We are just getting your medication sorted from the pharmacy, then you are free to go home. They do have a backlog so there might be a bit of a delay I'm afraid," she said apologetically.

"Okay ... thank ... you." I gasped a little to get my words out.

I returned to bed and texted Paul who would be collecting

me. My gaze moved from the clock to my phone as I flicked through videos on social media. The familiar rumble of the meal trolley appeared but there was nothing for me this time.

"I don't have lunch for you I'm afraid. Have you completed a meal sheet today?" a woman called through the open doorway.

"I'm going ... home today ... but still waiting ... for my medication," I replied.

"Oh I see, love. Are you hungry? I can probably find you something." She began rifling through a drawer in the trolley. "Cheese sandwich?" She held up a pack.

"Um ... no thanks." I couldn't face cheese sandwiches ever again.

"I've got a spare vegetable soup if you want it?"

"Great... I will ... take that... Thank you."

She handed me the soup with a small foil-sealed pot of chopped fruit.

"*Thank ... you,*" I whispered, my voice breaking.

Just after 2pm, I shuffled out to the nurse's station, holding my chest bone for support.

"*Hello ... it's ... been a ... few ... hours. Do ... you know...*" I stopped and gasped in air. "*Do ... you know ... when ... the medication ... is coming up?*" My voice was fading in and out.

The nurse glanced at the clock. "Gosh, I'm so sorry, it has been a while. I will call the pharmacy now."

"*Thank ... you,*" I whispered, still holding my chest to brace against the strain of being upright and talking.

"Are you having difficulty talking?" the nurse asked.

"*Yes, I ... seem ... to be ... getting hoarser. My ... voice ... keeps coming and ... going today...*" I stopped, exhausted just trying to complete the sentence.

"Is this a new symptom?" she asked, looking a little more concerned than inquisitive.

"*Yes ... today ... but ... the ... surgeon told me ... I have some ...*

bruising on..." I gasped a breath in to finish the sentence... "*my ... vocal cord.*"

"Did the doctors see you this morning on rounds?"

"*No ... last ... night.*"

"I will ask them to see you and check your breathing before you go as this is a new development. If they are happy with you, you can still be discharged. I will call them now." She picked up the phone on the desk and I shuffled slowly back into my room, deflated. I was tired and the bruising on my body was continuing to surface and ache.

I lay on the bed, staring at the rain clouds shifting slowly across the grey sky, listening to the endless ticking of the clock. The dinner trolley rolled by just after 5pm and didn't stop this time. I didn't care. I would eat when home and didn't want to delay my departure further by eating.

It was almost 7.30pm when the doctor finally arrived. "Hello, Ms Johnson. Sorry to have kept you waiting so long. I understand you are waiting to go home but you are having some issues with your voice and breathing. What's been happening?"

"*I just ... feel ... a bit ... breathless and ... my voice ... keeps ... coming and going,*" I whispered.

"Right, and when did this begin?" he said, unwrapping the stethoscope from around his neck.

"*This ... morning.*"

"Do you mind if I have a quick listen to your chest?"

I shook my head, leaning forward.

"A nice deep breath in for me," he said, gently placing the cold stethoscope on my chest.

"And again... Yes, I can hear some minor stridor when you breathe. It's a sound caused by an obstruction near the voice box. I believe this is due to the issues with your vocal cords. As you are coming back to see your surgeon in three days, I'm happy for you to be discharged tonight. I will make sure that the nurses give you the ward contact number and if you have any concerns before Wednesday, you can call through directly. Is that okay?"

"*Yes ... thank you.*" I nodded with relief.

"Okay good, you take care."

The doctor stood up and left the room. I'd waited all day for three minutes of his time, but I didn't care. I just wanted to leave the hospital and the whole experience behind me.

"*I'm allowed out now, can you come pick me up, please? Can you stay with me at Sunshine? I don't want to go home alone?*" I texted Paul, fighting back tears of exhaustion and relief.

My phone vibrated moments later: "*Of course, I will, and I will look after you, promise x*"

The journey to the hospital was at least half an hour which allowed plenty of time to get myself downstairs. I carefully picked up my bag, pulling it onto my back. I winced in pain. Although almost empty, the action reminded me how weak and bruised my body was.

I shuffled out to the nurses' station.

"You off then? Here are the ward's contact details. If you have any concerns, just give us a call. If you experience any difficulties with breathing, call 999." The nurse passed me a piece of paper.

"*Thank you ... for ... everything.*" I took the paper, and pushed it into my pocket and turned away, spreading my hand out across my breastbone to support my chest and neck. As much as I wanted to leave, the still-fresh wound left me feeling vulnerable to the world outside the hospital.

As I neared the end of the corridor, a poster on the wall caught my eye. I struggled to read the small print, but the image and title captured my gaze. '*You are not alone*' in bold, blue letters sat above a large blue and purple butterfly. It was just a poster on a hospital wall, but it meant something so much more to me.

I made my way to the lift and downstairs to the hospital entrance, my mouth salivating at the thought of a fresh coffee and cake from the hospital café. By the time I arrived at the entrance, it was after 8pm and the café was closed. Deflated, I eased myself into a chair to wait for Paul's text.

Occasionally the doors would open bringing in a visitor and each one stared at me as they passed. I sat in silence for fifteen minutes, my exhausted mind's thoughts tumbling over and over. Leaving the hospital felt confusing. I desperately needed sleep and a shower, and this place had been the source of so much trauma, but to leave the safety of the medical surroundings was equally frightening.

My phone buzzed alerting me to Paul's arrival. I pulled myself to my feet and gently pulled the bag onto my back.

"Oh, Emily...come here." Paul greeted me at the door and took the bag from my back, opening his arms to hug me. I was too sore to be held and too preoccupied with getting safely into his car. Billy sat in the back seat patiently waiting, before jumping up excitedly to greet me, his tail swirling furiously.

"I missed... you so... much," I whispered, unable to turn my body to touch him.

I manoeuvred myself in, bracing my chest with my hand, as Paul pulled the seatbelt across me. I was hungry and exhausted, and even the simplest of tasks felt overwhelming. *"Can you ... take me ... to a shop, please. I need ... something to eat."*

"Of course I will," he soothed, his face full of concern and sadness.

The world outside felt frightening, every minor bump in the road jarring my battered body. I needed to cry, to yell and sob and release everything my body was holding onto, but it wouldn't happen. My body hadn't the energy left, and my mind was preventing it.

After a brief detour to a late-night store, Paul drove me to *Sunshine.* I couldn't face returning home and my boys seeing me in that way. Paul propped me up on the sofa bed with several cushions. It was uncomfortable, but I had to remain sleeping upright for a few more days until the swelling subsided.

"*I smell ... of the ... hospital,*" I whispered, smelling my left arm, and still wearing my hospital identity bracelets. I felt dirty, covered in layers of sweat, and sticky remnants of blood and glue from plasters that had covered my arms, chest and feet. As tired as I felt, I didn't want to climb into the bed, nor lie on my fresh sheets without cleaning myself, but I didn't have the energy to wash either.

"Would you like me to wash you?" Paul asked gently as he placed his hand on mine.

"*No ... don't ... worry,*" I declined, shaking my head.

"Please, Emily, let me help you."

I was too exhausted to argue. Paul boiled the kettle and filled a bowl with water and fragrant shower gel. The scent filled the small space almost immediately. He snipped the hospital bracelets off, then dipped a face cloth into the bowl, the cloth dissolving into bubbles.

"Lie back," Paul said, as he gently stripped my socks from my feet, then my leggings. I could smell the subtle fragrance of the clean towel balanced upon his knee.

Paul dipped his hands into the bowl, burying them momentarily under a layer of bubbles, before bringing the steaming cloth back up between his hands and squeezing it. He took my left foot onto his lap and wrapped the warm cloth around my foot gently. The sensation disarmed me. I sank back into the pillow and closed my eyes and tears silently fell as he rid my body of the hospital smell.

I slept deeply, despite my upright position but awoke abruptly to a painful sensation and pressure in my neck just before 6am. I took some painkillers Paul had left beside me and settled in bed once more, waiting for the pain to subside.

It was still dark outside, and Paul and the dog were still sleeping on the other bed. I'd not lived with him for four years and the sound of his breathing was both comforting and at the same time, unfamiliar. I lay in the darkness running over the events of the previous days in my mind. I had so many unanswered questions, and so many emotions I was scared to explore. What had happened in the operating room? What did it all mean?

The sun was gently climbing and with its rising, the woodland began stirring and the familiar cheerful song of a robin filled the space outside the caravan. It was soon joined by others. The world was waking up with me.

I pulled up the blind just a little to observe another bird feeder Paul had hooked over a branch of the oak tree. A small grey nuthatch hung upside down on the feeder pecking at the generous breakfast of seeds and nuts. The tree was still full of vibrant green leaves. Unlike many of the other trees, it had not begun its autumnal shedding. I watched the foliage vibrating slightly with the birds' feeding acrobatics. Each leaf was gloriously backlit and outlined by golden sunlight. An unexpected wave of emotion forcibly hit my chest and I gasped. It was immediately met by pain at my sudden movement, yet the feeling was far more powerful than the pain. Five days earlier, I'd thought I was going to die. Now I was lying in my bed, alive, in my favourite place watching my birds feed once again. It was gratitude. I was grateful for being alive and able to witness something so simple, yet beautiful.

After an hour or so, Paul awoke and helped me up before dressing me. "Let me take you to the shower block and—"

"*No, I ... want to ... do this. I will ... be fine.*" I cut across him, preventing any further discussion.

I walked slowly towards the toilet block, crossing a gravel path covered in leaves that crunched underfoot. Autumn carpeted the footpath. It was the first time I had seen the trees in almost two weeks, their branches now almost bare, with just a few dark-red and brown leaves still clinging to them. The fallen leaves were deep in places, piled upon themselves where the winds had carried them. They tickled my bare toes through my open shoes, and I smiled at the sensation. The air smelt of autumn, rich and earthy, and each turn of the leaves underfoot uncovered damp ones, amplifying the scent. Like a toddler discovering her world for the first time, I soaked up the sensations with every sense. I was in awe of nature and my childlike wonderment carried me to the toilet despite my painful, stiff body.

Before leaving the toilet, I caught my reflection in the mirror. The sunlight streaming through the open skylight was unfiltered. My neck and chest were a putrid mix of green, purple and yellow bruising, blending against the grey pallor of my skin. The blue knots of the surgical stitches poked out from either end of the dressing. Seeing myself was shocking and triggered feelings I had been suppressing since my arrival in Critical Care. Tears filled my eyes, and a ball of emotions blocked my throat. I needed to release them, but I was scared to surrender. I knew it would be painful to sob.

I slowly returned to the caravan and carefully pulled the awning zip back down to keep out the fresh autumn air.

As I slowly climbed up the steps, Paul was waiting for me.

"Are you okay?" He'd caught the expression on my face. The physical pain was evident in my walk.

"*No,*" I whispered, looking at him.

"Come here." Paul pulled me slowly into his arms and gently placed my head on his chest.

The embrace was so comforting, it ripped my emotional wound open. My knees buckled and I sobbed through a hoarse wail into his chest as Paul held up my body. "*I was... so... scared...*"

"Come and lie down, you've got to rest."

Paul led me back to my bed before tucking me in and pulling up a stool next to me. We sat in silence as he held my hand, gently stroking it. Paul didn't need to say a word. I could feel everything he wanted to say through his touch.

Suddenly a flash of movement startled us both through the caravan window. A bird had found its way into the awning and was flying in frantic circles, its wings thrashing noisily. It landed on the back of my garden chair and settled in stillness, staring at us both with an intensity that was a little unnerving. It was a robin, its red chest rising and falling as it recovered from its attempt to escape.

I had listened to a robin's song several times whilst visiting the caravan and often observed it sitting in the tree as it cheerfully called for a mate. It had never ventured anywhere near the caravan. This was the closest I had been to one since childhood.

As a young woman, I'd learnt that a visit from a robin meant more to some people than just another feathered garden visitor. For centuries, some cultures had believed that the robin was a symbol of rebirth. And for some people, a robin appearing was a sign of a lost loved one visiting. Perhaps this one was both.

Paul stood up and opened the door to offer the bird a safe way out. The robin disappeared before Paul stepped into the awning. He'd let himself out.

I stayed for two more days, only moving to use the bathroom. It was the first time in decades I had allowed someone to care for me. I didn't have a choice. I felt physically and emotionally broken.

Three days after my discharge, Paul drove me back to the hospital for my stitches to be removed, before I could return home to my sons. Despite heavy bruising and stiffness, I felt much better for having rested, but my breathing was laboured, and my voice had become just a whisper.

Walking into the hospital was more challenging than I'd anticipated. I felt dizzy on the stairs and paused to grab the handrail to gasp for breath every few steps. People swerved around me on the busy stairwell. The effort to get to the clinic overrode a building anxiety in my chest that I couldn't understand. I'd never felt nervous there before. But the need to breathe and get to the surgeon masked the anxiety, temporarily.

After a short wait, I was led into the surgeon's office.

"Good morning. How are you feeling?" Miss Jones asked, smiling warmly.

"Um... I'm ... sore ... and it's ... hard ... to ... talk ... and breathe ... going ... upstairs." I strained to form the sounds of the words.

"That's understandable. You have quite a bit of bruising. When I tested your laryngeal nerve in theatre, the signal failed about 2cm from the end, so you have a weak left vocal cord which is probably not allowing the flow of air through. Can you try coughing for me?"

I tried the instinctive action, but nothing happened. *"No ... I can't,"* I said, bemused.

"I will refer you to my ENT consultant colleague and get you in to see her urgently to assess your vocal cords. I can still see it in my mind clearly from your surgery and I am confident it will heal and return to normal within a few months. I'm sorry things didn't go to plan in theatre."

"It's not ... your ... fault."

"You are my patient and—"

"*No.*" I stopped her. "*These things ... happen. Your calmness ... and kindness ... in the ... recovery room ... when I ... was bleeding ... really ... helped me.*" I didn't care about the patient-surgeon etiquette at that moment. I wanted her to know I didn't blame her and how much her calm reassurance made a terrifying situation a little easier.

Miss Jones nodded in appreciation and smiled, before standing up. "Let's remove the stitch," she said, coming around the desk and sitting in front of me as the nurse ripped open a package and passed her sterile scissors. She teased the edge of the dressing away. One snip and pull, and the long internal stitch was out.

She gently pushed the dressing back into place. "Keep the dressing on for another week and then you can remove it. Once it's off, you can start gently massaging your scar with a little Vitamin E cream, twice a day."

"*Okay ... thank you.*"

"Take care of yourself, plenty of rest now and my colleague will be in touch about your vocal cords. I will see you in three weeks for a follow-up." Her face filled with kindness.

"*Thank you...*" I said weakly before leaving.

I had made it through another appointment, another stage. There was something so reassuring about having these periodic appointments with her.

Paul pulled up outside the flat and unclipped his belt, getting out of the car to help me climb out and walk to the flat door. I had been away from my sons for a week, their longest time alone.

I turned around in front of the communal door, creating a verbal barrier to Paul assisting me any further. "*I'm ... fine ... honestly.*"

"At least let me carry your bag up to your door."

"*Okay,*" I conceded.

Paul walked upstairs ahead, and Billy chased him, eager to get home and hoover up any food crumbs he might find on the kitchen floor.

I steadily climbed the stairs and stood opposite Paul. "*Thank you ... for everything, for ... looking after ... me. I love you ... you know?*" I whispered. My voice felt particularly strained, raw emotion strangling it further.

"I love you too ... I always have. Please, just rest now."

"*I ... will, I promise.*" I watched him descend the stairs before turning and giving me a final wave goodbye.

I turned the key and pushed the door open, as Billy nuzzled in excitedly to the home he had not seen for a week. I dropped my bag, and the door slammed loudly behind me, making me jump.

The sound alerted Jack of my return. Within seconds, his bedroom door opened. "Mum, is that you?"

"*Yes ... it's ... me. Hello, Jack,*" I croaked and went to the bottom of the stairs. Our eyes met.

"Are you okay, Mum?"

Jack's familiar face and voice stirred something deep within me. A surge of emotion rose up from my belly, winding me. I spun around and sat on the stairs to steady myself and began to cry, the strange sounds escaping like a dog howling.

Jack stepped down and sat behind me, placing his hands on my shoulders. "*It's okay, Mum, it's okay now,*" he whispered, rubbing my shoulders gently.

I had cared for my son for nineteen years. Now he was a young man, sitting behind me, comforting me. Jack let me cry, even if he didn't understand why I was crying. The enormity of the critical bleed and the experience in the theatre had moved me in a way I was still trying to understand. Being reunited with my sons in familiar surroundings had returned a sense of safety and normality I had desperately missed.

I stood up and Jack took me by the elbow and led me to the kitchen.

"Can I get you anything, Mum?" he asked, staring at my neck. The natural light coming through the kitchen window clearly showing the extent of my bruising across my neck and chest.

"*No ... I ... just need ... to ... lie ... down,*" I whispered back, gasping.

Thomas had heard the strange sounds of me crying and appeared around the kitchen door.

He moved forward and put his arm around me gently. Seeing my other son provoked the return of the emotions and I wrapped my arms around his waist and began to wail again.

"It's okay. Mum, it's over now, you are home. It's all over," Thomas soothed as I settled.

"What do you need us to do, Mum?" Thomas asked, both sons staring at me, concerned.

"*Thomas ... can ... you take ... Billy ... out ... later. Jack ... you ... can ... feed ... him ... for me. Sort ... out ... some food ... or... a ... takeaway ... tonight. I'm ... going ... to ... lie down.*" I was drained and didn't have it in me to say anything else.

Jack opened the lounge door, watching me intently as I moved past him, before easing myself onto the sofa bed. Thomas hovered behind him with a glass of water and my phone in his hand. Neither were used to seeing me in obvious pain and so weak, and I could sense their fear.

"Get some sleep now, Mum. Call me if you need anything, okay?" Thomas said, passing me my phone and setting the water down beside me.

"Tell us anything you need, Mum. I will come down and check on you," Jack echoed.

"Thank ... you ... boys." I smiled gratefully as I watched them leave the room.

My sons. I love them so much.

SILENCED

24 SEPTEMBER 2023

As the days passed, my voice grew progressively weaker and changeable. I became hoarse and occasionally my voice layered itself mid-sentence with two sounds, sounding robotic. It was becoming increasingly hard to breathe, and going upstairs left me out of breath and sent my heart racing. Certain foods were becoming difficult to eat. Meat, bread, and cheese took several attempts to swallow, and I found myself spluttering from swallowing water down the wrong way. My body naturally attempted to cough to expel the liquid, but there was no power or force to formulate the coughing action.

Ten days after my surgery I stood at the kitchen bench, staring out of the window at the back of flats that filled my view. The mixture of brown and cream bricks had weathered during a century of coastal weather and were now dressed in a layer of dull smog. When the sky was overcast, it was as if colour itself had drained from the world. It was a depressing outlook, but it had been mine for eight years and I had grown accustomed to it.

Out of nowhere, the urge to sneeze arose and I instinctively grabbed my neck to support it, tensing to minimise the impact of the sneeze. A sharp pain shot across my neck and into my chest, as if I had pulled every muscle within it. The pain did not ebb, and my heart began to race in panic.

I ran to the bathroom, searching for signs in the mirror of something critical, but there was no blood. Yet something didn't feel right inside my neck.

I riffled through my desk for the hospital paperwork. It was Sunday and pointless trying the surgeon's office. I called the ward, and a friendly voice answered.

"*Good afternoon, Head and Neck.*"

"Hi ... my name is ... Emily Johnson and I ... was discharged last week ... after having my thyroid removed. I just sneezed... I couldn't stop it... It feels like I've hurt something ... inside my neck. I just wondered if that's ... normal?" It was far harder to speak in sentences that I realised.

"*Are you having difficulty breathing? You sound quite breathless,*" the nurse asked.

"I've got some ... vocal cord damage ... but I can breathe ... okay as long as I don't ... go upstairs. I'm waiting to see ... the ENT specialist."

"*It's probably tender from the surgery. Take some painkillers and if it hasn't improved in an hour, you can pop into A&E and ask them to refer you upstairs to us,*" the nurse reassured.

"Okay ... thank you."

I hung up and searched the cupboards for painkillers, before carefully swallowing the capsules. I lay down on the sofa and drifted off to sleep.

"Mum... Mum ... are you okay?" Jack's voice pulled me from my sleep.

I lifted my head, disorientated. A sharp pain burnt across my neck, waking me fully. "Pffft." I sucked air in through gritted teeth.

"What's wrong, Mum?" Jack's concerned face loomed in over me.

"I pulled ... my neck ... sneezing, that's all. I am just ... resting, nothing to ... worry about," I whispered.

"Do you want me to get you a drink?"

"No thanks ... I'm ok ... honestly." I smiled to reassure him as I lay back down and watched Jack leave the room.

Since my return from hospital, he'd watched me like a hawk. Every splutter or groan of pain, he was by my side, ensuring I was safe.

It was almost 3pm and the pain hadn't subsided despite the painkillers and sleep. I eased myself up off the sofa and went upstairs and into Jack's room.

"I am ... just going ... for a walk ... to get some fresh ... air. I will be ... about an hour ... or so."

Jack glanced up from his computer. "Alright. Are you sure you're, okay?"

"Yes, I ... just need some ... fresh air."

"Okay, be careful, Mum. Don't be long, will you?"

"I won't," I lied, smiling.

I had no idea how long it would take me in hospital but lying felt easier than telling the truth to someone who was already terrified I might not return next time.

I gathered my bag and headed out of the flat to walk the short distance to the bus stop. The exertion slowed me down, every step considered as I gasped for breath. I had several neighbours who would have given me a lift, friends too, Paul or my brother, but why would I disturb someone's Sunday afternoon? I could take myself.

The sun was breaking through the autumn sky; it felt warm and soothing on my face as I leant my body against the bus window. It was a short walk into the hospital emergency department from the bus stop.

I approached the nurse behind the screen. *"Hello ... my ... name ... is Emily Johnson... I've been told to ... come in."* I gasped in to catch a breath. "*I had thyroid ... surgery ... ten ... days ago.*" I gasped again. I needed the air to support my words, and it was exhausting. "*I ... sneezed ... earlier and I think ... I've hurt something ... in my wound area.*" I pushed my hospital letters under the gap in the screen. "*I've got ... vocal ... cord ... issues ... it's why I can't talk ... really.*"

The triage nurse glanced over my paperwork. "Okay, I will get someone to see you. If you could just take a seat over there for me, someone will call you shortly."

"*Thank ... you,*" I whispered before moving into the waiting room full of faces filled with pain, hands grasping sick bowls and red-faced children, crying and arching their backs in pushchairs. It was chaotic and overwhelming.

I eased myself into a chair and closed my eyes.

Please let me be somewhere else. Somewhere quiet.

The chair underneath me held me in a hug while my imagination pictured my bare feet resting on damp grass. I could hear the dog softly snoring, stretched out next to me by the caravan, birds singing in the trees, heavy and fragrant with blossom.

"Emily Johnson?"

I startled and opened my eyes. I stood up and followed a nurse through double doors into the emergency department. She looked tired and irritated.

"Sit there please," the nurse said, gesturing to a chair in the hallway next to an upright shelf as she walked away.

Another patient was wheeled in, moaning as he writhed from side to side.

"Right, here we go." The nurse reappeared wheeling a BP monitor and attached the cuff to my right arm. "That's fine." She recorded my blood pressure on a sheet before taking my temperature. "37, perfect. You are here because you have stridor, correct?"

I looked blankly back at her.

"You're breathing. You have stridor?" she repeated, seemingly irritated.

"Um yes... I have ... vocal cord ... issues from ... thyroid surgery. The Head ... and Neck ward ... asked me to come in ... and see them ... but said I had to ... come via ... here."

"Right." She sighed heavily. I could feel her exhaustion but took it personally. "If you go and sit in the waiting room again, I will let them know you are here and find someone to take you."

She ushered me back to the double doors and pushed a button, releasing me back into the bedlam. I chose a seat as far away from the girl with the sick bowl.

A nurse appeared ten minutes later and called me through the double doors again. "If you'd like to follow me, I'm going to take you to Head and Neck."

She led me into a corridor and towards a lift. "You are lucky to come straight up here. It's a twelve-hour wait downstairs at the moment." She sighed.

A wave of guilt washed over me for jumping a queue, mixed with relief that I didn't have to wait twelve hours. We reached the fourth floor, and she led me through another corridor onto the ward I had previously stayed on.

"This is Emily Johnson. I've brought her up from A&E," the nurse announced at the nurses' station.

"Ah yes we have been expecting you. If you could sit here, we are waiting for the registrar to come and see you."

I sat on a chair just outside the room I had stayed in. It felt strange yet familiar to be back, and in some way, reassuring.

A young woman approached me. "Hi Emily, I'm Dr Adams, if you follow me, we will go into a private room." The doctor smiled warmly and gestured for me to follow her back along the corridor. I traced her steps behind her, past the butterfly poster, into an empty examination room.

"Take a seat here. So, I understand you sneezed earlier today, and you've had some pain since. Is that right?" she asked.

"*Yes.*" Suddenly I felt very foolish for coming into hospital because of a sneeze.

"The staff were a little concerned with your breathing on the phone too." She turned to her computer and typed something. "Okay so you have an appointment on Wednesday with Dr Batten, the ENT."

"*Do I?*"

"Yes, I expect the letter will arrive tomorrow or Tuesday. Right, let's take a look at your neck." She spun around on her chair and felt around my wound under the dressing. "You have substantial bruising here," she said looking at my chest. "Where can you feel the pain?"

"*Across here ... and round ... here.*" I pointed to my dressing and around the right of my neck and under the ear.

"It's very tender and naturally, you would have tensed whilst sneezing and pulled everything in. It is very early days in your recovery. Your body has been through an awful lot of trauma with the two surgeries."

I felt tears filling my eyes. It was the first time in hospital anyone had acknowledged it had been a traumatic experience.

"I'm going to have a listen to your chest," she said, unwrapping the stethoscope hung around her neck. "Can you take a deep breath in for me...? And again." She moved the stethoscope around my chest. "And once more for me please." She removed it from her ears.

"Because the left vocal cord is weak, it collapses a little which can affect the airflow. It can restrict your breathing. You have a whistle; we call this stridor. When you see Dr Batten next week, she will be able to discuss treatment options with you. In the meantime, you need to get home and rest as much as you can, okay?" She stood up and opened the door.

"Okay ... thank you, doctor. Sorry to ... waste your ... time like this."

"No, absolutely not, you were right to come in and get it checked, especially after the bleed. I can understand why you were concerned. Here is the number for the ward and any further concerns, please call them, okay?" She passed me a slip of paper.

"Thank you." I took the paper and walked out into the corridor.

"You take care now."

"I will."

I walked through the double doors, stepped into an empty lift and burst into tears. I didn't have to pretend to smile in there. No one could see me. Losing my voice and ability to breathe properly was taking its toll and just another thing to try to cope with on top of everything else.

The following day, a letter arrived confirming my appointment with the ENT consultant. I was glad as my voice was reduced to a strained whisper. It was frightening and I felt very vulnerable. If I needed help, no one could hear me. I was unable to walk upstairs to the toilet without stopping and holding onto the handrail, to catch a breath. Every whispered sentence required gasps of air to complete them. When people phoned me, they couldn't hear me. "*Sorry, can you repeat that please?*" was becoming a standard part of every frustrating conversation.

The following day, Paul gave me a lift to the hospital refusing to let me catch a bus again. I made the mistake of telling him about my trip back to hospital on the bus alone. Both shocked and concerned, he insisted on taking me into my appointment this time. I refused but agreed to him waiting outside, anticipating another short consultation.

I found the clinic and checked in. A nurse led me straight through to a waiting room. She handed me a clipboard with sheets of multiple questions about my capacity to speak, cough, and swallow food and liquid. Shortly after I completed it, a nurse arrived in pink scrubs and sat in front of me with a small spray bottle with a long white nozzle.

"Hello Ms Johnson, my name is Kelly. Dr Batten is still in with her patient but in the meantime, I'm going to numb your throat for the procedure. Can you tilt your head back please?" she said in a matter-of-fact manner.

"*What procedure?*" I whispered, alarmed.

"Dr Batten will talk to you first and if she feels you require treatment, it will be done today."

Another nurse appeared and tapped the door, before entering the treatment room. My heart began to race anxiously. I had not mentally prepared myself for treatment.

"Head back," the nurse instructed.

I tilted my head backwards, and she squirted the noxious-tasting spray into my nostril. Its bitter taste hit the back of my throat and I shuddered. It was just as disgusting the second time around.

"It's not very nice, is it?" the nurse chuckled. "I'm going to leave you to numb for a few minutes and by then, Dr Batten should be finished with her patient."

Unable to ignore the feeling rising in my chest, I stood up. "*Where ... is the ... toilet?*"

"Along there on the left-hand side." She pointed to the end of the corridor.

"*Thank ... you.*" I turned towards the corridor and moved as quickly as I could to the toilets. I didn't want anyone to witness my building panic.

I closed the door and leant my back against it sobbing, silently. I felt terrified. And weak *because* I felt terrified at the site of nurses in scrubs. *What is wrong with me?*

My heart was beating loudly in my chest, and a suffocating pressure filled my lungs. I had to calm down and get out of there before anyone came looking for me. I went to the sink and turned on the tap, cupping my hands under the water and scooping it up, splashing it over my face. The cold water quickly snapped me back like a slap in the face. "*Pull it together, Emily,*" I whispered to my reflection in the mirror above the sink, patting my face dry with a paper towel. I lingered for a couple of minutes hoping the redness around my eyes would fade. I unlocked the door and returned to my seat.

A few minutes later, the doctor's door opened and a woman appeared. She was surrounded by three other staff, all in pink surgical scrubs. "Hello Ms Johnson. My name is Dr Batten. I understand my colleague has referred you to me for treatment for vocal cord palsy." She flipped through the sheets I had completed, scanning my answers. "You are having difficulties with breathing and your voice. Any difficulty swallowing food or liquids?"

"*Um ... yes... sometimes ... water, it feels like ... it's gone down ... the wrong way ... but I can't cough it up.*"

"Okay, so we can give you a small injection of Botox directly into the vocal cord itself and this will help strengthen it. I will give you a little numbing through your windpipe first. We will insert a camera through your nasal cavity so I can see the vocal cord. This should help improve your voice and breathing whilst the nerve is repairing. Do you have any questions?"

I shook my head. I was terrified into silence. My heart was thumping loudly in my chest. *Can she hear it too?*

"Okay, let's get you started."

She stood up, and the two staff hovering followed her back into her treatment room whilst another gestured me to follow. I walked behind her and sat down as directed, but everything in my body was screaming to run away.

"This is my colleague, Dr Borgen. She is here all the way from Denmark. Are you happy for her to watch the procedure?

"*Yes.*" I nodded looking at a tall, Danish goddess in pink scrubs smiling at me. "*Will ... this hurt ... my ... neck? It's ... still so tender?*" I questioned, holding my hand over the dressing.

"No, we will be going in here in the windpipe above your scar," the doctor said, pressing on my neck just above my scar.

"You really should have this dressing off by now and be massaging this scar," she said, feeling the wound underneath the dressing. It was tender and I'd not even touched it myself yet. I was too scared to.

"*Miss Jones told ... me to leave ... it on until ... tomorrow,*" I said sheepishly.

"Okay, if you can sit back in the chair. You can close your eyes if you wish. I'm going to pop the camera up your nostril."

I shut my eyes tightly, bracing myself for what was coming. I could feel my heart thumping rapidly in my chest, but I froze. I felt the familiar tickling sensation of the camera going in and being adjusted into place.

"You are going to feel a bit of pressure now and slight scratch."

I tensed myself against the needle as she pushed it through my neck, into the windpipe. It stung and dragged painfully momentarily, and I flinched.

"Well done, you are doing really, really well. Now, we are going to give that a minute or two to numb."

I nodded gently; my eyes still tightly closed and my fingernails gripping the armrests tightly.

"Last part now, Emily. I am going to inject the filler. This may make you want to retch, but you won't be able to, it's a natural reaction of the body but nothing to worry about."

I felt a pressure in my neck, but no pain, but within seconds, I involuntarily gagged. I could feel tears running down my cheeks, despite my eyes being firmly closed. I could not move. Sheer terror and a camera still held me pinned to the chair.

"Okay, nearly finished. I am going to remove the camera now."

I felt the line retracting from my nose, tickling as it left.

"All done."

I opened my eyes to see the three staff staring at me and began to silently cry.

"Oh dear, you were nervous, weren't you?" The doctor squeezed my hand, still gripping the armrest tightly.

I'm not weak. I am strong really, honest, I am, I just feel so traumatised. It's only been ten days. Ten days! I screamed inside as I stared at the staff who were looking at me sympathetically.

"*It's not that... I'm still getting over intensive care...*" I barely managed a whisper.

"Yes, I'm sure. Right, can you say your name for me?"

"*Emily Johnson,*" I strained silently. My voice was gone.

"You are going to be hoarse for the next forty-eight hours, so no raising your voice, but you should start to see an improvement in your speech and breathing in the coming days. Unfortunately, this is a temporary treatment. I will review you in three months and we may have to repeat the treatment again."

"*Okay, thank you,*" I mouthed as I climbed out of the chair and walked towards the door, she was holding open for me.

I held back until I reached the safety of the corridor then covered my face with my hands and sobbed. I hadn't anticipated how anxious and overwhelming it would feel coming back into the hospital for treatment. I felt foolish for crying in front of the doctors over what to them, was a simple procedure under local anaesthetic.

I made my way to the hospital exit and out to Paul who was in the car waiting for me.

"How did you get on?" he asked, leaning across the car to

open the door for me. I looked at him and burst into tears again, pointing to my neck with another dressing over the injection site.

"*It was horrible, I felt so scared. I feel so stupid,*" I mouthed silently.

"Shh, it's okay, come here." Paul gently pulled me across the seat into his arms and held me until I stopped crying.

NOT ONE, BUT TWO

3 OCTOBER 2023

A WEEK AFTER THE PALSY TREATMENT, I RETURNED TO hospital to see the surgeon for another post-op check-up. My hospital visits had become routine, yet since the surgery, each visit was preluded by an overwhelming feeling of anxiety I couldn't understand. After so many appointments, it *should* have been getting easier.

"Good morning. Come in, please." Miss Jones welcomed me from behind her desk. This time there was no committee to greet me, just the surgeon and the nurse who showed me in. "I see you came in last week and saw Dr Batten for your vocal cord treatment. How is your voice and breathing?"

"Better, thank you... I am still very hoarse... It's weak but improving," I replied huskily.

"Excellent news, I'm sure it will fully recover in time." She manoeuvred around the desk. "Let's have a look at your neck. Can you tilt your head up?" I looked up to the ceiling as she observed my neck, before touching it gently. "You have some scar tissue forming, start massaging it twice a day to help break it down."

She returned to her seat. "Now, as you know, we sent your

remaining thyroid tissue to pathology for further testing, and a small nodule showing evidence of papillary thyroid carcinoma was found in the left lobe..." she continued.

"Is this... a different type of cancer?" I asked, stunned, without waiting for her to finish.

"Yes, it can happen sometimes, although it is unusual. This one probably wouldn't have caused you any issues for some time."

I had two types of thyroid cancer?

"I have referred you to Dr Singh in the Oncology department, his team will be taking over now to facilitate your radioactive iodine treatment. They will be in touch with you in due course. You will also remain under my care, and you have Katie's contact details if you have any questions or concerns." She removed her glasses and smiled at me.

I knew I wasn't just a number to her. I felt her dedication to her profession. I was a woman who had cancer, and she was doing everything she could to cure me.

"Thank you."

I stood up as the nurse opened the door, signalling it was time to leave. I rode the bus home silently. Only one thought rolling over and over in my mind this time: *I'm so lucky it was found!*

SHEDDING
OCTOBER 2023

My body was healing slowly and adjusting to life without a thyroid. After my second surgery, I had been placed on a higher-than-usual dose of thyroid-replacement hormones to suppress thyroid-stimulating hormones (TSH) in my body which could accelerate the growth of remaining cancer cells. The side effects of such a high dose were exhausting a lot of the time, and different to when I wasn't producing enough thyroxine in between surgeries. I felt wired and hyper but exhausted too, yet struggled to fall asleep. My heart raced constantly. It impacted my digestion, and I suffered frequent bouts of diarrhoea. I used to be a woman who needed socks, a hot-water bottle and a blanket around me to watch television in the winter. Or a jumper in spring because my hands and feet always felt cold. Now I stood in my kitchen in just my bra, with the window wide open and a chilly four degrees outside to wash the dishes. I couldn't feel the cold anymore, and I couldn't cool down. I was burning up from the inside out, and it went on around the clock. My medication had cranked up my inner thermostat and every function was sped up and overworked.

One unexpected side effect that wasn't so bad – I was very

giggly at times, almost childlike in my bouts of uncontrollable laughter. Some of that could be attributed to my unadulterated joy at being alive, although it wasn't all sunshine and rainbows.

About four weeks after my surgery, I noticed my hair was beginning to fall out at an alarming rate. Not in patches, but all over. Every time I brushed it, or pulled it into a ponytail, the brush would be full of hair. Long, chestnut tangles would catch in my clothes, or in my bed, on the floor, or the kitchen bench and almost every dinner I prepared for my sons came with a side of my hair.

My hair was shedding everywhere and it had become very dry and coarse. I began to dread washing it, for it was then the extent of loss was most apparent. As I pulled conditioner through my hair, it would come out in handfuls. For years my hair had been the only part of me I remotely liked and even then, I had loathed the frizzly curls, straightening them for over twenty-five years.

The year before my cancer diagnosis, I'd made peace with my reflection and began embracing my curls. My hair straighteners were finally retired to a cupboard, and I enjoyed wearing my hair curly. Now, every wash reminded me my hair was falling out. I hated myself for being so upset by my hair loss. It felt trivial and selfish – other people had it far worse than me. At least I didn't need chemotherapy and be at risk of losing it completely. But I couldn't help it. Staring at balls of hair in the bathroom sink made me cry. It was part of *me,* and it felt like I was losing a piece of my identity.

My hairdresser suggested it may be from the surgery and the aftermath of the traumatic circumstances surrounding the critical bleed. Stress is a leading factor in the development of temporary hair loss after surgery, but hair-thinning was also a possible side effect of too much, or too little thyroxine.

One evening, whilst in the bath, I lay back and sank under

the bubbles, allowing the water to flood my ears. I could hear my heartbeat amplified through the water. My hair floated around my shoulders, softly touching my skin with a gentle rhythm in time with the bobbing water. I pulled my hands up behind my head and gathered my hair in, gently holding it.

"It's going to be okay, you'll come back stronger one day. It's all going to be okay," I said quietly, soothing myself. My hair was part of me, and it was falling out for a reason. I needed to remember to be kind to every part of me.

ONCOLOGY

26 OCTOBER 2023

I TOOK AN UNEXPECTED CALL FROM THE HOSPITAL NEAR the end of October. The oncologist had a cancellation and could fit me in the following day. I took the appointment willingly. I wanted to know when the next phase would begin and free me from the treatment limbo state I was residing in. It was hard to relax into recovery. I yearned for the radiation treatment to be over, yet I feared it too, and how sick it might make me feel.

The next morning, I put on my favourite long dress with heeled winter boots. Autumn had arrived in full force just days before and high winds had stripped the last of the leaves still clinging to the trees. I dressed up for the occasion. It gave me back a small sense of confidence and control, something cancer had taken from me.

I'd sat beside my father at his first oncologist appointment. Twenty years had passed since his death and here I was, his little girl, now a fifty-one-year-old woman taking this trip for myself, only this time alone. Unlike him, I didn't want anyone with me.

"Ms Johnson?" a nurse called across the waiting room.

I looked up, knowing what was coming. I had watched the nurse publicly weigh everyone after they had checked in.

Two years earlier, this action would have mortified me. I would have removed my coat, my boots, in fact, any layers that could affect the accuracy of the weight – anything to make me seem lighter to the nurse, the waiting room full of eyes, but more importantly, lighter to me.

I never weighed myself anymore, it was unfamiliar territory to be weighed freely, and so publicly and not be inclined to ruminate for hours over the numbers. This very action had been an obsession of mine for almost forty years, an addiction I satiated up to fifteen times a day during its worst phases, each time hoping the scales were incorrect and my weight was less in reality. Those days were behind me.

I hopped on the scale, coat, boots and all, without hesitation. With my weight recorded, I sat back down and waited to be called. As the minutes ticked by, I grew more anxious. The daytime cookery show playing silently on a large television hung on the wall did little to distract me from the reality of the situation.

What if I am the same as Dad? What if they didn't get it all?

My stomach turned over anxiously. I glanced over at a large corkboard fixed to the wall in the corner of the waiting room. It was filled with thank-you cards and letters, pinned across each other, well wishes from patients and family members for the oncology team.

In the centre, a card captured my gaze. A card covered with butterflies.

"Emily Johnson."

I turned around.

"Hello, follow me..." The nurse trailed off before leading me to a nearby office where my oncologist was waiting.

"Good afternoon, Ms Johnson. Come in, please sit down. I

am Dr Singh." A middle-aged man smiled warmly as he extended his arm to the chair opposite his desk. His soft voice disarmed my nerves almost immediately.

"If it's okay with you I'd like to go through a few things first so we can understand what you have been through so far and take things from there. You had your first surgery on the 15th of June, and you had your completion on the 14th of September."

"That's correct, yes."

"So, we found a 4.5cm follicular thyroid cancer which was removed. On the second surgery, we found another type of thyroid cancer and that has been removed too. As far as we know, all the cancer was removed but we would recommend radioiodine treatment to get rid of any microscopic cancer cells which may be remaining, as well as any normal residual thyroid tissue. The reason we want to remove all the normal thyroid tissues as well as the cancer, as both produce a protein called thyroglobulin and we can measure the protein in your blood. If we get rid of any thyroid tissue, there should be no protein in your blood. If there is, then we know something is happening and we can investigate.

"You will need to have two thyrogen injections over two days before admission to the hospital. Your blood will be tested on the third day, and as long as it is okay you will be admitted to hospital to swallow a radioactive iodine capsule. Once you've had the radioactive iodine, you will become radioactive. Don't worry, you won't turn yellow and glow or anything!" He paused and chuckled and I laughed along with him, nervously.

"But you will have to stay in hospital in a special isolation room. They will measure your radioactive levels regularly; once it is safe; you will be allowed home. You might be here for two or three days. Who do you have at home?"

"I have my two sons and my dog. I am a full-time carer for my son..."

"Do you have close contact with him?"

"Yes, I do, every day."

"I see, unfortunately even after you go home, you will have to avoid close contact for a few more days after your discharge. I will ask the Nuclear Medicine team to contact you and explain how best to manage your isolation.

"I was thinking of booking myself into a hotel after I'm discharged to isolate," I said, eager to have a holiday for the first time in years.

"It's best to discuss this with the Nuclear Medicine department as they will be able to advise you further. Now, generally speaking, radioactive treatment is quite well tolerated. You might feel tired and experience some soreness in the neck area. You might also experience a dry mouth for a couple of weeks and a metallic taste in your mouth. I will give you a leaflet on the radioactive iodine treatment as this will tell you a little bit more about what to expect." He passed me a leaflet. Another one to add to the folder of information at home.

I'd already reached the conclusion it was better not to read leaflets and just have my own experience, whatever that may be. Up until that point, what I had read had underplayed the side effects of surgery complications and life without a thyroid, granted I hadn't had the smoothest of journeys.

"You will need to go on a low-iodine diet for two weeks prior to this treatment. Here is a list of things you can eat and what foods you should avoid." He passed me a sheet of paper.

I glanced down at the list, scanning over the 'avoid' column first. Three quarters of my regular diet was in that column.

"The Nuclear Medicine department will contact you with a date for your radiation treatment. It will probably be at the end of November as we only have one lead-lined room, therefore we can only treat one patient at a time. The chances of the cancer having spread elsewhere is quite small, but we can't rule it out.

"After the treatment you will have a full body scan, and the team will discuss the results at our meeting in January. I will see you in February with the results. We will do some more scans nine months after your radioactive treatment and if those scans are all clear, you won't need any further treatment. I know it's a lot to take in and understand but we shall begin with the radium treatment first and then follow up with a scan and will discuss the results and treatment plan from there. Now then, is there anything you want to ask?" The doctor turned away from his computer and faced me, smiling with his gentle eyes.

"Yes, I have a few questions." I had prepared a list. "For my tumour to have been this large, could I ask, in your opinion, how long it had been there?" I could speak without gasping but I was still hoarse.

"Well, with follicular thyroid cancer, it is very difficult to say. It is not an aggressive or rapidly progressing cancer so it may have been there for some time. However, some thyroid cancer might be more aggressive so until you have the radioactive treatment and scans, we can't be sure. It is difficult to say how long it's been there, but I would have thought it has been there some time."

"As in months or years?" I asked. 'Some time' was too loose for me. I needed to know when it began.

The doctor sighed gently. "Certainly months, I can't say about years."

"Okay, thank you. And to have two types of cancer, is this normal?"

"We do see it occasionally though it's rare. The significant cancer you had was follicular, and the papillary cancer was smaller."

I was no clearer why I had two types of cancer, or how long they had been there, and there was nothing more he could say to clarify it.

"And what could have caused this?" I was asking questions that were impossible to answer.

"Most of the time, we don't know why. Sometimes people have had radiation exposure when younger, or if there is strong family history of cancer. It's generally speaking one of the rare cancers – most of the time we don't know what has caused it."

"Is it hereditary? Is there a greater chance my sons could get this because I have?" I asked cautiously.

Please say I haven't passed on any more genetic gifts to these kids.

"It's unlikely if there is no other family history with thyroid cancer."

Relieved, I moved on. "I've had three recent surgeries, and my hair is starting to fall out, is this down to the surgery or thyroid medication?"

"I think your hair loss will be partly related to the medication but in most cases, it will stop and settle down. You are probably taking more than your body would have normally produced but we need to keep your TSH suppressed until you have the scan in nine months and once we know it is all clear, we may be able to reduce that dose." He spun back around to his computer and began typing something and silence hung between us for the first time.

"Can I ask you one last question, please? If any other thyroid cancer cells have spread around my body, will this treatment get them?"

"As I was saying, the radioactive iodine is to get rid of any microscopic cancer cells. If the cancer has spread to other parts of your body; it might show on the first body scan but generally speaking, it doesn't show up. When we repeat the body scan nine months after your treatment that will show us if it's clear or not."

"But the chances of it having spread is very small, isn't it?"

"Yes, but it happens sometimes."

"But I keep having all these complications that were meant to be very low risk, I can't help worrying..." My dad's story was in the forefront of my mind.

"I understand your concerns. The chances of this having spread are minimal but I'm afraid I can't rule it out," he said, sympathetically, tipping his head one side slightly. I nodded in acknowledgment.

"Here is the consent form. It confirms you are having radioactive treatment to reduce the risk of any reoccurrence. Side effects can include tiredness, nausea, swelling and soreness in the neck, a dry mouth, and a metallic taste. I have given you the leaflet about the treatment. If you can read through and sign here for me just here." He passed me the form. I glanced through it and signed before passing it back to him.

"When you come into hospital to stay, you will be in an isolation room, with your own en-suite bathroom. You will be given food at mealtimes, but you will need to look after yourself. The Nuclear Medicine team will advise you what you can bring because whatever you bring into the room can become radioactive and will need cleaning. I will see you in February once you have had your treatment and body scan. If you have questions, you can contact Katie and here is the number for the Nuclear Medicine team too." The doctor passed me a piece of paper as the nurse stood up.

"Okay, thank you." I stood up and followed the nurse, who was waiting by the door. Another important appointment was over.

A couple of days later, I bumped into Lexi near my local supermarket, and we walked to a nearby bar for an impromptu catch-up. It was quiet and somewhere we could talk. My days of shouting to be heard across background noise were over. Although I could now speak, my voice was still very weak, and I couldn't project it. I turned to Lexi and faced her. It was the only way to make myself fully heard. We caught up on each other's lives and then she paused and took my hand.

"How are you *really* doing?"

Suddenly all the emotions I had been holding in since my oncologist's appointment broke through. I began to cry and couldn't stop the tears. I was still stuck in the trauma of the emergency-surgery situation. Inwardly, I was struggling with flashes from that scene, visual memories that would resurface throughout the day and paralyse me momentarily with anxiety. But outwardly, I was always cheerful, so skilled at putting on the brave face I thought people around me needed me to wear. My positive cancer story was well rehearsed, but Lexi's question gave me a space to be vulnerable and honest.

"Some days, I just can't believe it's all happened. Most of the time I'm okay and then every now and again, I realise what has happened and my world feels out of control. I'm scared... What if it has spread...?" I stared at Lexi searching her face for reassurance. "People keep telling me I am so strong and brave, but I don't feel it, not today. I don't feel brave at all... I'm sick of being strong!" I burst into tears again.

Lexi squeezed my hand. "You are sick from *being* strong for so long."

Lexi held my hand and let me cry. We both ignored the stares coming from behind cloudy ales of old patrons who were perhaps not used to such public breakdowns. I sighed deeply afterwards as I wiped my tear-soaked face with my sleeve. I just needed to say to someone that it was really hard some days, and hear that it was okay to not be strong or feel brave every day.

The following week I had a particularly difficult couple of days and spent most of that time in bed, resting. The fatigue had been overwhelming and all I could manage was a quick dog walk outside the flat before returning home, out of breath and with an invisible fire burning inside. I stripped down to my underwear and got into bed.

Unable to sleep but too tired to summon the energy for anything else, I lay there all day, something I *never* did. My inactivity irritated me, and I felt guilty for not being more productive. The fatigue pushed emotional buttons too and I kept bursting into tears. I was frustrated at myself, and my body for its slow recovery. I had read other people's recovery accounts on thyroid support groups. Some patients bounced back quickly into their normal lives. Why couldn't I be like that?

After spending a second day in bed, I'd had enough of my own sweaty body by the evening and ran a bath. Standing up to shower felt like an energetic battle, baths felt just a little bit easier. It had been four days since I last bothered to shower. My hair was dry and the curls matted, but I couldn't face washing it. All I wanted to do was lie in the bath and not move.

In the past, I would often escape to the bath and secretly eat during my days of binge-eating. I'd wrap two or three chocolate bars in my pyjamas and disappear into the bathroom, past the hallway mirror I'd covered up years before, so I didn't have to look at my own reflection. I'd fill the bath with bubbles so I could bury my overweight body beneath them.

My disordered relationship with my body began when I was thirteen, around the same time my dad left the family home following my parents' separation. It began with a seemingly harmless diet to slim my teenage body, but the behaviours escalated, and I began withholding food.

The reasons behind the behaviour were far more deeply rooted. I wanted to punish myself because I believed I was unlovable, but probably most of all I starved myself to capture my dad's attention. It was a toxic, disordered relationship that endured through most of my adult life, as I struggled first with anorexia and then binge-eating disorder. During the merry-go-round of diets and binges, I spat verbal venom at my body every time I finished a binge, or had to see it, especially when naked and stepping into the bath, words I'd never dream of saying to others. I saved that poison for myself. I hated every part of my body for not being good enough. I wrote about this and how I found acceptance and healing in my second book, *BELLY*.

It was almost 10.30pm and I needed to sleep. I'd been lying in the bath listening to music for over an hour, topping up the water from time to time. I dislodged the plug with my toe, feeling the water slowly drain away. Its departure pulled my body downwards with a pleasant heaviness, leaving only bubbly residue resting on islands of my flesh. I stared at my knees and thighs filling the bathtub. I could feel my heart beating, faster than it should, a steady thump in my chest reminding me how hard it was working. It was working *for* me. Perhaps it was the song playing, or the moments of still observation – I'm not sure which, but something provoked a powerfully emotional surge of recognition, and I gasped.

"I love you! I love *all* of you! Oh God, *I love you!*" I blurted out joyously, cupping my breasts in my hands and staring at the things I had loathed my whole life. "Ha!" A half-cry, half-laugh escaped my mouth unexpectedly.

"And I even love you!" I giggled gently as I ran my finger over the nipples I had spent decades hating. They'd fed my babies, they had a life-giving purpose. They weren't ugly or different. They were a part of me.

"I love you, hairs on my chin ... and grey hair ... and wrinkles

... and you too, arms." I lifted my left arm and squished the loose flesh underneath. I had *hated* these arms for being fat and kept them hidden for years. Arms that carried every burden my life had given them without complaining.

I took my fleshy belly with both hands, and I held the skin tightly and, in that embrace, I was holding myself. Every organ, every bone, every sinew, every cell of my body. It was me; it was *all* part of me and in that moment, I knew, without question or doubt, that I deeply loved every single part of me.

"I'm so sorry for all the things I ever said to you..." I cried aloud, almost laughing whilst simultaneously bursting into tears. I lay in the empty bath until my body and tears had dried, basking in the life-altering epiphany of something that had eluded me for almost forty years.

GRATEFUL

3 NOVEMBER 2023

"Hello, come in please." Dr Atkins greeted me warmly. The familiarity immediately put me at ease. He ushered me into his office, and I sat down. "How are you feeling?"

"Well, it's been a lot to deal with..." I trailed off, desperately wanting to maintain my composure. I had something important I needed to say.

"I know, I've just been reading your notes. Gosh, you've had a tough time lately, haven't you?" His acknowledgment was comforting.

"I am still struggling with my voice, though it is getting better. I still feel breathless but that's to do with the vocal-cord palsy. My heart is racing all the time too."

"Let's just check your blood pressure and heart anyway," he said reassuringly, as he wrapped the cuff around my arm and pumped up the band until it squeezed my arm uncomfortably. "Your blood pressure is fine, but your heart rate is still very high. I'd like to get the nurse to run an ECG just to be sure, but to be honest, reading everything that's been going on in your notes, I think your elevated heart is probably a lot to do with trauma. You have gone through a lot in the last two months."

"I *feel* traumatised." My voice quivered dangerously. He had given me the space to acknowledge how I was feeling out loud. "I can't cope with the idea of going back to work yet. I'm signed off for another two weeks, but I just feel like I'm dragging myself through the days. I'm not coping... I was thinking about taking extended sick leave until my treatment is over. I just can't..." I trailed off. My emotions were threatening to overspill, and I was worried if I began crying, I might not be able to stop.

"It is not a question of thinking about taking time off, I'm going to insist you do. I'm signing you off for three months and by then you will have had your radiation treatment, and we can review it then."

A wave of relief washed over me. "Thank you ... so much."

"I will send you a link via text with your medical certificate and if you ask the girls on the desk, they can book you in for the ECG. In the meantime, I want you to look after yourself and rest." He turned to me and smiled warmly.

Now was my opportunity. I leant around under the chair picked up my backpack and placed it on my lap. "I just wanted to say thank you. If it weren't for you, I would never have known I had cancer, and things could have turned out differently for me." I pulled out a gift bag and card.

"Oh that really wasn't necessary," he said, a little embarrassed. "It's my job to help you and I'm just as surprised and pleased that I found this."

"I know it's your job, but this is my life, and I'm so grateful to you," I said, choked up as I passed him the bag filled with chocolates, wine and gourmet biscuits. I had tried to cover all bases. "It's just a little something to say thank you."

"That's so kind of you," he said, peeking into the bag.

"It's the least I could do," I said, standing up.

Dr Atkins stood up and opened his office door for me. "Take care."

"Thank you." I turned around and left.

A couple of days later, I took a trip on the bus back to the hospital and left gift bags with the Critical Care unit, the anaesthetist, and surgeon's office. I didn't see them; I didn't need to. Everything I needed to say was written in the thank-you cards.

BUT, WHY?

4 NOVEMBER 2023

"Why are we here, Mum? Like... what is the point of it all?" Jack asked, lying on his stomach on the lounge floor, staring up the window. Jack had spent years locked inside his own mind, inside the flat. The isolation had led to bouts of deep introspection.

I breathed in deeply, stretching my toes on the sofa next to him. "I honestly don't know, Jack."

I didn't have the answer for Jack, but what I did know was I wanted to live my life now. Having cancer strengthened that desire to *really* live. Aside from the trauma, I was still trying to process what had happened in the theatre during the emergency. No one else understood, least of all my son. The strange experience was mine alone and I couldn't give anyone objective proof that it had happened, only give my account of the events.

Why *are* we here? I had been asking the same question since childhood. As a teen I was fascinated by the stars and planets. Whilst my friends were out discovering alcohol and boys, I was painting the moon and beach landscapes and wondering how they came to be. I had been searching my whole life for something I could never find and my experience in theatre drove a renewed and insatiable desire for those answers.

Jack's questioning that night sent me spiralling into an existential crisis fuelled by more than my cancer diagnosis. My out-of-body experience in theatre had shaken me to my core, and I felt lost, drifting without an anchor to ground me. The questions of the purpose to my existence rolled over in my mind and I would sit ruminating, trying to find answers to impossible questions.

I spent hours searching online, getting nowhere closer to the answers I was seeking and found myself coming back to meditation as a starting point. I began to practice again and in those few minutes of meditation, the questions stopped. I couldn't feel my body, just a subtle energy inside that felt both familiar and comforting and, in that stillness, there was no cancer, or fear, or searching. Just peace.

Meditation became a daily practice, every morning before I let the noise of my life in.

Just after waking, whilst still sleepy, and before reaching habitually for my mobile phone, I would sit up. The slightly uncomfortable position would guarantee I wouldn't drift back off to sleep. I closed my eyes and followed my breath in and out and as I did, I silently whispered inside my mind.

Breathe in... Breathe out.

Naturally, thoughts appeared, and I had to focus on breathing to bring my mind back from distraction, but in time it became easier.

Breathe in... I

Breathe out... am

Breathe in... I

Breathe out... am

I added sentences onto the end of my breaths:

I am in perfect health.

I am cancer free.

Every day, I get stronger and stronger.

During meditation, I really felt those words. I didn't feel pain. I had no vocal issues, or breathlessness or tightness in my surgical site. I started to look forward to my practice every day, for it offered me an escape from the reality of my healing body and surroundings.

I began adding images to my statements. I saw myself sprinting with Billy and reaching the end of the lane by the caravan, jumping for joy in my healed body that was gaining strength each day. I captured the image in my mind like a photo and held onto the essence of joy I felt as I leapt into the air full of life.

I imagined myself sitting in the oncologist's office. I felt the fabric of the chair that held me. I heard him telling me it was good news, that there was no evidence of any cancer. I imagined the relief I would feel when he said those words and I let that feeling amplify until it filled my entire body. I explored the image in my imagination in detail over and over until it felt real. In my mind, I was there, in perfect health.

I did my best to carry those feelings with me throughout the day. It wasn't easy. My body reminded me regularly that it was still healing, but I knew that meditation was somehow helping me physically, and mentally. I went to sleep at night listening to guided health meditations, more often than not, falling asleep before I could complete them but certain my subconscious mind was listening to the empowering statements of perfect health.

MOPPING UP

14 NOVEMBER–4 DECEMBER 2023

In preparation for my radioactive iodine treatment later in November, I began my low-iodine diet (also known as the LID) to reduce the amount of iodine in my body. The body requires iodine to produce thyroid hormones. These hormones control the body's metabolism, energy, and other essential functions. Iodine is found in various foods, most predominantly in dairy products, eggs, and food sources from the sea such as fish and seaweed. Some of the plant-based dairy alternatives are now fortified with iodine too. Although in the UK iodine is not routinely added to salt, in the US and other parts of the world, it is, making it even harder to avoid. By restricting my intake for two weeks, any remaining thyroid cells would be craving iodine by the time I took the radioactive iodine pill and would readily absorb it, bringing the radiation directly to the cancerous source.

I dreaded starting the diet. I'd spent almost four decades on one restrictive diet or another. The LID meant completely altering my food intake and put me right back into restriction and scrutinising food labels. All the things I'd learned to love once again were now forbidden: no milky coffee, no Greek yogurt, no cakes or milk chocolate, or eggs, biscuits, or pastry. No soy sauce, no fish. The list felt endless.

I had to plan all my meals and snacks. I researched as much as I could and wrote the days up on a whiteboard. It challenged me to get creative with food, but it wasn't easy or much fun. I lived on black coffee, plain meat, salads, and fruit. I became hyper-vigilant over ingredients, scared I might slip up and accidentally eat the wrong thing and compromise my treatment.

The first couple of days on the diet affected my digestion. I had diarrhoea, but by the end of the first week, the diarrhoea was the least of my problems. I felt drained and exhausted and extremely bored of food. I had no idea of the value of a varied diet and in cutting out all dairy foods, I was missing a large part of my regular energy source.

The highlight of the diet was discovering a week in, that meringues were considered low in iodine. Eggs are one of the highest sources of iodine, but most of it is in the yolk. I'd sit night after night munching through sweet crunchy meringue crumbled over tinned fruit as a dessert. It was hardly gourmet food, but believe me when you are on the LID diet, that combination seemed like a Michelin star-worthy dessert. I craved hot, cheesy pizza on fresh dough and frothy milk in my coffee. And a bar of creamy milk chocolate!

Every day I crossed off the date with a red marker knowing that I was a step closer to a dreamy pizza. My mouth would salivate at the thought, yet I was very disciplined and stuck to it rigidly. I had to be, for if I hadn't prepared my body for the radiation treatment, it might not be as effective and it wasn't a process I wanted to repeat.

The night before my hospital admission, I slept fitfully, spooned next to Billy. I wanted to feel his warmth and listen to his snores. I wanted to savour his familiar smell. The treatment would prevent me from being in close contact with him for some time. The separation would be hard for us both.

The alarm startled us both at 7am. I busied myself dressing and packing the last few bits, distracting my mind from the latest instalment of cancer treatment. This was one I was dreading. The thought of putting radioactive matter inside my body really scared me.

I forced myself to eat dry toast. I wouldn't be able to eat anything until late afternoon. Lining my stomach with something felt like protection from the poison I was scheduled to swallow.

Jack appeared at the kitchen door. "What time are you leaving, Mum?"

"Paul is picking me up at 8.45," I replied through a mouthful of toast.

Jack outstretched his arms in a rare gesture of contact. I wrapped my arms around his waist gently and felt the warmth and life of this soul I'd fought so hard to conceive and keep alive.

"Take care, Mum, I will be thinking of you. It's going to be okay. Just don't lie to us about anything this time, will you?"

Jack had researched my treatment and side effects, just as he'd searched the statistics on my cancer. He needed facts. Jack needed to know I would be okay.

"I won't, I promise. It's perfectly safe, I just have to stay away from you afterwards for a bit," I said, lingering in his embrace.

My phone buzzed on the kitchen counter, interrupting our hug. Paul was waiting for me.

"I'm outside, but no rush, take your time x"

I grabbed my bag and the dog who was eagerly awaiting seeing his dad. He was like a child we co-parented. "Bye, Jack."

"Bye, Mum. I love you..."

"I love you too, Jack." I smiled, before turning to the front door and opening it.

Paul was in the communal hallway of the flats and as he climbed the stairs, I could see tears in his eyes.

"Oh, please don't cry. You will start me off," I pleaded, throwing my arms around his neck.

"It's just hard, you know... It's so hard to see you go through all this."

"I know, but I will be fine."

Paul took my suitcase and the dog, and I turned to lock the door.

"Go on, I will meet you in a moment."

I went back inside and scoped around the kitchen, looking at all the plugs, triple-checking everything was unplugged, and switched off. I really didn't have time to get caught in checking rituals.

"Bye, Jack!" I called up the stairs once more, leaving before he could reply.

I left the flat and climbed in the car. It was grey with thick, drizzling rain, the kind of weather that dampens enthusiasm on the best of days. It was a sombre reflection of the day to come.

The twenty-minute journey was unusually quiet. There was nothing to say. I didn't want to reveal how scared I felt, to anyone, not even myself but as my mind wandered to that place of fear, I couldn't stop the silent tears.

Stop it, you need to be strong!

"Are you okay?" Paul enquired quietly, having seen me wiping my face with the back of my hand.

"I'm fine, it's just..." I couldn't say it and didn't need to. Paul knew.

"I know. The last two hospital stays felt like surgery to me. But this treatment, this ... is what people with cancer do." Paul said it for me, his voice quivering.

"It's okay. Nothing's going to happen to me this time, I promise," I reassured us both.

We pulled up outside the hospital and I leant across the front seat for a final hug. I'm not sure who was comforting who more, but we both took that embrace and held onto each other.

"Bye, Billy. Mum's going to work." I climbed into the back-seat and ruffled Billy's head, squishing his cheeks gently. "I love you. You're the best puppy in the world." I kissed his warm, soft head. It was just as hard to leave him.

I climbed out of the car and looked behind me one final time, waving at Paul and Billy, blowing a kiss as they drove away.

After a blood test, I navigated the hospital basement warren and found the Nuclear Medicine department. Even the name scared me. I was led to the cancer in-patient ward, cheerfully decorated and welcoming. A friendly nurse ushered me into an empty waiting room as my admission paperwork was prepared.

After a few moments, a nurse arrived with menus for that day. I scanned over them. I was still on my low-iodine diet which only left braised chicken or cottage pie and fruit for dessert. It was the same for both lunch and dinner. How bad could it be? At least someone was cooking for me for a change. Just the sound of braised chicken turned my stomach, though. I selected cottage pie and fruit, twice.

Shortly after the nurse left, two men arrived in blue scrubs.

"Hello Miss Johnson, my name is Emin, and this is my colleague, Harry. We are the nuclear physicists here and I am going to run through what we are going to be doing today."

They both sat down beside me, Emin held a collection of papers. He was around my age. He spoke with a gentle Turkish accent, softened by his years working in England. He had a thick, dark moustache and when he smiled, his eyes disappeared into warm wrinkles of kindness. Harry was younger, with a mop of blond wavy hair and cheerful manner. Both men immediately put me at ease.

"We will be taking you to your room shortly and our boss, Lucy, will be bringing in your radioactive iodine around 11.30am this morning, so nothing to eat or drink from now on. Now then, there are some things we will need to run through in the room—"

A nurse opened the door, and we all turned to look at the interruption.

"The room is ready now if you want to bring the patient through," the nurse said, looking at me.

"Okay, let's go. We can continue in your room."

Emin and Harry stood up. I gathered my belongings and followed behind them onto the ward. My room was at the very end of a long corridor. It was now apparent I was a patient on a Cancer Treatment and Palliative Care ward, and it was probably the first time I'd felt like a cancer patient during the whole experience.

"Here we are," Emin announced as he led me into a basement room.

There was a view of sorts from the high window behind the bed. A set of concrete steps outside led upwards to somewhere unknown, blocked by a gate and foreboding '*NO ENTRY*' sign. Two brick walls sat either side of the steps with several pipes and vents protruding from them. The angle of the room permitted a limited view of the sky. Being down in the basement level, I hadn't anticipated any view at all, so the small glimmer of wintry sky was a welcome surprise.

The room was a little bigger than normal. A large, vinyl photograph of a sunny beach wrapped around one wall in a cheerful mural. The en-suite bathroom had a similar beach scene covering the wall opposite the toilet. Despite the murals, it was still a hospital room with unforgiving fluorescent lights and plastic sheets on a mechanical bed. The familiar hospital smell awakened a simmering anxiety, and my stomach turned over nauseously.

Emin pulled a board across the entrance of my room blocking the door. It looked like a whiteboard on wheels, but this was a thick lead wall, positioned to protect him and the other staff who would deliver my food. I would be otherwise left alone as my radiation levels could affect anyone who came into contact with me.

"This is a lead board, and I will stand behind here and measure your radioactive levels twice a day," Emin said, stepping behind the board to demonstrate.

He pulled a high table on wheels from the left-hand side of the room and pushed it up against the edge of the lead board forming a barricade between us both. "The staff will place your food and water on here. Once they leave your room, you can collect it. Your meals will come on paper plates, and we will give you a set of cutlery. You must keep them and wash at the sink yourself, then reuse them.

"If you have any food scraps from your meals, you must put these down the toilet and flush it away before binning the plates in the yellow bin there." Emin pointed to a large yellow bin in the corner. "You will need to shower at least twice a day, including washing your hair and drink plenty of water to flush the radium out of your body. When you use the toilet, please flush it twice and wash your hands thoroughly before touching anything."

I nodded in agreement without saying a word. It was beginning to feel overwhelming.

"Tomorrow you can start sucking on sour sweets to encourage the salivary glands. The radium can pool in them, and this will help you flush it out. Occasionally people can feel sick with this capsule so we can arrange to give you an anti-sickness tablet if you like?" Emin paused.

"Yes please." The last thing I wanted was to heave up radioactive debris or strain my neck, still tender and swollen from surgery.

"Okay, I think that's everything. Do you have any questions at all?"

"No, not that I can think of."

"Okay, good. We will be back with Lucy around 11.30 to administer the capsule." Emin grinned and Harry, who had been silently listening, joined him.

I liked these two men. Emin had momentarily minimised my terror of swallowing radiation with his matter-of-fact instructions delivered with an infectious grin.

I unpacked my toiletries and the old clothes I had brought in with me and settled on the bed. Lexi had given me a little gift for hospital with instructions to open it there and dispose of it before I left. On the front was a gift tag: "*Now you have a hand to hold in hospital Xx*"

Intrigued, I unwrapped the tissue paper. Inside was a pink woollen glove, stuffed with cushion filler. She had stitched a heart on the front and on the side, was a blue label. On it '*A hand to hold xxx*' was beautifully hand-stitched. Like a child with her comfort blanket, I hugged it to my face for comfort.

This space would be my home for the next three days. In the corner of the room was a sink with surgical soap and paper towels, along with washing-up liquid and a tub of surgical-grade wipes. Next to the sink sat the large bin, lined with a yellow industrial bag. '*DO NOT EMPTY – RADIOACTIVE WASTE*' was printed in unmissable bold letters reminding me why I was here.

The small en-suite bathroom wasn't any less clinical. A tiny sink, soap and towel dispenser were squeezed into one corner and alongside sat another yellow labelled bin. Everything I touched would go in these bins to be decontaminated from radiation, before being destroyed.

The shower screen reached the top of my thighs and concertinaed into a folded frame, with a white vinyl shower curtain that separated me from the toilet. The shower screen was cracked, and the edges were caked in opaque limescale. The grout around the shower head was thick and discoloured from countless repairs. It was tired and worn. The room was depressingly dim and claustrophobic. It quickly became apparent this wasn't going to be the relaxing escape I hoped it might be.

I sat on the bed waiting, fidgeting constantly in nervous anticipation. A tap on the door diverted me from my thoughts and a young man in a mask appeared.

"Hello Ms Johnson, I'm Dr Benson and I'm just going to ask you a few questions about your general health." His voice was muffled by the surgical mask. He lifted my wrist and felt for my pulse. "Okay, good. Now if you can just lean forward and take a deep breath for me."

I felt the cold disc of metal from the stethoscope through my jumper as he moved it around my back.

"And another deep breath in for me ... and breathe out. Excellent. I will write up a prescription for your anti-sickness medication," he said, his eyes softening with a smile I couldn't see before he turned and left the room.

Fifteen minutes later, a nurse appeared with a pill in a little white paper pot. "Here is your anti-sickness medication. If you wait for the Nuclear Medicine team to get here, they will advise you when to take it." She left and closed the door behind her.

Suddenly I didn't feel brave or strong, despite everyone telling me I was. Despite the science behind it, I feared this poisonous medicine and lying in a lead-lined room with screens and yellow and black radioactive warnings everywhere, amplified the fear. My heart began to race. I screwed my eyes shut tightly.

I am safe. I am safe. I am safe.

Over and over, I repeated the mantra silently, attempting to soothe myself.

I heard a rumbling noise approaching my room and the familiar jovial tones of Emin. He and Harry had returned, along with the head of the department, Lucy, who was pulling a small grey metal trolley. On the back of the trolley sat a small white can and plastic syringe in the middle of a large blue tray. All three staff were wearing lead vests. My heart began to race faster again.

"Hello Ms Johnson," Lucy greeted me jovially.

Wearing protective gloves, she placed the tray on the table over my bed. It was edged with yellow tape and the familiar black radiation warning logo – '*CAUTION – RADIOACTIVE MATERIAL*'. Next to the lead canister was a small white bottle, the size of a travel-shampoo bottle, sealed with a matching green lid. It was labelled '*DUMMY CAPSULE*'. I was getting a fast lesson in radioactive capsule administration.

Emin and Harry positioned themselves behind the lead screen pulled across my room entrance.

Lucy smiled. "Right then, here it is. I'm going to show you how we extract the capsule using this dummy one," she said, taking the pot and unscrewing the lid, before picking up the plastic tube. "We put this tube inside the pot, and squeeze, and this will pull the capsule up into the tube like this." I watched the dummy pill appear in the plastic tube.

"Then I will pass it to you, and you will need to put the other end of the tube in your mouth and tilt your head back. The capsule will fall down the tube into your mouth."

She continued tipping the tube as I watched the pill slide

down to the other end. "You need to take a drink of water immediately and swallow it, okay? Now if you can't swallow it the first time, don't panic and spit it out. Once these capsules touch skin, or the inside of your mouth, the warmth will start to dissolve it, and we don't want you spitting radioactive iodine all over the room!" Lucy laughed heartily. "If you can't swallow it first time, just take another sip of water and try again. Do you have any questions?"

"No." I shook my head.

"Okay, then, here we go." She unscrewed the green cap from the lead container and squeezed the long plastic tube inside the can. A bright-yellow capsule appeared, untouched by human hands. She immediately passed the tube to me, and without stopping to think, I tipped the larger end into my mouth and grabbed the glass of water. I felt the capsule hit my tongue. I've swallowed dozens of capsules during my lifetime but this one terrified me.

What if I panic and choke on it? What if it melts on my tongue?

I had visions of my tongue bubbling away and disintegrating.

I gulped a mouthful of water within seconds and tilted my head back and swallowed. "Done!" I exclaimed.

All three doctors breathed again.

"Well done," Lucy encouraged. Her anticipation of a smooth administration was palpable. "It will start dissolving in your stomach almost immediately so nothing to eat or drink for at least an hour. You may start feeling sick in a few hours, if you do, please take the anti-sickness medication. At about 1.30, you can eat your lunch and start drinking lots of water."

"We want this to flush through your system so if you need to pee, don't hold onto it, go straight away so it doesn't pool in the kidneys or bladder. Make sure you flush twice and wash your hands thoroughly. Please shower a couple of times today and wash your hair too."

Lucy manoeuvred the trolley around the lead board and towards the door before turning around and looking over the screen. "They call us the mop-up team. The surgeons remove your thyroid and as brilliant as they are, occasionally there is microscopic thyroid tissue left. Our job is to go in and mop that up." She smiled and wheeled the trolley towards the door.

"I will be back in about ten minutes to take your first reading," Emin said before he, Lucy, and Harry left, closing the door. The faint rumble of the trolley disappeared along with their muffled voices.

And just like that, it was done. It was a strange and unnerving feeling knowing this toxic capsule was dissolving in my stomach. A substance that killed people, caused mutations and malformations, a substance that *caused* cancer, was now in my stomach on the sole mission of destroying any that remained of mine.

I picked up my phone and looked at the news, I needed distraction.

Ten minutes later, I heard a faint tap at the door. The lead screen mostly covered the glass panel almost blocking my view.

"I'm back!" Emin called, his familiar face appearing over the lead screen. He leaned his arms on the screen holding a yellow box and a tape measure. "Could you come to the end of your bed for me please? I'm going to pass you this."

He fed a retractable tape measure towards me. "Now hold this up against your chest, I need you to be at least a metre away. This is a Geiger counter. It will measure the amount of radiation you are emitting."

"Does it make a sound?" I asked curiously. I'd seen these devices on films.

"I can turn on the sound for you." He clicked a dial, and the machine began to crackle loudly.

This was no movie set, this was my body, crackling with dangerous radiation. It was both curious and terrifying.

Emin leant against the wall and filled out a chart on a clipboard, before turning back to me. "I will be back at 8.30pm to measure again. In the meantime, rest, and have a relaxing afternoon." He left, closing the door.

The room fell silent. I turned around and looked out the window and the brown moss-covered brickwork and grey concrete steps. The small scrap of visible sky was as grey as the concrete below it. I climbed back onto the bed, scantily covered in one white sheet and a thin blanket that barely covered the blue hospital bed beneath. The plastic pillows in white slips were flat and uninviting. Despite the beach mural, nothing could disguise the fact it was a hospital room on a cancer ward, and I was alone.

I picked up my phone and earbuds and put on a show I'd been saving to watch in hospital.

Just after 1.30pm, someone tapped the door. "*Here's your lunch, lovely. I will put it here. You can collect it after I'm gone.*"

A lady's arm briefly appeared at the side of the screen and placed a paper plate and wooden cutlery down on the table that blocked me in. At least I had no washing up to do.

"*Enjoy your lunch,*" she said cheerily and closed the door behind herself.

I collected the food and carried it to my table. I was hungry and keen to dilute the nuclear liquid gurgling in my stomach. The rice and pie were barely palatable, but I ate almost all of it. Someone was cooking it and bringing it to me. All I had to do was put the plate and cutlery in the bin afterwards. It was a luxury I wasn't used to. I had been cooking for myself since I was seventeen, and cooking for others for just as long and I welcomed the break from that role.

The afternoon passed, the time marked by the number of episodes of the show I was watching.

Before long, the nurse was back with my dinner: a carbon copy of lunch, delivered from behind the lead screen, this time with a disposable plastic cup of gravy. The boiled rice looked as if it had been left over from lunch and reheated to a dehydrated grey pile.

I picked through the dinner. It was even less palatable second time around. I scraped the remainder in the toilet and flushed, twice. Watching the food fill the toilet bowl and swirl with the water was nauseating. I stepped on the yellow bin pedal and threw in the plate and cutlery and shuddered as it slammed shut.

I forced myself through drinking two litres of water in three hours. The downside meant five trips to the bathroom, each with two flushes and fastidious handwashing. Emin would be back in less than two hours to measure my radiation levels again and I had to shower before then. I was grateful of the opportunity to rid the radiation from my skin. I couldn't see it, nor feel it but I knew it was there. I had heard it.

The shower was mercifully hot and powerful. I closed my eyes and stood under the water, letting it fall over my hair and body. The papery thin shower curtain stuck to my back, making my skin crawl. I let my mind disappear, to a shower in a fine hotel, somewhere far away from this basement hospital room. A few moments of escapism distracted me from the task in hand.

I opened my eyes and stared at the thick, aged sealant around the taps, aware once again of my real surroundings and the slippery shower curtain still glued to my back. I scrubbed my body, from head to toe, twice in thick soapy shower gel. I wanted this stuff out of my body.

Emin appeared just after 8.30pm. I was dressed and my wet hair hung around me proving I was doing as I was told.

"I'm back again!" he announced cheerfully, armed with the yellow box, tape measure and clipboard. "Can you come to the end of your bed and do the same," he said, feeding me the tape measure.

I pulled the metal end and held it firmly to my chest as he turned on the Geiger meter and I waited for the crackle. It was a little quieter.

"Oh, that's dropped!" He sounded surprised, as he noted down the measurement on his clipboard. My two and a half litres of water and scrupulous scrubbing was having the desired effect.

"I will be back tomorrow morning around 8.30 to take another measurement from you. Get some rest. Goodnight." He grinned enthusiastically.

"Night."

I watched him close the door and heard his footsteps retreating into the quietness of the ward, knowing he was my last human contact that evening. I climbed into bed and settled down, pushing my earbuds in and continued to watch the show on my phone.

Just after 10pm, an alarm sounded, I could hear it over the audio on my earphones. I paused the show to listen.

"*Can I get some help in here!*" a voice called from next door.

My heart began pumping faster, thumping in my chest. I knew the sound of the alarm and what it meant.

"*Come on... Come on, come on!*"

Although muffled, I could hear through the lead-lined wall separating me from the other patients, and I knew they were trying to resuscitate someone.

Suddenly a swarm of staff were outside my room and in and out of the room next door.

Please let them be okay... Please let them be okay, I silently willed.

I could hear my heart pumping over all the noise. It was the loudest sound of them all.

I grabbed my woolly hand, laid it on my stomach and gripped it with my right hand. I needed a hand to hold. I put my show back on and turned up the volume, trying to block out the situation unfolding outside. A team of doctors were milling about in deep discussion. I could see the top of their heads, from their eyes and above and occasionally they glanced in at me and our eyes met. I heard them organising a bed in Critical Care.

An hour later, they transferred the patient, and the ward fell silent once again. I settled down on my plastic pillows and pulled the covers up. I was cold and shaken by the events next door and nausea was creeping in. I wasn't sure if it was the radium or adrenaline, but I didn't want to risk vomiting. I swallowed the anti-sickness pill and turned off the light.

The night dragged by, and I barely slept. A new bed with minimal covers and plastic pillows interrupted any hope of deep sleep.

At 6.50am, the lights came on outside on the ward and I could hear the nurses talking and the sound dragged me from the shallow sleep I'd finally fallen into.

Shortly afterwards a lady tapped the door and appeared with a paper plate and a small packet of jam and margarine and a slice of cold dry toast. I rarely ate breakfast and never at 7am but I grabbed the opportunity. I had barely picked at the dinner the night before. Thankfully, I packed some fruit in my bag and ate a banana with the piece of bread.

Emin would soon arrive to take another measurement. I showered and changed just in time, and he appeared a little early.

"Good morning. How are you feeling? Did you sleep well?" he asked enthusiastically.

"I didn't sleep great, but I feel okay though felt a little sick last night, I took the tablet about eleven," I replied.

"Oh. You didn't sleep?" He cocked his head in surprise.

"No but never mind, I'm not going anywhere today, I will rest!"

Emin fed the tape measure towards me silently. This was the third time, and I knew the drill. The crackle was much quieter.

"Good, it's going down!" he said, muttering numbers under his breath as he filled out the chart. "Now, I want you to drink plenty of water and start sucking some sour sweets. This will stimulate the salivary glands. I will see you this afternoon, and hopefully I will have some good news about when you can go home tomorrow." He beamed.

"Going home ... tomorrow ... already?"

"Yes, your readings are coming down and hopefully tomorrow you will be under the safe levels so we can discharge you.

"Oh ... I'd better call the hotel and see if I can come a night earlier then!" I said, feeling a glimmer of excitement at the thought of a comfortable hotel bed and some decent food.

"You are going to a hotel ... not home?" Emin asked, surprised.

"Yes, I'd planned to. I spoke to someone in your team three weeks ago and they said it was okay."

"I will talk to my boss. I'm not sure it is possible to go to a hotel for legal reasons as you are radioactive. I will come back soon." Emin left, closing the door behind him.

My heart began to race. *No hotel?* I didn't have a back-up plan. I didn't want to go home but I had nowhere else to go.

About ten minutes later, Emin returned, accompanied by Lucy, and delivered the news I had been dreading. Staying in a hotel was a complex matter for legal reasons, she said. The hospital would have to declare my situation and risk of radioactive contamination to bedding, cutlery and the bathroom, not to mention staff. Exposing hotel staff to my radiation wasn't something I was prepared to do so I resigned myself to returning home. There was nothing else I could do.

When they left the room, my mind went into overdrive. *Was there anywhere else I could go?* I didn't want to go home to my cramped flat. There was no way to escape contact with my sons and with only one working toilet, it meant I would have to share. I cancelled my hotel booking, at least that way I could avoid a charge for a room I couldn't sleep in.

I paced the room anxiously. This last-minute change was not part of the plan.

Lexi! She lived alone and had a spare room. She had offered to help me so many times. I could ask her ... but it's such short notice. No, I will leave it and go home.

In less than a minute, I'd talked myself out of the idea. I settled back down; my only conversation was the one in my own mind, and it was a lonely one-sided chat. Aside from the occasional nurse check-in at the start of a shift and my food delivery, there was no one to talk to. Emin brought a sense of safety and lightheartedness into the room with him and each time he left, I found the isolation harder to deal with.

I'd foolishly thought my inpatient treatment would be a pleasant break, lying in a bed all day with no responsibilities. All I had to do was shower and eat food that would be brought to me. It sounded a welcome change from my busy life. But the reality was shaping up very differently.

My days were normally full of interactions: text messages,

phone calls, bumping into neighbours, strangers stopping to pet the dog. My life living in a town centre was busy and connected. I dashed into my local shops daily. I knew everyone and they knew me. I was never short of conversation or company. I hadn't predicted how isolating it would feel to be in a room alone. I had my phone for company, but after thirty-six hours with only that, I was becoming agitated.

I showered, lingering far longer that I usually would. I had no desire to return to the bed in a room with a basement wall for a view. The thick shower gel splashed against the curtain, foamy purple suds trailing down the grey vinyl wall. My sense of smell seemed different. The sweet shower gel nauseated me slightly, its scent seemed far more pungent than usual.

I looked down at my feet, buried under the bubbles that slowly swirled and disappeared down the large, raised drain. The floor, an industrial blue speckle, felt slimy. I shuddered at the sensation, closed my eyes, and put my head under the warm water, the hot needles dancing on my scalp. I carried my mind away, to a warm shower on the edge of the beach I stared at from the toilet seat during each visit. I'd just come off the beach. My skin was warm, my hair tangled and stiff with salt. Traces of sand gathered beneath my feet. I stayed there for a few moments, escaping.

I got dressed in the same radiated red shirt and leggings and returned to my bed, staring at the bag of sour sweets lying on the table. Sweets had never been my 'thing'. Everything containing sugar, yes, but not sweets themselves. I tore the bag open and put a sour gummy on my tongue. I winced instantly. The taste was foul – bitter and sharp but laced with a sweet hit. My face contorted in disgust as I sucked the sweet, but it had the desired effect – my mouth instantly filled with saliva. I forced myself to swallow. Despite whatever noxious substance was coating the gummies, they were also laced with sugar, and I gobbled them up one by one until my stomach and mouth ached.

I lay on the bed watching the clock. Lunch would arrive in two hours and soak up the toxic concoction swimming in my stomach. I put on a pair of rubber gloves I'd brought in with me and pulled out the writing tablet. It felt strange to type in gloves, but they created a protective barrier between me and the keyboard. I began to write about the room, the treatment, and my feelings, and it flowed for almost two hours. Putting it all down on digital paper helped in some way.

A tap on the door startled me from my writing.

"Hi, I have your lunch. I will leave it here for you." A different lady's face and arm partially appeared around the screen before disappearing again, followed by the sound of my door closing.

"Thank you ... so much!" I called after her as I jumped up to collect my food. I meant it, grateful for the human contact.

I glanced down at the day's lunch offerings. It was the same meal for the third time. It had clearly been batch-cooked in a large catering kitchen days earlier and the edges of the food had become progressively drier and grey. They had forgotten to add the boiled vegetable of the day. It was no great loss – boiled, unsalted carrots – but I was so bored with the food, even that felt like a culinary injustice.

I picked through the food, barely eating anything – just enough to soak up the sugary liquid gurgling in my stomach – and flushed the remains down the toilet.

I lay on the bed watching the clock thinking of my dad all those years ago, having radiation treatment and surgeries for cancer. What would he think of his daughter now on a similar journey? Did he feel what I felt? Was he as scared? I already knew the answer to those questions. Dad had resigned himself to his death, but it wasn't an easy fate to accept. He had turned towards religion for comfort in the months leading up to it. Occasionally a priest would visit him and read passages from the Bible, and he would take comfort in the scripture. But Dad died suddenly without warning and through a dreadful misunderstanding, I'd learnt he was terrified in his last moments.

I remember the call at 3am and taking a taxi to the hospice alone, shortly after, still numb with shock. It wasn't supposed to happen, he wasn't meant to die.

I arrived at the hospice and was greeted by two nurses who were waiting for me.

"Your father passed away very quickly. He didn't feel any pain," one nurse reassured me before turning and walking towards a phone that was ringing on the reception desk.

I remember looking across at the other nurse and asking if he knew he was dying and her response floored me.

"Ah, actually, he was very scared," she said, tilting her head and giving me a look of sympathy, as if her words would offer me comfort. I could tell that English was her second language. Perhaps her words had become lost in translation.

I was enraged. "What... What...?? Why would you tell me that?" I cried angrily.

The other nurse heard the commotion and led me to a family room. She sat me down and that's where the inevitable happened. The acceptance of his terminal diagnosis which I'd held behind a wall of denial for so long, broke. I sobbed, my body convulsing in waves of grief until there was nothing left inside me. I was devastated by my dad's sudden death, and incredibly angry at cancer. The insidious disease took my dad from me. It never gave me the chance to say goodbye. Knowing he was scared still haunted me at times, all those years later, for it was me who left him alone to die. I swallowed hard against the guilt stuck in my throat.

The room had grown dark in the late November dusk and the energy even darker through my sombre reminiscing. "*I'm sorry, Dad,*" I whispered into the emptiness, wiping away tears with my sleeve.

I got up, breaking the silence of my own thoughts and stood by the large window behind the bed. I wanted to shut out the heavy darkness outside and reached for the plastic chain attached to roller blind. It tugged, caught on something at the back of the ledge.

I stood on my tiptoes to release the tangle from its obstruction and a transparent plastic sheet peeled off the windowsill with difficulty, as if it had been glued down. The action released the chain, and the blind fell down noisily onto the ledge. I reached up, feeling around for the plastic sheet until my fingertips found it, and pulled it down. It was a thick sheet of malleable window stickers, the kind you peel on and off. I gasped at the design. I know the ledge was way above head height, but how had no one noticed them when the room was regularly decontaminated after each patient?

"*I know it's you. I know you hear me. Thank you for being here, Dad,*" I whispered, smiling through tears as I ran my fingers over the collection of colourful butterfly stickers. I sat back down on the bed and gently wept. I was *never* alone, not really.

Why had I always felt so alone? For years, I'd searched people's behaviour for confirmation of what I felt so deeply inside. I wasn't even conscious of it. I alienated myself over the years and loneliness had become a self-fulfilling prophecy. But somehow Dad's butterfly gift reminded me I didn't have to do everything alone. It was time I stopped repeating that narrative to myself.

I picked up my phone and texted Lexi, "*Hi, I'm not allowed to go to a hotel after all. Legal reasons. I might be discharged tomorrow. Is the offer still there for me to stay with you for a few days? XX"* Lexi would still be at work so I knew it would be some time before she would reply.

Dinner arrived and it was the same pie with a plain jacket potato and boiled carrots. I took a mouthful of potato and carrots, grateful for a change from the grey rice. The potato was raw in the middle. I burst into tears and dropped the wooden cutlery onto the plate, abandoning the meal. I ate the chopped fruit reluctantly through tears, like an exhausted toddler following a tantrum. I scraped the food into the toilet and flushed it away.

I distracted myself with another shower. I couldn't summon the enthusiasm to wash my hair for the third time in twenty-four hours. It was long and tiresome to dry without a hairdryer, so I wrapped it up, stepped into the shower, and washed my body unenthusiastically. Afterwards, I dressed and climbed into the cold bed. I felt imprisoned, mentally, and literally. Only one night remained, and I could leave this place and eat some real food!

Emin arrived for the last measurement of the day. As expected, my reading had dropped again. "Excellent... Get some sleep and I will see you in the morning. Goodnight."

"Night." I watched him leave.

I leant over and picked up my phone. Lexi had replied:

"Of course you can stay. I am so glad you asked me. I will look after you. Just text me when you know what's happening. Love you xx"

"Thank you so much. Will text in the morning. Night. Love you too xx"

I bit my lip, preventing the tears of relief and pulled all my clothes over the bed covers. The warmth of the extra weight felt like a comforting hug and enabled a more restful sleep.

I awoke to the ward lights being turned on around 6.30am.

An icy wind whipped sleet against the window on the dark November morning as I raised the blind. I had a couple of hours until Emin would arrive to take the last measurement – time enough to shower and wash my hair for the last time.

Opening my bathroom door after my shower, I was greeted by snow swirling in a gently flurry around the basement yard. We rarely saw snow in southern England and so when it appeared, it always delighted me. I stood by the window looking up at the small patch of heavy grey sky. I loved the silent sound of snow falling. It temporarily muted life and made me feel like a child again. It didn't last more than a few minutes, but it was a welcome glimmer of joy.

In the still semi-dark room, I laid my red t-shirt out on the bed, staring at it. I'd worn it for each hospital admission. I'd worn it in critical care. If clothes could hold energy, this top held trauma and pain.

I folded it up, along with my leggings and underwear and a pair of old socks I'd been using. I stood on the pedal and opened the yellow bin. "Goodbye, cancer," I said to the clothes, dropping the folded bundle in the bin and took my foot off the pedal, causing the lid to slam shut, loudly. It was a crude ceremonial goodbye, but I felt relief discarding the fabric memories.

My breakfast arrived a few minutes later. It was my seventeenth day on the low-iodine diet. I sat eating my cold, dry toast with a scraping of margarine and jam, thinking about all the things I wanted to eat when I was free from hospital: hot, fresh pizza from my local Italian pizzeria, with creamy mozzarella and garlic-infused olive oil. It may have only been 7.11am but my mouth was salivating.

After breakfast, I cleaned my teeth for the last time, before binning the toothbrush and my small disposable bag of travel-sized toiletries. I hated waste, it felt so strange to dispose of half-used things, but I didn't want to risk bringing any more contaminates home. Emin had forewarned me to dispose of everything I wouldn't be taking and leave my belongings on the bed to be cleaned. I laid out my small case, phone, charger, and writing tablet. Everything else was binned.

Emin tapped the door just after 8am. "Morning, how are you feeling today – are you ready to go home?"

"I think so," I replied, assuming my position at the end of the bed as Emin fed the measuring tape towards me. I held the end tight to my breastbone.

He mumbled something under his breath reading the Geiger meter. "Good. It's under the limit. You can be discharged today! I'm just going to prepare your paperwork, then you will be free to go, but I will come back first to talk about your discharge and clean your belongings."

"Thank you," I replied, both relieved and a little anxious watching him leave the room.

How radioactive *was* I? I wanted to spare anyone ever having this disease and I certainly didn't want to be a cause of someone else's cancer down the line.

I texted Lexi and arranged a lift with Paul. The short ride to Lexi's house would be safe if I remained behind the passenger seat in the back of the car, maximising the distance from each other.

Emin returned with Harry ten minutes later. Both men were dressed in white boiler suits, wearing masks, gloves, and protectors over their shoes.

"Here is your discharge card. You must remain isolated another seven days until the 6th of December," Emin said. "Use your own cutlery, plates and towel and you must flush the toilet twice after each use. Clothes and bedding should be washed twice, and this will clean any residual radioactivity. You need to carry this card with you for three months. This confirms you have had radiation treatment." He passed me a yellow card. "If you go through airport security or a ferry terminal, you may set off the radiation alarms and it can be tricky to explain why." He chuckled. "Do you have any questions?"

"When can I eat normal food?"

"You can eat normally from today." He smiled and his eyes disappeared into his warm expression.

"Ahh." I sighed, relieved the diet was finally over.

"Okay, if you can step outside for us – we are going to measure the radiation and clean your belongings." Emin pulled the mask up and over his face.

I stepped outside the door onto the ward for the first time in three days, feeling nervous and unsafe. Despite my isolation and discomfort, the room had been my safety zone during the radiation treatment and now I felt both vulnerable, and a danger to others.

I watched as they carefully removed the yellow rubbish bags from the hazardous waste bin and Emin ran the Geiger counter over the contents. I could see remnants of food and banana skins squashed against the side of the bag and my stomach turned at the smell of rotting food already filtering into the doorway. Emin placed it inside another bag and tied it firmly before putting it on the lead trolley. They disappeared into the bathroom and returned with the other yellow bag moments later and laid it next to the other one.

They returned to my bed and the few possessions that remained lying on it.

Emin ran the wand over my bag and phone then stopped and turned towards me. "Could you move away from the doorway? I think your levels are affecting the reading." His request was a terrifying reminder that I was still radioactive.

I stepped away from the door and stood in the corner at the end of the corridor, away from everyone. I turned to the wall and silently wept. The reality of my cancer treatment was beginning to hit me.

I listened to their muffled conversation as they worked to decontaminate my belongings ahead of the deep clean that would follow my discharge.

A few minutes later, Emin called me back to the doorway. "Okay, everything is clean now, you are free to leave," he said, passing me my possessions, damp from being cleaned with special wipes.

"Thank you ... for everything," I said, taking my things.

It felt surreal, as if I had been caught up in some strange sci-fi film as I stood staring at the men wearing biohazard suits because of something emanating out of my body. "Bye."

"Bye!" they echoed in unison.

I turned and walked along the corridor, leaving Emin and Harry to begin the decontamination process.

I wonder if they will find the butterfly stickers this time.

I passed the busy nurses' station and opened the door at the end of the Oncology ward. No one noticed me leave. I'd just completed my cancer treatment and got up and left. No one said a word.

I walked through the bustling hospital entrance avoiding every woman or child on the way. It was over, and I felt completely alone. Guilt stepped forward and filled the void.

Stop feeling so sorry for yourself, my inner troll reminded me coldly.

Paul was waiting in the usual parking space and this time there were no hugs. I climbed into the car and said very little as if my words would carry the poison out of my body and contaminate the car.

"Are you okay, Emily?" Paul asked softly.

"I'm just glad it's over. Could you take me to a shop on the way please?" I asked, diverting the conversation. I didn't want to venture into my feelings.

"Of course I will."

Paul pulled up outside a shop. "What would you like?"

"Can you get me a croissant and a bar of chocolate, please?" It was just after 9.30am. The pizza could wait.

I climbed out the car into the icy wind, spitting with sleety rain. I didn't want to linger in Paul's car, worried I might somehow contaminate it. I shivered in the wind waiting for him, salivating at the idea of warm, buttery pastry.

Paul appeared a couple of minutes later, grinning, with a brown paper bag in his hand and a large chocolate bar. "Here we are," he said proudly, passing me the bag.

I could feel the warmth of the fresh pastry through the bag. I tore it open and took a bite of the croissant, closing my eyes to shut off my senses and savour the taste. After such a plain diet, the rich, buttery taste shocked my palette as it melted in my mouth.

"Oh ... it's amazing!" I cried to Paul who was eagerly awaiting my reaction. I savoured every last crumb, collected by my finger from the bottom of the bag. It had been worth waiting three weeks for.

We climbed back into the car and Paul drove the short distance to Lexi's house. She came to her door to greet me, having waited, watching for the car to pull up. Paul lifted out the case and we stood a few feet apart.

"*Thank you ... for everything. I love you,*" I mouthed silently.

"*I love you too,*" Paul whispered. "I'm so proud of you for going through all this."

"Thank you. I will text you later. Maybe we can go for a walk with the dog in a couple of days if I stay away from you both?" I suggested, wanting another opportunity to see him again.

"Yes of course. Billy will love that – he misses you."

Billy... I'd missed him so much.

I waved goodbye and turned to Lexi who was waiting at the front door for me.

"Hello, come on in, I will take you to your room."

Lexi led me into her house out of the bitter air and I kicked off my shoes, before following her up the stairs.

"This is your room," she said gently, gesturing me into her spare room.

I pulled my case in behind me and took one look around the room and burst into exhausted tears. Fresh tulips sat in a vase by the bed, and a tray laid on it ready to rest my writing tablet on. Next to the tray sat a parcel of fluffy new socks. Lexi had fashioned a swan out of a towel and beside it, placed two chocolates just like they did in fancy hotels.

On the bed was a stuffed-toy dog, just like Billy. She found it in a charity shop the night before and had sewn a label on the dog with his name, *Billy*. Lexi put so much thought into preparing for my last-minute stay and her kindness was overwhelming. I began to sob.

"Oh I hate that I can't hug you!" she cried as we stood metres apart. Lexi was crying too.

"Thank you so much ... for everything," I said through my hands, covering my face.

"Thank you for letting me help you, I know how hard it was for you to ask me and I'm proud of you for accepting the help. Get some rest now and come down whenever you want."

I climbed into the clean, warm bed, still fully clothed, and closed my eyes, sinking back into the fluffy pillow. I curled my legs up to my chest and pulled the thick duvet up to my nose. I felt safe at last, as I closed my eyes and drifted off to sleep.

"Would you like some soup or toast?" Lexi's voice called up the stairs, rousing me from my dream.

I glanced at my phone. Almost two hours had passed. "Yes please, I'll come down now." My stomach felt unsettled from the pastry earlier.

After lunch, we sat down to chat, separated, and confined to opposite ends of Lexi's lounge as I perched on the floor by the wall. I was allowed to spend ninety minutes in the same room as long as we remained adequately distanced. I felt exhausted and sick. The soup had done little to settle my stomach, and it wasn't long before diarrhoea began. My body felt poisoned from within. Every trip to the bathroom meant bleaching the toilet, after double-flushing then washing my hands twice, then cleaning the sink down. It was tiring.

I climbed into bed about 7pm and grabbed my temporary Billy, tucking him under my arm like a child as I fell into the most comfortable deep sleep I had experienced in days.

The following day my mouth tasted strange, as if coated in a film of something with a lingering metallic taste. I looked at the nightstand. The chocolate Paul had bought me was there, unopened. Despite my griping stomach, I tore it open and popped a square in my mouth. The initial sweet creaminess excited my senses, encouraging me to eat another, then another until I had eaten half the bar, but the sweet taste was soon replaced by an unpleasant metal flavour. "Ugh." I put the rest of the bar back on the nightstand and sipped some water. Even that tasted like rusty nails.

Lexi had left for work, so I went downstairs to the kitchen to make toast, shivering as I waited for the kettle to boil. I stared through the window into the back garden.

I miss my little caravan, my birds and my view. I can't wait to get back to Sunshine.

It was eerily still outside, blanketed in frost and silenced by thick, grey cloud. I perched on a stool watching the stillness. The only sounds were my own as I devoured toast smothered in jam, with black instant coffee to mask the foul taste in my mouth.

The combination of chocolate and breakfast had been a mistake on a fragile stomach, and I spent the remainder of the morning cleaning the bathroom after myself. It seemed my rush to return to a normal diet after three weeks restriction had been thwarted. My body just wasn't ready for it, nor the toxic radiation still working its way through my digestive system.

Lexi returned at lunchtime, and we spent the afternoon watching a movie, sitting as far away as possible from her, near the log burner roaring warmly against the minus-four degrees outside.

The following day, Paul arrived to take me to a nearby park. With him he brought me a surprise – a hot flat white from a local coffee shop and Billy! It was difficult to stand apart from Billy, he didn't understand my distance despite his attempts to jump all over me.

I took the lid off the coffee and breathed in the fragrant steam escaping into the frosty air. I was giddy with anticipation, and quickly took a sip. "Oh Paul!" I exclaimed, tears welling up as I swallowed the rich milky coffee. "It's amazing!" I cried.

I had a newfound appreciation for everything, and coffee had never tasted so good, or creamy, after three weeks of dairy abstinence. The coffee was also strong enough to disguise the lingering metallic taste.

We walked a metre apart, through a local park in heavy freezing fog that hung in the air, shrouding the trees in white frost draped over every object. Delicate spiders' webs, coated in tiny sparkling diamonds, decorated the bushes of the wintry landscape. We walked slowly, Paul, Billy, and me with my hot, steaming coffee. We chatted comfortably, our words escaping our mouths in clouds of mist that froze and hung between us. Life was teaching me to saviour even the simplest of moments.

Paul walked me back to Lexi's place; half an hour had been enough in the bitter weather. I felt exhausted. In three days, I would return to my sons and Billy, so I needed to make the most of my isolation time and Lexi's easy company.

Over the following days, my stomach settled a little and I was able to eat some soup and toast. I really enjoyed staying with Lexi, and for the first time in many years, I gave myself the time to exclusively care for me. I napped in the afternoons, read a book, watched movies, and took long baths. It was exactly what my body, and soul, needed.

The following Monday, Paul arrived to pick me up. My isolation was over, and it was time to return home.

As I was leaving, I turned to Lexi. "Thank you ... for everything."

"Oh, come here, I don't care about distancing anymore!" Lexi pulled me into her arms, and we shared the hug we'd both been longing for, for days. It was as if I had never felt a hug before and I savoured every second of it: the warmth of her skin, the soft touch of her hair on my cheek and subtle fragrance of her perfume.

"Thank you... I've loved having you here. I love you," she spoke softly into my hair as I squeezed her back in acknowledgment.

"*I love you too,*" I whispered.

We pulled apart and I climbed into the back of the car, turning to wave at Lexi until she disappeared from view through the rear window.

I had one more hospital appointment to attend before I could return home. It was the whole-body scan, along with CT scans that would show how effective my radiation uptake had been. Paul parked nearby and I returned to the Nuclear Medicine department. It was 4 December, trip number 23, and the last for the year.

I was led into a room housing the largest piece of hospital equipment I'd ever seen. It looked like a giant metal doughnut connected to a three-metre-long conveyer belt. It was a Gamma camera and would scan my body from various angles.

A radiographer instructed me to change into a gown that had been left on a chair, before disappearing into a control room and drawing the privacy blinds on the large glass window. Two radiologists returned a few minutes later.

"If you could get on here and lie down," one of them instructed, patting her hand on the long, conveyor belt-style table.

I climbed on and lay on my back. She secured my arms inside a wraparound cover to stop me moving whilst the other radiographer explained the procedure. It comprised of three stages and would take around fifty minutes altogether.

"Do you have any questions?" I shook my head. "The first machine will come down from here," she said, pointing towards the flat machine in front of the circular shape. "It might feel like it's coming very close to your face. Don't worry, it doesn't touch you. Try to keep still and if you feel uncomfortable just call us," she reassured, before leaving the room.

I rarely felt claustrophobic, but I was beginning to feel uncomfortable. The machine jolted into action, the mechanical whirring and movement nudging me closer to the doughnut shape and the large box slowly began descending over my head. I closed my eyes and tried to distract myself from the noise.

It stopped momentarily and I opened my eyes. The machine sat less than an inch from my nose. Terrified, I squeezed my eyes shut tightly. It lasted several minutes, though I had no way of accurately measuring time. Even so, they were exceptionally long, uncomfortable minutes, filled with mechanical clicks overhead and shuddering table movements.

"That's the first part over," the radiologist announced, entering the room. "Everything okay there?"

"Yes, thank you. Do you have any music you can put on?" I had seen a small radio when I was changing.

"Oh yes, sorry. I will put it on now." She switched it on, and the room filled with a loud advertisement for a supermarket. "The next part will take around twenty minutes, lie perfectly still, okay?"

"Okay."

There was something strange about being instructed to lie still that made me highly conscious of any movement and made me restless and desperate to wriggle. Suddenly the machine shuddered in a forward motion. I closed my eyes and welcomed the burst of familiar music that came onto the radio loudly. *"Ohh, I don't want a lot for Christmas, there is just one thing I need..."* It was still three weeks to Christmas, and there was only one thing I wanted: to be cancer free.

The remainder of the scan was lengthy but less claustrophobic and I kept my eyes closed throughout. The music successfully distracted my mind as I sang along in my head to the familiar tunes.

The door opened and the music went off mid-song.

"All finished. You can get up and dressed now and leave the gown on the chair." The radiologist released the strap around my arms. "You have an appointment with your oncologist in February and he will discuss the results with you then."

"Okay, thank you."

I climbed off the long table and moved towards my clothes on the chair. After the radiologist left the room, the blinds came down once again and I dressed, thinking about the results. My appointment was at the end of February, still over three months wait to know if there had been any spread of cancer, and even then, I still wouldn't really know for another eight months. A heaviness sunk over me. I was exhausted both physically and emotionally. The wait felt like another unbearable load to bear.

I took one last look at the machine, marvelling at the technology despite my sinking mood. I turned and left the machine behind me and walked out of hospital for the last time in 2023.

NOW WHAT?

5 DECEMBER 2023

Arriving home felt strange. My surgeries and radioactive treatment were over and after the full body scan, I simply got up and walked out. There was no conclusion for me. No bell to ring because I didn't have radiotherapy or rounds of punishing chemotherapy. But why? Had it not been a hard enough cancer journey?

Shut up! Stop complaining. Other people fight this disease harder than you! my inner troll scolded me.

I felt so guilty thinking those thoughts, even silently. I still feel guilty for even writing this, but I owe it to other thyroid-cancer patients because I know from the forums, many feel the same.

I had won the cancer lottery, I knew that. I didn't have chemo; I still had my own hair, and my cancer had been miraculously caught and removed. But ... I still had cancer. I'd gone through six months of my own cancer hell. I'd had three surgeries, been in Critical Care, lost my voice and endured radiation and my body was trying to adjust to losing my thyroid. I'd watched my children, my mum and Paul fight with their own emotions and sometimes struggle to cope with watching me suffer. Their emotional pain hurt me just as much as my physical pain. More in fact, at times.

I didn't look like a cancer patient. People kept telling me I looked well. I presented myself well to the world, and to myself. I was trying to keep my mindset in the positive. But behind the smile and freshly washed hair was a woman struggling. A woman who couldn't make it to lunchtime without needing to lie down. A woman who cried in the bath alone because the trauma of hospital events sat within her, and she couldn't hold a conversation about anything without her feelings overwhelming her.

Up until then, cancer had completely taken over my life. Life revolved around hospital appointments and the small goals I set myself between each surgery. Each appointment was a date to reach, and it distracted me from the reality of what was happening. I knew what lay ahead and it gave me a sense of control at a time when I had little control over anything. There had been a feeling of safety to the organised hospital visits. Now I was on my own and cast adrift with no anchor. After the noise of treatment, now there was nothing but silence. Everyone's lives were carrying on as normal around me. People were excitedly preparing for Christmas, but I wasn't. It was then that the cancer diagnosis finally caught up with me. I had thyroid cancer. Now what? I felt lost.

I received a letter a couple of days after my discharge inviting me to an appointment at my doctor's surgery. My cancer support worker had arranged a session with a physio who specialised in working with cancer patients. It was another appointment goal post to cling onto.

Melanie was a bubbly woman whose warm manner immediately put me at ease. The first forty-five minutes of my appointment was spent telling her my story and how stranded I felt. I fought to hold the emotions in.

"Emily, everything you are feeling is perfectly normal," she reassured. "I speak with lots of patients who feel the same and very bewildered after treatment ends. Your body is physically still in recovery, and you have at least a month or more of the immediate symptoms from the radiation alone. The radiation takes about six months to work fully and as those cells die off in your body, that process uses up lots of energy and can make you feel very tired. But perhaps even more so, mentally you are just beginning to process having a cancer diagnosis and the impact on your life and those of your loved ones."

"But I feel guilty, like I should be just getting on with it. People have it worse than me..."

"It's perfectly normal to feel all those things and you are not alone. But you don't need to feel guilty. You have been on your own cancer journey and your feelings are valid."

I began to cry, the kind of tears that spring up and fall without you making a sound. I wiped them with my coat sleeve without acknowledging them. "I thought I was going to die in that theatre..." I stopped. I couldn't say anything else.

"How would you feel about getting some counselling to talk through your feelings?" Melanie offered. It was apparent to her I was struggling with the events of the last six months.

"I'd like that." I nodded, wiping my nose. I still couldn't speak to anyone without crying and I needed help to make sense of it all, especially the events of the emergency surgery.

"I will make a referral for some counselling through a local charity. I'm not sure what the waiting time is but they will be in touch with you to let you know."

"Now tell me a little about exercise – are you managing to do anything? I'm going to suggest that you start some gentle stretching exercises, even starting in a chair as it's been a few months since you were able to exercise. There will be some muscle atrophy where you haven't moved."

For the first time, I recognised it had been six months since I had moved my body, *really* moved it, and that realisation made me sad. I'd been so focused on my recovery and symptoms; I'd not even thought about exercise.

I left the appointment with a therapy referral and exercise suggestions, but I also left with the validation of my cancer journey that I needed. I left the guilt in her treatment room. I no longer needed to carry that with me.

A couple of days later, I received a text from Lexi. She had witnessed my sense of bewilderment from finishing my treatment whilst staying with her. She knew how estranged I felt from normality and how I was finding it difficult to cope.

"I've just got back from my meet-up group. One of the women is a bell ringer at St Michael's Church. Tomorrow night at 7.30pm they are going to say your name and they will ring the church bells for three minutes to mark the end of your cancer treatment. You deserve more than one bell ringing, now you will have a whole church full. I love you xx"

I slid down the cupboards onto the kitchen floor clutching my phone and cried. It meant far more to me than just a beautiful gesture.

THE END OF DARKNESS
22 DECEMBER 2023

I climbed the ladder to the loft and flicked on the light. It was unseasonably wet. Wintry rain was hitting the roof noisily. In the corner was a camp bed, still unmade. The covers just as I had left them two months earlier.

I felt sad for the woman who'd climbed from her bed early one morning in September. She'd left for surgery, unaware of what would happen and how her life would change. I stripped the bed and folded down the camp bed. The loft was no longer my space. It belonged to an old version of me, a woman who needed to escape. One who'd hidden bags of food there and verbally abused herself. It was the scene for many a binge. She was gone now. I'd replaced her. Now I had my own space with a garden, a view, and the trees, with birds and when this was all over, I would carry on rebuilding my life in my little caravan.

I glanced around at the boxes of memories stacked between layers of fibreglass insulation. Some had travelled all the way back from Australia. Some had made that journey twice. I hadn't touched these things for years; they served no purpose. They were just memories I couldn't bear to part with. The critical bleed had highlighted the unpredictability of life.

I thought about my sons having to sift through torn boxes of my memories, much of which was junk, and I didn't want them to have that burden should anything happen to me. My clutter didn't have to become theirs out of obligation. So, I began the operation of sifting through the mess and ruthlessly culling. I set up a box for each of my sons and filled it with special memories of them. The pregnancy ultrasound images. Newborn baby tags from hospital. Their first drawings, and locks of their baby hair. Just a few sentimental items that I hoped one day, after I was gone, would remind them how much I loved them from the moment I knew they were coming to this earth.

Amongst one of the boxes was a faded photo. It was an old picture of my dad, leaning up against a large stone, one hand tucked into the pocket of his flared jeans. His hair was long, his beard and moustache thick and in keeping with the fashion of the early 1970s. Dad had a slight smile upon his face as if he knew it would make a cool photo as he bathed in the golden sunshine of a summer storm afterglow. The purply blue sky looked heavy behind him, with thundery clouds framing the large stones and lintel that rested above them. I ran my fingers over the photo, trying to feel him.

I had so few memories of my father as a child, but the photo triggered a memory long since buried. Dad had taken me to Stonehenge in Wiltshire in the late 1970s. I was no more than six or seven years old at the time. I remembered the stones and climbing over the mound that encased them. It was just me and dad. A rare trip together. I don't know why he took me – we never went anywhere together – but this place must have meant something to him.

I unfolded some paperwork. It was my dad's last letter to Ryan and me before his death and a makeshift will with his final wishes. He had annotated his will just before he died. The writing was barely legible, and it made me sad. I remember how his hands trembled in the weeks before he died. I scanned over the letter reading the details of the dissolution of his minimal assets, the final paragraph, so difficult to read:

"Ryan and Emily, I love you so deeply and I am so proud of you both..."

I folded the letter and put it back in its box. It was too painful to read on.

A couple of days later, I was laying in the bath listening to a podcast when my phone pinged next to me. It was a text from Paul:

"Do you feel up to going on a trip to Stonehenge for the winter solstice? I could drop you nearby, so you won't have to walk far. I've never been. Something to think about anyway x"

Stonehenge in winter? It had only been ten days since my hospital discharge – I'd be ready to lie down by lunchtime. The thought of an early morning hike to Stonehenge in the middle of a British winter felt impossible, but the odd timing of Paul's suggestion intrigued me.

I immediately searched the history behind the winter solstice traditions and seasonal pilgrimage so many people attend. For centuries, many cultures have believed the solstice symbolised renewal – the end of darkness and the rebirth of the sun. It seemed somehow fitting but I was more curious to revisit a place that seemed to have held some importance to my dad.

"I don't know, let me think about it, right now I can't walk upstairs to the toilet without feeling tired! Let's keep an eye on the weather. if it's raining, I'm not sure I can do it with the way I feel x"

December 22 was still two weeks away and the weather and

my health would be the deciding factors on whether I attempted it.

During the days that followed, my fatigue worsened, and I noticed my sense of taste was declining each day. I had shared the much-anticipated pizza with my sons when I returned home and yet I could only feel the pizza texture in my mouth, not taste much of it at all. I was bitterly disappointed. By day thirteen, I'd lost my taste completely, other than the faintest hint of vinegar from a balsamic dressing and a mild hit from hot chilli sauce that I forced myself to put on everything. Everything else was tasteless, with a metallic aftertaste.

I hadn't realised how much taste, along with texture, was important to me. Eating was a sensory-stimulating, pleasurable experience and I'd been denied a particularly important part of that. After the low-iodine diet, I'd craved tasty, familiar food, and this loss seemed like a cruel slap in the face after the cancer treatment. I found myself eating more than usual just to taste something, and when I couldn't taste anything at all, it made me feel extremely low.

I had learned to accept the fatigue over the last six months. I'd adjusted my life around it. I knew I couldn't fight it and lying down under a warm blanket and watching television wasn't all that bad. However, the loss of taste was difficult to accept. After decades of denying myself certain food groups, I now *loved* food. I loved to cook and bake, and now I couldn't taste the fruits of my labour. I gave up trying and bought soup and dressed it with chilli sauce every day just to taste something.

A week later, Katie called me to check in. She'd arranged for some blood tests in the new year to check my medication levels. My previous results indicated my dose was too high, my TSH levels were over-suppressed, and my oncologist was recommending a drop in dose. Long-term over-suppression at those levels posed a risk to my heart and bones. It was a balancing act to get synthetic thyroid medications at optimal levels. Ask anyone with thyroid disease and they will agree it's an equally fine balancing act to get natural thyroid hormones to optimal levels too. The 'normal' range on blood tests used by doctors to gauge dosage can leave many people feeling far from 'normal'. My endocrinologist warned me that some people never feel well after surgery. The tiredness, constipation or diarrhoea, loss of appetite and weight gain were all part of that adjustment, and I had no choice but to accept my new normal.

Katie confirmed my body scan results wouldn't be reviewed until their team meeting in early January and I would have to wait until the oncologist could go through them in February. There was nothing more she could do to expedite that wait. We wished each other a pleasant Christmas and I resigned myself to tasteless festive season.

It had rained daily for the first two weeks of the month, but remarkably, the winter solstice fell on the only dry day forecast for the following ten days.

A text startled me from a film I was watching:

"Are you in?"

"Yes, why?"

The day before the solstice, Paul arrived unexpectedly to see me. I rarely saw him in the week. Impromptu visits weren't something we usually did.

"I'm outside if you want to pop down to say hello?"

Paul never came inside. No one did. Just mental-health workers and an emergency plumber in between lockdowns. I'd withdrawn myself and allowed mental illness to take over my home. It was tired, things were broken. Paint was chipped and the fifteen-year-old carpet, worn. I was embarrassed by my home and the way I lived.

I grabbed my keys from the hook by the door and headed down the stairs and outside. Paul was sitting in his car. He smiled and waved at me, before pointing to the phone nestled next to his ear. I could see he was talking to someone.

I climbed into the car quietly, so as not to interrupt the conversation.

"*Sorry,*" he mouthed silently. I gathered from the conversation it was his friend, Gregg. Moments later, the conversation ended.

"Sorry about that, Gregg called. What are your thoughts on tomorrow? I've checked the weather, and it looks dry. I can walk okay today so I think we can do this if you feel up to it?" Paul said, hopefully.

"Um..." I paused momentarily, staring at the windscreen watching large raindrops collide and run down the glass. It was the kind of wintry sky where heavy clouds hold a grey blanket over the day until the sun sets behind it without ever getting a chance to break through. "Okay, let's do it!"

One thing cancer had taught me was to stop putting things off. Yes, I would be tired and yes, I might struggle, but I was going to at least try to see the sunrise and see why this place had meant enough to my dad to want to share it with me.

"You should ask Gregg if he wants to come," I blurted out from nowhere, unsure why I suggested it.

"Really?" Paul looked at me surprised. "Okay, I will text him later. Right, I will pick you up at 5am tomorrow. Try to get a good night's sleep and if you don't feel up to it, we can just watch the sunrise from the car."

I leant over and kissed his cheek. I missed being his wife. I missed seeing him every day. But we had salvaged a strong friendship from our separation, and I was grateful for that. Mental illness had torn us both into bits and we had spent four years on our own journeys, rediscovering those shreds of ourselves and healing them, piece by piece.

Later that evening, Paul texted. Gregg had agreed to join us and offered to drive us both. They would pick me up at 5am. I settled into bed early and after one final weather check, drifted off to sleep.

I naturally awoke and checked my phone at 4.21am, just a few minutes ahead of the 4.30 alarm I'd set. It was cold and dark.

Why did I agree to this?

A part of me wanted to back out of this madness and pull the duvet over my head and settle next to the dog's snores, but both Paul and Gregg would already be on their way to me.

"*I must be mad,*" I whispered into Billy's ear who stirred from his cosy place by my side.

"Come on, let's get up," I said, scooping his warm body into my arms and carrying him to the kitchen. He stood bewildered at the early morning awakening as the kettle boiled loudly beside us both.

I hurriedly dressed in the warm clothes I'd laid out the night before and slipped his lead on. After a quick walk outside, I tucked Billy back into bed. He nuzzled back down and sighed heavily.

I looked up at the framed picture of my dad sat on the kitchen shelf. I wanted to take something of my dad with me, but what? The picture was too big to carry around. I wanted to feel close to him and to take him there too, but I didn't need a talisman. I *was* him. I carried a part of him within me ... always.

I grabbed the small flask of coffee I'd made earlier and three cups. Gregg's company was an unexpected addition to the adventure.

It was almost 5am when I slipped quietly outside to wait. It was unusually mild for so late in December, but I knew I might be grateful of the layers of warm clothing on a blustery Salisbury plain.

Gregg and Paul were sitting outside waiting and the low

hum of the van in the silent street sparked a little excitement inside me. I was going to Stonehenge after all these years.

We set off on the hour-long journey, chatting enthusiastically and catching up on the events of the previous six months. I'd last seen Gregg just prior to my diagnosis. We'd bumped into each other in a coffee shop. A lot had happened in that time. It was easier to speak about it sitting side by side in the darkness and I realised it was the first time I had spoken in detail without breaking down. I had an optimism that morning. Something of the symbolism of the darkest day passing felt hopeful.

As we neared Stonehenge, the traffic ground to a halt, and we sat stationary for twenty minutes listening to the windscreen wipers periodically swipe away the drizzle. We had just over an hour until the sun would rise but none of us predicted the volume of traffic we would encounter. Squally winds blustered drizzly rain across the plain and hopes of seeing a sunrise faded the longer we sat in a queue. It was clear the small carpark was already full, and the traffic backed up and at a standstill for miles.

Gregg diverted to an alternative route, and we left lines of red lights behind us. Between Paul's immobility and my fatigue, we couldn't park up and walk for miles as others appeared to be doing.

We slowed once more, caught in another line of traffic that wasn't moving, the bright lights of the visitors' centre visible on the horizon like a glowing taunt.

"Why don't you two hop out here? I will find somewhere to park and walk," Gregg suggested. He was a seasoned walker and up for the challenge.

"Really?" we sang in unison. It seemed unfair to leave the driver stuck in a queue of traffic.

"Please, you two go. I will catch you up," Gregg encouraged.

We hopped out of the van into the blustery darkness, lit

only by the line of car beams sitting in a row. Gregg swung the van around and disappeared into the darkness. I led the walk; my pace was slow, and the ground was unsteady. Paul followed behind with his walking stick. Drizzle danced in the headlights of cars sat idling.

It wasn't long before we reached the large glass building that housed the visitors' centre. We found a bench outside and sheltered from the wind. The rain had stopped, and on the horizon, a pale-grey crown of sky signalled the sun was rising soon.

Miraculously, Gregg appeared just ten minutes after us. He'd parked in a village some twenty minutes away and hitched a ride. We joined the thousands of others walking the stretch to the stones. Shuttle buses passed us by from time to time, but somehow it felt like a rite of passage to slowly walk through the fading darkness on a pilgrimage of sorts to the stones. Pagans and druids passed us in the silent procession, only interrupted by the rattle of bells adorning their fur coats and crowns of flowers. And amongst the worshippers skipped excitable tourists, and people with drums, and wearing horns, holding staffs with bells. Over a million people visited Stonehenge every year. Many millions of footsteps would have walked this very path during the five thousand years these stones had stood. My dad's, too.

We arrived just minutes before the sunrise at 8.08am. The giant stones stood ominously against the cloudy dark sky. Thousands of people gathered around them, yet it felt oddly peaceful, and the cold wintry air hung heavy with anticipation.

We weaved amongst the stones. People were leaning against them, eyes closed, bathing in something unseen. Couples embraced lovingly; noses pressed against each other. Drums began to beat; bells rang out and horns sounded across the air as a wintry ball of golden hope broke the horizon's darkness. It lit up the sky and the formidable rocks that towered above us, the dark moss covering them, brightening a little in the weak dawn light.

We headed into the stone circle and joined hundreds of people who had braved the winter morning to welcome back the sun. A group of women dressed all in red with crowns of flowers broke into song, singing words of thanks for the Earth and all its bounty and for the sun that sustained us. Despite the crowds it was serene, filled with a tangible feeling of peace. I scanned the stones, searching for my dad's. As the celebrations slowly ended and the crowds thinned, I was able to find it.

"Show me your dad's picture again?" Paul called out. He and Gregg were on a mission to help me find the right location.

I pulled out my phone and showed them both. They studied the stones' positions and gently moved me into the right place. I stood in the same spot, recreating my dad's pose and Gregg took a picture of me.

"I just need a minute!" I called to Paul.

"*Take your time*," he whispered, leaning in, before joining Gregg and moving into the crowds of scarlet red feathers, flowers and beating drums.

I placed my hands on the slant in the rock, the natural dip held them. I closed my eyes and felt the cool, rough texture beneath my fingers and paused until the noise and crowds faded away. "*I'm here, Dad. I love you; you know. I always loved you*," I whispered.

"*I'm here with you, Emily*," I heard, as clearly as I had heard those words in the theatre that day. My body tingled and a warm, overwhelmingly loving energy ran through my fingers radiating throughout my body.

"*I feel you*," I whispered through tears, holding onto the rock, not wanting to let him go. My dad had stood in this spot decades before. I was touching the very stone his hands had laid on and for the first time in twenty years, I felt as if I was touching him. It was the closest I'd felt to him since I was a child.

The noise of drums and laughter and song faded back in as if someone had turned up the volume once again. I opened my eyes and wiped my tears as I turned around, scanning the crowds for Paul and Gregg. They'd moved outside the stone circle. Paul saw me and they both walked towards me.

"Come here. Are you ok?" Paul said, wrapping his arms around me.

"Uh huh." I nodded. "I felt him, Paul. I felt my dad and I heard his voice. He is with me... I..." I stopped. I didn't want to sound foolish in front of Gregg.

With perfect timing, bagpipes cut in across the air and the familiar melody of *Amazing Grace* blended in with beating drums, horns and bells. All manner of costumed people of mythical folklore weaved in and around us, dancing and celebrating the rebirth of the sun.

"Can you give me a minute?" I shouted to Paul across the music. "There is something I need to do."

I turned around and walked towards the large sarsen stone nearest me without waiting for his reply. I put both palms on the rockface and looked up towards the lintel towering metres above me. The surface was covered in pale-green moss that incubated my hands from the cold. I closed my eyes and pushed away the sounds of the crowds until it was just me and the stone.

"*It is the end of darkness. I've come here to start over. I have come to say goodbye to cancer. Please take away the darkness and return me to the light,*" I whispered to the stone.

I felt the heaviness of the earth through my feet. No shoes could prevent the sensation. A trail of energy rose up through my body, dancing in my stomach like ... butterflies.

I am cancer-free. I am in perfect health, I chanted over and over silently.

"Thank you," I whispered, before opening my eyes.

The sun had climbed above the stones and the blustery winds had blown away the clouds to reveal ribbons of weak blue sky. Paul and Gregg were standing on the fringe of the crowd, shivering as they waited for me. Chilled from the biting wind, it was time to leave this place behind.

I pulled out the flask of coffee and three steel cups from my backpack, pouring the sweet milky coffee that steamed in the early morning air. "Here's to the end of darkness and return of the sun!" I grinned at Paul and Gregg.

"To the return of the sun!" we sang in unison, clanging our steel cups together, and sipping the hot, sweet coffee, offering a little warmth to our bodies.

Before we boarded the shuttle bus back, I turned to look back at Stonehenge one last time. It had been a strange and mystical morning, and I was glad that I'd come.

Gregg left us in the warmth of the visitor centre café whilst he hitched a ride back to his van. Within half an hour he was back, and we climbed into his van and headed home, each of us silently processing our personal encounter with the stones that morning.

As the men reminisced about their past and many a shared adventure gone by, I listened quietly, thinking about the day. I had felt my dad. I had felt *something* tangible yet inexplicable as I privately prayed to the stones. We had all witnessed the sunrise on the only dry day in between two weeks filled with rain, and we wouldn't have made it without Gregg joining us last minute. Each piece of the journey fitted together seamlessly, as if the universe had ensured I made it there to see the return of the sun.

As we neared home, my phone buzzed in my pocket. I pulled it out. No caller ID. I hesitated. I was sandwiched in the front cab of a van between two men, and it would be hard to hold a conversation in such a small space. Something made me answer.

"*Hello, is that Emily?*" a friendly voice enquired. It sounded familiar.

"Yes, that's me," I said, cautiously.

"Hi Emily, it's Katie from the Endocrine Clinic. How are you?"

"I'm good, thank you. How are you?" I wanted to race through the pleasantries. My stomach turned over anxiously. I was still high from my solstice experience and her call grounded me with an earthly bump.

"I wanted to let you know we reviewed your scan results at our meeting yesterday. I'm not sure why but they have looked at yours early. I have spoken with Dr Singh, and he has agreed for me to let you know that there is no sign of any metastatic spread in your body at this stage."

"Oh, my goodness, thank you ... so much!" I spluttered, taken aback.

"I just thought you would like to know before Christmas. Dr Singh will see you in February as planned but, in the meantime, have a lovely Christmas and I will be in touch with you in the new year after your blood tests."

"Merry Christmas, Katie." I ended the call, glancing from Paul to Gregg who couldn't help but overhear the conversation.

"That's fantastic news. I'm so relieved." Paul placed his hand over mine and squeezed it tightly.

"I'm so pleased for you," Gregg added.

I closed my eyes. *Thank you,* I silently offered to whoever was listening to me.

Within minutes Gregg pulled up near the flat and Paul and I climbed out of the van, standing still to wave goodbye as he drove away. I turned to Paul and stared at him momentarily, unable to speak. He offered his arms as a place of safety, and I stepped forward into them and burst into tears.

"I just can't believe I got that call today, now, after this morning. I wasn't meant to hear until February. Why did it happen today?!"

I walked Paul to his car, and we got in. Paul held me as I cried tears of relief and joy, trying to process it all. Maybe it really was the end of the darkness for me and the return of the light.

RESTLESS

JANUARY 2024

In mid-January, after almost six weeks with no taste, it slowly began to return. But something just as troubling replaced it. I began waking up every forty-five minutes. More often than not, my body was also burning hot, like a hot flush, only throughout my whole body.

I'd kick the covers off, and despite the bitter temperatures outside and no heating on, I would still be sweaty and restless. The hot flush would fade after a couple of minutes and I would fall back asleep, but the disruptive hourly awakening lasted all night. After three weeks of disturbed sleep, I was exhausted and my ability to cope with even the slightest irritation vanished. I was dragging myself through the days. I knew I couldn't continue in that way and scheduled a GP appointment.

The doctor was my age and shared she was also in perimenopause. She understood the impact the lack of sleep and hot flushes were having on me, on top of everything else.

After reading through my notes, she turned to me and sighed heavily. "The last few months have been bloody shit for you, haven't they? I can see you are overwhelmed right now. I want you to go home and be kind to yourself. You don't have to be some sort of superwoman, you know!"

I will always remember her candid words, mostly because they made me smile, but also because she acknowledged how difficult the whole experience had been for me. The last few months *had* been really tough, and I was exhausted and overwhelmed. My hair was brittle and thinning. I'd lost my appetite completely, gained weight and felt constantly tired. I didn't recognise this version of myself anymore.

The doctor prescribed a mild antidepressant to use as a sleep aid. After a couple of nights of trying them, I slept marginally better, but the side-effects forced me off them. I tried over-the-counter sleeping tablets, magnesium and melatonin but nothing helped. I gave up trying and stuck it out.

After three months it slowly improved but I felt I'd physically aged a decade during that time. My hair became very dry as if it had been chemically fried. The nerves in my toes hurt and I developed dark purple patches on my palms and groin that itched and peeled. My bones and muscles ached, and I felt every fifty-one of my years. But the body is one vessel, and ingesting radioactive material not only affects the cancerous cells, but the healthy ones too. It wasn't surprising that my body was feeling the effects.

IT'S GOOD TO TALK

FEBRUARY 2024

For five months, my mind had been suspended in the trauma of my emergency situation, and beyond that, the whirlwind of the cancer diagnosis itself. A few weeks after the physiotherapist referral, I received a call from a local cancer charity offering me some therapy sessions. I felt a little apprehensive about the first appointment, I knew it would involve opening up about my experience in front of a stranger. Having had therapy before, I knew that to benefit from the sessions, I needed to be honest with my feelings.

I arrived early for my first appointment and stood outside. The building was an ordinary-looking house that had been converted into charity offices. The only indication it wasn't a residential home was the large sign in the front garden advertising it was a hospice-care and bereavement-counselling charity.

The word 'hospice' stirred a dormant beast. I'd placed my dad in a hospice against his wishes. The medical staff suggested it and I remember feeling a little relieved, but extremely guilty for feeling it. I'd angered my dad in his dying weeks. *How selfish, Emily.* I felt the guilt returning. I had so far survived my cancer, Dad hadn't. Should I even be here, when other people were dying from their cancer, or mourning the loss of a loved one?

Before the guilt could settle in, the front door unlocked, and a lady opened the door.

"Emily Johnson?"

"Yes."

"Come in, sorry to keep you waiting."

Jane was around my age, perhaps a little younger. Her manner was warm and her voice gentle. She showed me into what would have been a lounge, with a comfortable sofa, a side table with an obligatory tissue box and an armchair for the counsellor. The artwork on the wall was large and colourful. I felt at ease almost immediately.

"Take a seat," she said, gesturing towards the sofa.

Once we'd both settled, she began explaining the confidential nature of our sessions. Nothing would be discussed outside the room, no notes were being made, and that wouldn't change unless I indicated I was a danger to myself, or others. She encouraged me to relax and say whatever I wanted to say, and that invitation broke the ice.

"Okay ... where do I begin?" I smiled nervously. "I went to the GP in April last year and he spotted a lump on my neck. The ultrasound and needle biopsy were inconclusive, so I had a partial thyroidectomy in June to remove the mass and it came back as follicular thyroid cancer. Then I had a second surgery to remove the other lobe and that came back with a different type of cancer, papillary cancer." I paused to breathe.

"But I had a situation in theatre..." I stopped and covered my face with my hands to block her from seeing my face twisting into a silent sob. I'd ripped the scab off the trauma, and I couldn't speak.

"It's okay," Jane said quietly, passing me the tissue box. "Would you like some water?"

"No ... I'm fine, thank you."

"I had ... a situation..." I continued, then stopped again. "I will go past that and come back to it." I couldn't dip into it anymore.

"That's okay, take your time."

"In late November, I had radioactive iodine and a full body scan, and my next oncology appointment is at the end of February." I was crying again. "I've had a lot of symptoms since my surgery and radiation, but I feel so guilty. I don't look like I've had cancer, and everyone keeps telling me I look so well but I don't feel it. People don't understand. I'm not sleeping..." My voice was breaking.

Jane had been periodically nodding. It was evident she was listening, and her gentle manner enabled me to return to the emergency surgery.

"I was in recovery after my surgery and just waiting to go up to the ward, when I began to bleed from my neck. They had to open my wound and stem the blood flow and take me back to theatre. I was awake when it happened... The alarm was going off and all the staff were around me..."

"Oh gosh," Jane sounded surprised.

"I ended up in Critical Care. But ... I had a strange experience in theatre before they put me back to sleep and I can't talk to anyone about it because the doctors aren't interested in spiritual experiences. I'm still trying to make sense of it. I ... can't stop ... replaying it all because I was awake and I... I felt ... my blood coming out..." I began to sob again. "And then I had some heart issues which were so frightening." It was all tumbling out and I felt relieved to say it aloud to someone else.

"Have you had heart problems before?"

"No, never and they couldn't understand why my heart kept

racing. I'm sure it was the shock on my body, but they said it wasn't that. I thought I was going to die in the theatre ... but then I had this feeling... Someone else was with me like it was a near-death experience, only I was awake, and I don't know how to express it, or make sense of it..." I stopped. I had said too much and felt foolish.

"So, the out-of-body, kind of spiritual experience you had – did that feel comforting?" Jane asked without a hint of judgment.

"*It was amazing...*" I whispered, smiling at the memory of the incredible love. Tears were running down my face. I didn't even attempt to catch them. "It was so peaceful," I said, staring behind her at the wall, suspended in my thoughts.

"Was there someone with you or was it just a feeling?" Jane asked gently.

"Well ... at first, I felt them. It was my dad. He died over twenty years ago from cancer. Then my grandfather came in. I could see them both in my peripheral vision in the theatre and they made me feel so calm.

"I was awake, and I remember everyone moving around prepping for the surgery, apart from the woman who was applying pressure to my neck. I just felt so serene and surrounded by the most incredible love and it was as if the room got whiter somehow. I heard things being said to me and... Sorry." I stopped and looked back at Jane, studying her face for signs of judgment.

"No please don't apologise, it sounds so traumatic what you've been through, yet also lovely and comforting too," she reassured, her face filled with genuine curiosity.

"Can I tell you what I heard? You won't think I'm crazy, will you?"

"Of course you can, not at all, no."

"They... It said... '*It doesn't hurt here and nothing else matters, only love,'* and I felt as if the whole room filled with love. That's the only way I can describe it," I said, crying again. I knew it sounded ridiculous to anyone else, and I felt foolish for repeating it, but saying the words again aloud, stirred something deeply emotional inside me.

"And you heard it as if they were standing next to you?" Jane asked.

"Yes ... I know it sounds unbelievable. I heard it in my head, but then it was like something bigger, like God, or the universe was holding me... It was amazing. But it sent me off questioning the meaning of life: not just the cancer, but why am I here? Why are we all here? I couldn't answer those questions, and it scared me. I'm still trying to make sense of it all."

I stopped to breathe again. I needed to get all this out and I only had twenty minutes left. "In the surgery, I had some damage to my vocal cord and had to go back in about ten days later for an injection. I was a mess, anxious you know, and the staff just thought I was a bit nervous. And I wanted to say no ... I feel traumatised..." I stopped, covering my face with my hands, and burst into tears again.

"Yes, it is trauma, isn't it?" Jane said, allowing me to feel my emotions without trying to contain them. "It's huge what happened to you, very impactful and all your feelings are very valid."

After a minute or two of crying, my body settled, and I continued: "I had inpatient radiation treatment and after it was over, I just left the hospital – it was as if none of this happened. I felt lost that the appointments were over. I didn't know how to continue with normal life as so much had happened. I felt exceptionally lucky in many ways. I'd seen my dad's version of cancer; it was a long and painful death and mine was found by chance. It was treatable and so I feel lucky and grateful but also like a fraud because of that."

"It certainly has happened, you have been through all sorts, it just isn't the same process a lot of other people go through. It was a different type of surgery and treatment, so you don't feel like you have been through what people understand a typical cancer journey would be," Jane confirmed, carefully acknowledging my words.

"I had a life-affecting – and life-affirming – incident in surgery but I only have my account of it, if that makes sense?" I searched her face for confirmation.

"Yes, and it's yours and you felt it and heard it, and it doesn't matter what anyone else feels or thinks about it, it's yours," Jane said softly, gifting me my experience back without criticism.

I nodded in silent recognition. "I feel like I should be back to normal, that I should slot back into life, but these massive things have happened..."

"Yes, they have and it's so hard, it's so overwhelming. There are so many things that have happened, and you have lots of questions," Jane reassured me as I continued to sob into my hands. "You did have cancer, you had two cancers, it was very real. What happened to you was pretty significant. You've gone through a lot of loss too, including losing your voice and taste. It matters to you, the details matter to *you*, the feelings you have been left with matter to you," Jane said gently, each sentence solidifying something I needed to hear.

"I just feel a bit stuck in that situation. Every time I try to talk about it, it's all too much. I can't get past it."

"Well, we can work together with that. Today's session was really about you telling me what happened and how you are feeling. Now we can start to pick it apart and pull out the bits that you are really struggling with and put in some strategies. Let's get you booked in next week. Is the same time next week, okay?"

"Yes, thank you." I nodded before standing up. I was uncomfortably aware I had run over by almost ten minutes.

Jane unlocked the front door, and I stepped out into the garden. I turned around to her. "Thank you for listening. It's really helped."

"You're welcome. Take care and see you next Friday," she said, before closing the door behind me.

I shivered against the icy rain. I felt drained and exhausted from crying, yet a little lighter. It felt liberating to openly speak about what had happened to me with someone who didn't know me.

RELEASE

14 FEBRUARY 2024

In 2013, I travelled to India alone. I was running away from life, licking my emotional wounds from a seventeen-year marriage that had ended in divorce and a subsequent relationship heartbreak. It was my first escape as an adult, alone.

My last solo travel had been to Italy at the age of fifteen. Mum sent me there as an exchange student in the early days of my anorexia recovery. In between those two solo journeys, I had lived my life for others, always as someone's something. I'd been a girlfriend, lover, wife, carer, mother but never just me. My Indian adventure was my first gift to myself in decades.

Once there, I treated myself to a few one-to-one beginners' yoga classes. It was challenging, and my body hurt. I wasn't used to twice-daily exercise, but I left India with a personalised daily practice and the words of my yoga instructor, Minesh, firmly ringing in my ears: "*If you do this practice every day for the rest of your life, you will never suffer neck or back ache.*"

I kept it up for a couple of years until mental illness snuck its way into my family and my daily yoga practice fell to the wayside, along with every other aspect of self-care.

By 2022, I had been in the throes of a full-blown eating

disorder for five years. Binge-eating disorder disconnected me from my body and I loathed the shape of the obese body I lived in. Even if I had carved time to get on a yoga mat again, I wouldn't have. I was so far removed from the woman who went to India, I didn't recognise myself anymore. I didn't want to feel that body as it was, let alone stripped down and vulnerable on a mat.

The week after my first therapy session with Jane, I was sitting in *Sunshine* watching heavy wintry rain soak the trees, when a desire to move my body came from nowhere. I stood up and stretched my arms above my head as far as they could reach, before pulling them down and bringing my hands together in front of my heart as if in prayer. I pulled my right foot up and pressed it to my left leg, just above the knee and stood, staring forward at the trees outside. I wobbled, unable to hold the pose, but just for a second, I was that woman in India. I caught a glimpse of the long-lost woman inside me.

I crouched down and settled on my hands and knees and arched my back slowly, curling my spine. The movement triggered a surge of emotion that overcame me, and I burst into tears. I pulled myself up and rested my bottom on the back of my heels, taken aback by the unexpected release.

What am I feeling? I don't feel sad, I questioned silently. I couldn't pinpoint the sensation but immediately recognised it had been generated by the yoga position.

I stretched my arms down and forward onto the floor resting my tummy on my bent knees and laid my forehead on the floor. It hurt my back so I moved my legs outwards, opening my hips as wide as I comfortably could. The stretch felt momentarily pleasurable through my inner thighs. I used my fingers to creep forward on the carpet gathering a few further centimetres of stretch.

As I was reaching forward, another surge of emotion rose

from what felt like the depths of my stomach. I dropped my head on the rug, sobbing loudly. This time I surrendered to the experience. I lay there for a moment or two, shocked by the ferocity of the release, before pulling myself upwards to my feet. My body felt lighter, looser in some way, though my head felt heavy from the crying.

I sat down to steady the feeling, wondering what had just happened. It had been powerful and not something I was able to prevent or control. Subsequent stretches never evoked that primal release again. Whatever it was, it felt like it had been released from deep within my body.

The following week I returned to see Jane and the counselling session felt much more upbeat with far fewer tears. I told her about my meditation practice and my experience with the yoga stretches. Jane acknowledged how beneficial both appeared to be for me. Even she could see the shift within me. It was reassuring to speak with a practitioner who understood the trauma I had experienced may have become trapped in my body and she encouraged me to continue with both practices.

We loosely arranged a further appointment the following month, once I had my medical records, should I feel the need to see her. She could see during the session that exploring the medical information might help me to process it differently. I left my session feeling more empowered and peaceful than I had in a long time.

BACK TO ME

26 FEBRUARY 2024

At the end of February, I had my second appointment with the oncologist. I knew from my call before Christmas that there was no sign at that stage of any disease spreading in my body, but somehow, I still needed to be told that face to face. It felt like such massive news.

I arrived at the Oncology Outpatient department and found a seat. At times, it felt surreal to find myself in hospital or say those words: *I had cancer*. I felt like an impostor in the clinic, by far the youngest and healthiest-looking person sitting waiting to be seen.

Within moments of sitting down, I was called into the doctor's office.

"Hello, Ms Johnson Have a seat. So, you had your radioactive iodine treatment and body scans, haven't you?" Dr Singh dove straight into the conversation without hesitation.

"Yes, that's right, I have."

"We discussed your results in our meeting, and it all looked okay. There was no evidence of any metastatic disease anywhere, apart from some uptake in the neck which we would expect, that's why we give you the radioactive iodine. The team have recommended that we do some more scans in nine months from your treatment, so around August time. You'll have a whole-body scan but this time you will be seen as an outpatient and won't have to be admitted for isolation as the dose we use is much lower.

"You will be given two thyrogen injections, this time the first one will be on a Monday, the second on Tuesday. Then on Wednesday, you will have a radioactive iodine injection, rather than a capsule and then you will come in for the body scan on Thursday. You will also have an ultrasound of your neck around the same time and some blood tests. If your blood tests and scans are all okay, we won't need to do any more at that stage.

"I will book your scans for August, and we will discuss the results in our September team meeting, I will see you in October to discuss the results but so far everything looks good. We just need to make sure the scans in August look okay too." The doctor spun his chair around to face me. "How did you find the radioactive iodine? Was it all right?"

"Um..." I paused. "Well, it was an unpleasant experience and knowing what you are swallowing was hard. I lost my sense of taste for a few weeks."

"Did you get the dry mouth?"

"A little, I had a metallic taste, then I lost my taste altogether, but it came back after a few weeks."

"Yes, that can happen. So, as I said the scans look okay which is good so I will see you in October after you have had the next scans. Do you have any questions?"

"Yes, before I had this diagnosis, I was going swimming and having a sauna regularly. Am I okay to go back to the sauna now I've had my radiation?"

"Well, it shouldn't be any problem in terms of the thyroid cancer."

That was the green light I had been waiting months for.

"Do you have any further questions?"

"Yes, so when you said there was uptake in the neck, what do you mean?"

"Sometimes there is some normal thyroid tissue which is leftover after the surgery, so that's why you have the radioactive iodine to get rid of the normal thyroid tissue. Whether there is any microscopic cancer in there or not, we won't know as both the cancer and normal tissue take up the radioactive iodine. When you have the body scan in August, whatever was there, should have gone."

"Okay ... well ... thank you and see you at the end of the year."

"Yes. See you then." Dr Singh smiled with a warmth that reminded me of my granda. I liked him. I liked both of my consultants. They made me feel like a person, not just a hospital number with cancer.

I got up and left his office. It had taken six minutes to hear him say what I'd been seeing in my imagination night after night for weeks; a scene I created for comfort.

There was no sign of any metastatic spread.

This was *huge* news, but there was no fanfare about it either. It was just a statement absorbed into a conversation, a powerful, life affirming sentence that had been lost amongst other words. I felt both elated and lost at the same time because it still wasn't over, not yet.

I made my way to the hospital exit and to the car where Paul was waiting anxiously. As soon as I saw his familiar face, I burst into tears, unsure why I was crying. Happiness and relief in part: it was the best possible news I could have received. Yet I felt exhausted and drained too. It was the knowledge that I had to repeat the miserable diet and injections, and I still wouldn't be given the all-clear for a further eight months. After Paul dropped me home, I ran a bath and climbed in and allowed myself to feel it all, in solitude.

The following week I rejoined a local hotel pool. One Tuesday lunchtime, I went to the empty locker room at the deserted pool and changed into my swimming costume. It was the same one I'd swum in almost ten months earlier, before I knew I had cancer. I didn't pull a face at the woman standing in the mirror. I didn't scold her for the cellulite that now covered her thighs, or the extra weight that was stubbornly sticking to her body in recovery from cancer. Instead, I looked at the red line across her neck and I put my hand over it, soothing her and admiring her bravery.

She was a warrior. A cancer survivor.

I pushed the door open to the pool area and popped my towel on the sun lounger, before stepping under the shower and letting the warm water fall over my body as I closed my eyes. I managed five minutes in the hot sauna. It would take time to build up my resistance to the heat again.

With my muscles warmed up from the sauna, I climbed down the pool steps and eased myself into the shallow end of the empty pool and moved into a gentle breaststroke. I felt the muscles across my shoulders, my thighs, my stomach, my calves. I could feel them awakening, pulling me, helping me power through the water slowly. Every part of my body was waking from its dormant state.

After the second lap, my neck ached around the scar from holding it in position above the water, so I rolled onto my back and allowed myself to float. The water carried all my weight, and my hair bobbed and floated all around me.

My God, it feels so good to be back, to be carefree and weightless.

It felt so good to be *alive*. I started to cry at the realisation. Bit by bit, I was coming back to myself.

In early March, a local cancer charity emailed with an invitation to a fundraising morning tea. They were hosting the monthly event five minutes' walk from my flat. The Dorset Cancer Care Foundation had helped me twice, once replacing my broken fridge, and later awarding me a grant for a writing tablet that allowed me to write chapters for this book whilst staying in hospital, and at *Sunshine* as I recovered after my surgeries. Sometimes I would lie and just write the events of the day for ten minutes. It helped enormously, for at times the brain fog was so overwhelming, parts of this book would have been hard to recall and write.

The fundraiser started an hour before my first shift back at work following my radiation, but I wanted to at least say thank you in person to the charity, even if I couldn't stay for long.

I arrived shortly after it began, not knowing what to expect – it was the first time I had been to a public event centred around cancer since my dad passed away. I wasn't prepared for the wave of emotion that overcame me, being surrounded by people who had survived cancer or loved someone who perhaps hadn't. It reminded me I wasn't alone, and never had been throughout my cancer journey.

I found the staff member who had arranged my grant. "Hi Polly, my name is Emily Johnson. We spoke though email. I just wanted to say thank you for helping me with the fridge and writing tablet grant last year."

"Emily! Oh yes, I remember you!" Polly exclaimed, clasping

her hands together in delight. She turned to another lady who had joined us. "This is Emily, she is a recipient. I just *love* meeting our recipients!" She beamed. Polly's exuberance and joy was infectious.

"Hello," I said, shaking Jenny's hand firmly.

"She's writing a book about her cancer journey with the writing tablet we funded," Polly explained.

"Oh, how wonderful. You will have to share it with us when you publish it," Jenny encouraged.

"Oh, I definitely will, though it may be a while yet. I can't stay today unfortunately as I'm about to start work – it's my first shift back in months – but I really wanted to say thank you and support you today," I said, smiling at them both.

I really was grateful, but it was more than gratitude. I felt a sense of belonging with people I'd only just met.

"Ah bless you, you take care and thank you for coming." Polly and Jenny returned to their fundraising duties.

I moved to a table filled with cakes and sweet treats and grabbed a napkin, wrapping it around a large cookie. There wasn't time to sit down with coffee and cake, and I didn't want to be late for my first shift, even if it was working from my kitchen.

As I was gathering up my coat and bag, an impeccably dressed woman approached me.

"Hello, I'm Margaret, I am one of the trustees. I hear you are one of our beneficiaries." She beamed.

"Hello, yes I am, and I just wanted to say thank you for you kindly helped me with the grants, for the fridge and tablet to write about this journey."

"You are so welcome, I'm glad we were able to help you. When it's ready you must let us know and we will have a launch for you. Sometimes our beneficiaries come back and give a talk about their lives. Would you like to do that?" Margaret asked.

"I'd love to do that," I agreed enthusiastically. Despite my fear of public speaking, it was the least I could do.

"I think people will love to read your story and your book would be very helpful for people going through this journey as I don't think anyone really understands it until they go through it themselves."

We stood for a few minutes as Margaret spoke about her own cancer journey some twenty years before. Still, after all that time, her eyes filled with tears as she recounted her husband and daughters' reaction to her cancer diagnosis.

"It was lovely to meet you, Emily. You take care and make sure you rest too. It's time to be a little selfish now in life." She winked and smiled.

"I will, and it was pleasure to meet you too. I will hopefully try to get to another fundraiser soon." I picked up my coat and headed to the lift, snapping bits of the cookie, and nibbling on it as I waited for the lift to arrive.

I arrived home fifteen minutes before my shift started, with just enough time to make a coffee and finish off the rest of the cookie. The fundraiser had been a welcome distraction from the fear of overwhelm creeping over me. What if I couldn't juggle work with recovery?

My work team became home-based during the Covid lockdowns, and we stayed that way thereafter. I could log in from my kitchen and work at my pace with no pressure during my phased return. I had been offered more support than any other job I had ever been in, and I knew that I was exceptionally lucky to have that. My first shift was reduced to just four hours and by three and a half hours in, I was flagging and all I wanted to do was curl up and sleep. It was only 3pm.

When the shift was over, I closed the laptop and burst into tears. How could four hours sitting working at a laptop make me feel so tired? How would I cope with a regular shift?

Rather than being proud of myself for returning to work whilst still living with the side effects of cancer and radiation, I zoned in on the negatives. I should have gone into the shift with realistic expectations instead of criticising myself. I needed to stop trying to be a superwoman, just as that doctor had said.

I didn't take a nap. Instead, I slipped into my swimming costume and walked to the pool a few minutes away and lay on my back floating, without even trying to lap. I let the water hold me up and wash away the fatigue. By 4.30pm I realised I hadn't managed to fit in my daily meditation – something that had become as routine as cleaning my teeth.

I left the pool and went into the empty sauna and lay down, closed my eyes and allowed myself to breathe into a meditation.

I am in perfect health.

I am cancer-free today and for the rest of my long life.

Every day I get stronger and stronger, I recited over and over, and I could feel my body relaxing.

I am can—

The sauna door flung open abruptly, catching a young man by surprise and pulling me out of my meditation. The sauna was a snug space at the best of times, so whilst lying down, I'd claimed half the area as my own private meditation space.

I immediately sat up and swung my legs around. "Sorry," I murmured, echoing his apology as he squeezed himself past me and into the corner of the sauna. We British have a habit of apologising for absolutely everything. And nothing.

Despite the lack of light, I could see he was in his late twenties. His tattooed muscular body occupied half of the cramped sauna, along with me. I returned to my upright meditation position in the dimly lit sauna, closed my eyes and began again silently.

Breathe in... Breathe out...

Every day I get stronger and...

My mantra was interrupted by my fellow hot friend sniffing beside me. Being in the company of strangers in a confined space for more than a few moments either ends in awkward silence or encourages interesting conversation. For some reason, the sauna wasn't quite as warm as usual and it was his observation of the temperature that sparked a conversation.

Not as warm today, is it?" he remarked.

"I'm not sure, I've just recently joined."

"Ah have you? That's good. It's normally a bit warmer in here but I like it anyway. I come after the gym. I can just chill in here."

"Yes, I find saunas very relaxing."

"Only trouble is, it's a bit quiet isn't it? Too quiet really. Sometimes I overthink, about work and stuff. My head is so busy all the time, I wish I could learn how to settle it down, you know? I want to learn how to meditate. There's this Buddhist centre near where I live, but I've never had the guts to go in. My girlfriend keeps telling me to try it. I've tried watching videos and that, you know, but when I try, my mind thinks all these thoughts."

"Mmm," I agreed. I knew from having sons it was often easier for them to open up if they sat next to me to speak rather than opposite where they'd be forced into awkward eye contact. "It can be hard to switch off, can't it?"

"Yeah."

"I use this technique, and it's helped me when I've been stressed and found it hard to focus my attention. I close my eyes and follow my breath, and, in my mind, I say, breathe in... breathe out. If your mind wanders, it's okay, you just come back to acknowledging your breath. Maybe try that – it's simple but it works."

"Yeah, I will, thank you," the young man said, and I believed he might.

The heat was becoming overwhelming, and I felt a little dizzy. The pause in conversation seemed an appropriate time to leave. "That's me done." I eased myself off the hot wooden bench.

"Nice to meet you, what's your name?"

"Emily, nice to meet you..."

"Alex," he said, pushing his fist towards me, inviting a bump – the millennial handshake.

"Nice to meet you too, Alex." I smiled in the darkness, bumping his fist back with mine before opening the heavy sauna door and walking into the welcoming cool.

I stepped under the cold shower, recoiling at the shock of the icy water hitting my baked red skin. A flash of dopamine-fuelled energy tingled throughout my body. It was almost unbearable but equally exhilarating.

I feel alive!

I eased myself into the empty pool and floated onto my back, my mind drifting to Alex. Not his twenty-something-year-old inked body, but his mind instead. I felt sadness for him. He was a young man in his prime. He had a girlfriend, a job, he kept fit and seemed confident, yet he couldn't quiet his own thoughts.

I wish I could help him somehow. I wish he could remember who he truly is. I want people to feel what I feel now about life, I thought, as I spun my body around, stretching my arms in front of me, gently dividing the water in a soft breaststroke. I could feel the cool water caressing my skin and all the pain in my neck and back had melted away from the heat of the sauna. I knew the time spent there, being gentle with my body, needed to become a non-negotiable part of my cancer recovery.

BOB

MARCH 2024

As winter merged into spring, I spent more of my free time at *Sunshine*, writing. When not working, I would catch a bus with Billy and sit outside the caravan looking across fields that were often flooded from heavy rain. The trees were just beginning to bud with new leaves and the woodland was alive with many species of birds who sang, searching for a mate.

Amongst the blackbirds and blue tits, house sparrows and nuthatches was a regular visitor - a brightly red-breasted robin who favoured the same branch each time. High in a tree that was dressed in an ivy coat, he sat and sang the most enchanting song. I always greeted him and thanked him for coming. I named him Bob. Not very original I know, but it suited him. Bob had been visiting me since I left Critical Care, though he never ventured near me or came back into the awning.

One day in early March, I brought some meal worms with me to the caravan, hopeful of a closer encounter than our distant tree conversations. "Hello Bob! Look what I brought you," I said, cheerfully holding the plastic container up towards him, trying to tempt him down from the tree.

Bob flew down and sat on a bush nearby, his head slightly

cocked to one side watching the worm's movement. With a flash of red and brown wings flapping above the container, he came then retreated, still unsure of me or a safe place to land.

The temptation of a tasty fresh meal brought Bob back again, once, then twice, hovering above the worms in a burst of fluttering wings. Bob landed on the container momentarily, just enough time to take a worm before disappearing down the bank into the woodland. I gasped, grinning with excitement at such a precious encounter. Bob returned moments later.

"*Bob ... you came back!*" I whispered, holding the container of worms as far away as my arm would stretch.

Bob flapped and hovered with uncertainty before landing on the side of the container long enough to eat one worm, then two, then three.

"*Good boy, Bob,*" I whispered to the magnificent little bird. "*You are safe, I'm not going to hurt you.*"

Bob's legs were tiny, but his little feet masterfully clasped the plastic container maintaining his balance. His chest was a bright orange-red with a white streak below. Bob's little black bead eyes stared at me intently, assessing the danger this strange animal with the tasty worms may pose.

That encounter was the beginning of the most magical few months with Bob. Each time I visited the caravan, he would appear on his branch, and after a while he brought his mate, Mrs Bob (even less original, I know). Mrs Bob was a much more nervous robin, she stayed in the tree and observed Bob's brave stealth missions of worm-gathering.

Bob's trust in me grew quickly and within three weeks he began to fly alongside me when I arrived at the campsite. At times he would fly in front of me to catch my attention and land on my foot, or knee if I were sitting outside. It wasn't long before he would sit on my hand eating the worms. Sometimes he would just sit and look at me, his delicate feet resting on the edge of my palm. There is something deeply moving about gaining the trust of a wild creature and being able to observe them so closely.

As their mating season began, I was privy to the most precious courtship rituals. Bob would gather worms and feed his mate first, before returning to take one for himself. Mrs Bob was his priority, and it wasn't long before she was nesting.

During the breeding weeks, Bob would feed constantly, all day long, grabbing four or five worms in his beak at a time before disappearing into the dense foliage. He would sit on the fence outside the caravan window waiting for worms, and if I didn't appear fast enough for his liking, he began to let himself in. Bob was making himself right at home, and often followed me around the awning or hop up the little steps into the caravan and perch on the table or chair, waiting. If I was making a coffee, I'd pop the container of worms on the side and let him help himself.

The feeding frenzy died off after three or so weeks and shortly after, the robins brought their babies to me. Three little plump, speckled chicks with their parents appeared outside the caravan. I threw worms on the ground and the family of five hopped about, feeding. Bob was teaching them how to catch their own worms.

Within days, the chicks disappeared off into the woodland to mature and find their wings. The robins returned to their branch in the tree and a few weeks later the courtship rituals began all over again.

IMPOSSIBLE TO FIND

APRIL 2024

Something had been gnawing at me for some time since my emergency surgery and even though I had some counselling, I still needed to see what happened from a medical viewpoint during the critical bleed.

I requested my records and within a month they arrived by email. Most of them made no sense to me, though I searched online for the explanations of many acronyms. I don't know why I needed to go through them, or to what purpose it served, yet in some ways it was helpful to see the medical references, the timing of my surgeries and medications given to me. It was all recorded in detail: the time of my arrival in surgery, the anaesthesia, the knife-to-skin, the surgical completion, and transfer to recovery and Critical Care. Most people wouldn't want to know, but that afternoon's events had been reduced to two sentences in a paragraph in the follow-up letter to my doctor. So much confusion remained about the spiritual experience but in reality, those answers couldn't be found in medical notes recorded by doctors and nursing staff.

Alongside the medical notes, were copies of the images including my initial ultrasound, my CT scan and all the images from my whole-body scan. It was both confronting and fascinating to see cross-sections of my body with a brilliant orange glow filling my neck area showing the radiation uptake in my neck tissue. And the grey mass outline of my whole body with dark spots in my neck, stomach, kidneys and bladder, showing traces of the radioactive iodine working its way through my digestive and waste system.

There was another picture included in the mix – a detailed, clear image from my waist up, showing my bones, lungs, heart, intestines and stomach surrounded by visceral fat. I stared at my outline, a stripped-down version of the body I'd loathed most of my life housing the vital organs that were keeping me alive. It was probably the starkest reminder that my body is a remarkable feat of biological engineering, and I felt privileged to have the unique opportunity to see the inside of it, despite the circumstances. The other images were of my thyroid and tumour taken from stills of the ultrasound. I got to see the cancer itself. It was a surreal and poignant moment.

I waded through over four-hundred pages of my medical history, much of it I knew already, but the most important part to me – the surgical notes – were handwritten and difficult to read in their scanned format. I contacted the medical-records department who advised me that I could either speak to my surgeon's secretary or my own GP. Speaking to my surgeon didn't feel like an option to me. She was an extremely busy woman, and my request felt trivial and a waste of her valuable time. Instead, I arranged an appointment with my doctor's surgery in the hope they could explain to me what happened that day.

Although acknowledging the bleed was a very frightening experience for me, and a situation that I must have felt I had no control over, the doctor was unable to elaborate any further and steered me back to the surgeon's secretary.

As I was listening to my doctor's suggestion, a realisation hit me: I wasn't going to find the answers I *thought* I needed. It felt uncomfortable in that moment. The idea of pursuing it felt like picking at a scab that had only just healed. I didn't want to look backwards anymore. It didn't matter what my records said, or what any medical practitioner could say to me – nothing would change the fact that the critical bleed was a terrifying ordeal for me. Through therapy and my meditation practice, I had worked hard to leave that incident behind me.

That afternoon, I decided my search for more detailed information needed to end.

FINDING MY VOICE

15 JUNE 2024

I STEP INSIDE THE GRAND BALLROOM. IT IS FILLED WITH decorative round tables, beautifully set for a fine-dining experience, and adorned with bouquets of fresh flowers and balloons rising above, dancing gently under the ballroom ceiling. I take a deep breath in. There must be two hundred or more guests, dressed in their finest clothes, gentlemen in dinner suits with bow ties and women in shimmering gowns that skim the floor as they glide across to be seated.

The compere takes the microphone and calls our attention and a hushed murmuring settles as people find their seats. I take my seat next to Lexi, my plus one. We join the surgeons and businessmen, and women in their finest clothes and we smile at each other as we greet.

My mouth is so dry I can barely speak. I can't focus on anything, knowing I'm about to speak.

At least it's at the start of the evening.

I pour myself a glass of water, then a second and third and not even the fourth is quenching this arid tightness in my throat.

What if I get it wrong? What if I cry? What if...?

As the charity video ends, my picture appears on the two large screens on either side of the stage. It's time.

Breathe. You can do this, Emily, I remind myself.

I'm called to the stage and introduced. The compere warns them how scared I am as I giggle nervously in agreement.

I climb the stage alone and walk across it.

Please don't trip.

It's been a long time since I wore heels.

I place my papers on the lectern in front of me and look out to the audience. My hands are trembling. The stage lights blind me, and I can't discern the crowd behind the glare. It's probably easier this way.

"Good evening," I begin and a sound man rushes towards me from the back of the room. The microphone is too high. I wait as he lowers it. He nods at me to continue.

A strange calmness settles over me. I don't feel scared anymore. This is my story, and I know it inside out. Before I came on stage, someone well-versed in public speaking told me to speak from the heart. I don't know any other way.

There isn't a sound in the room, just the beat of my heart thumping in my chest.

"Good evening. I'm Emily and like many people here tonight, I have seen my world turned upside down by cancer. Cancer strikes when it is least expected, stopping us in our tracks and throwing our plans and dreams into disarray.

"Thankfully, here in Dorset, we have the Dorset Cancer Care Foundation and people like you who are making a real difference in the lives of local people fighting cancer, by taking away some of the financial pressure which often accompanies the disease, as in my case.

"I would like to share with you how I came into contact with the DCCF and met some of its wonderful fundraisers – and also felt the benefit of its help during my still ongoing cancer journey.

"In April 2023, I'd just got back on my feet after several years of living with disordered eating. I am an author and had just published my second book – life was finally on the up. And then my world was tipped upside down after a routine visit to my doctor.

"Whilst I was speaking to him, he noticed an unusual symmetry around the front of my neck and referred me for an ultrasound. They found a mass on my thyroid and took a biopsy immediately. The results were inconclusive, so I was scheduled for surgery to remove half my thyroid for further diagnostics.

"A year ago today, I had that surgery. I wish I could go back in time and sit down with that woman on her hospital bed. I would tell her that not only would she get through the many challenging months that lay ahead, but a year later, she would tell her story to a roomful of people – you. I know it would have offered her comfort and hope during a very frightening time."

I pause and look out at the lights to the people behind them. I want to hold onto this moment, just for a second for that woman in her hospital bed. An emotional ball builds in my throat and threatens my composure.

Speak from the heart, Emily, you can do this.

I clear my throat. "After a nerve-wracking three-week wait, I was diagnosed with follicular thyroid cancer. The tumour had just become invasive. My surgeon said the timing of its discovery was excellent. I was extremely lucky it was found. I had no obvious symptoms and no idea I had been living with cancer for some time.

"In late June, my cancer support worker introduced me to the Dorset Cancer Care Foundation. My fridge kept breaking down and as I was unable to afford to replace it, the charity very kindly paid for a new one. It was a huge relief for me. I was telling a staff member of my wish to write about my cancer journey. She encouraged me to apply for a grant for a writing tablet I could take to my hospital appointments and write on the go. They agreed, and so my writing began.

"In September, I underwent a second surgery to remove the rest of my thyroid. Unfortunately, a few hours after my surgery, a vein in my neck ruptured and I was rushed back into emergency surgery. I spent three days in intensive care recovering from the critical bleed. Ten days later, I lost my voice completely for a few weeks due to nerve damage supplying the voice box. Even worse was to come."

Breathe, Emily, breathe.

"My second operation revealed I had another type of cancer – papillary thyroid cancer. Having two types of cancer in the thyroid is rare. I was still trying to process the first cancer diagnosis.

"In November, I went back to hospital for in-patient radiation treatment. It was a frightening and lonely experience. I took my tablet with me and captured the experience, writing in plastic gloves to minimise the radioactive contamination. It was a lifeline and really helped to pass the time alone.

"I have spent several months recovering from cancer and used that time to continue working on my writing – something that would not have been possible without the support of the DCCF. I cannot finish my book just yet, the last chapter is not yet written, because I am still living it."

I stop and look out to the lights, swallowing hard.

They must be listening, there isn't a sound.

"At the end of August, I am going back to hospital, and in October, I see my oncologist. It is at this point I will hopefully get the all-clear.

"I would like to take this opportunity to thank you all for coming tonight to share in this wonderful event. And for listening to my story. The money you help to raise this evening will go directly to ease the financial burden of many Dorset people who are already struggling under the weight of cancer.

"Through your kindness and ongoing generous support of the Dorset Cancer Care Foundation, you help people like me in Dorset communities and make our cancer journeys that much easier. Thank you again and have a wonderful evening."

I pick up my papers and walk across the stage and the room erupts into applause. They are clapping for me, *Belly*, a woman who spent her life feeling like a nobody, never quite good enough for my dad, or anyone, really.

I return to my seat to a standing ovation. I wipe away tears a little awkwardly and sit down and look around at a room full of smiling faces still on their feet, clapping loudly at me, *for me.* I feel embarrassed but strangely lighter, like a weight has been lifted from me. I feel free. I've found my voice again, for the first time in years.

Later that evening, when the music begins, I kick off my shoes and dance until the night's end and the carriages appear. Barefoot and beaming, I spin myself around singing along loudly, a swirl of turquoise fabric from my long gown chases my spin.

I think of the woman I was exactly a year ago tonight. *Look how far you've come!* I remind her proudly.

NOT HIM, PLEASE

12 JULY 2024

"JACK, CAN YOU FEEL THIS?" I INTERRUPTED JACK MID-sentence, gesturing for him to confirm my findings.

Jack stood up and stroked Billy's right leg. "Yes, I can. You need to call the vet now, Mum, get it checked." Jack had also felt the grape-sized lump.

"It's probably a bite, if it's there tomorrow, I will call the vet."

The next day, the lump had almost vanished, but a quick online search confirmed I should probably get it checked by a vet anyway. The following day I took Billy to the clinic. Although the lump had shrunk to almost nothing, the vet could feel it and the sudden disappearance was a cause for concern.

A week later, Billy went in for sedation and testing. The lump required removal, and I gave permission for the operation to go ahead.

That evening, Billy was able to come home. Paul collected me en route to the vet. Billy limped towards us, his tail wagging excitedly as we both stared, shocked at the large surgical wound.

The vet walked towards us, extending his hand, shaking mine first, then Paul's warmly. He explained the surgical procedure, and what he'd found. To ensure the tumour was completely removed, a large amount of surrounding tissue from Billy's leg had also been removed. He'd looked at a sample under a slide. It was a mast cell tumour, a type of cancer.

We listened to the vet, but I didn't hear a sound, not after he said *that* word. I went through the motions and thanked him profusely for helping my best friend.

I left the vets and walked towards Paul's car, before climbing in and bursting into tears, burying my head in my hands. "Not Billy ... no ... no ... not him, *please*," I sobbed.

It felt so unfair. So painfully raw. Not even a week had passed since the anniversary of my own cancer diagnosis.

Paul dropped me off and I carried Billy inside. His anaesthesia was wearing off and he was clearly in pain. The reality of his cancer diagnosis was sinking in. I had to tell Thomas and Jack. I needed to minimise their pain because I didn't have the answers to the questions they would have. I didn't know if the cancer had spread, or if it was life-limiting. Only the online statistics I'd foolishly searched. I had to wait for results to know the grading of his cancer and whether he would require further treatment. I couldn't carry the burden of their worry along with my own. So, I lied to spare them. I told them it was all gone.

Billy didn't sleep for two nights, and neither did I. I stayed up all night comforting him, telling him how much I loved him, how sorry I was for all the times I'd not taken him to the river or beach – his favourite places before I bought *Sunshine*. Billy had been by my side through the hardest years of my life. He'd loved me unconditionally, during years when I couldn't even like myself. I couldn't imagine life without him.

I silently cried into his neck fur, savouring his warmth and smell. I wanted to ease his pain. He didn't deserve this. Like me, Billy had no symptoms, and his lump had been discovered accidentally.

The first results came back four days later. They were inconclusive and the lab required a couple more days for further testing. I couldn't eat or speak to anyone without crying. I couldn't focus on anything, but I kept my fears hidden from my sons.

The days dragged by and the anxiety of not knowing was suffocating. For the first time, I understood how Paul and my sons had felt watching me go through my cancer treatment.

When Billy was back on his feet, I took him to *Sunshine* for an afternoon. When I whispered it to him, his little eyes lit up. Despite his pain, his enthusiasm for an adventure to his favourite place hadn't waned.

We sat in our healing corner together, Billy on my lap, as I gently put my hand over his stitches, still fresh and healing. "*You're the best puppy in the world. You'll always be the best puppy in the world to me,*" I whispered by his ear. "*I love you so much.*" I pulled the blanket over him and held him like a child as I silently wept. I needed to hold onto these precious moments with him.

Twelve days passed and still, the results were unavailable. The delay caused me to shift gradually from a state of overwhelming anxiety to acceptance of whatever the outcome might bring. I realised I couldn't change it, but I could give Billy the best life from here on, filled with adventures and everything he loved.

It took two weeks to receive the results. Billy's cancer had been caught early and was thankfully contained with clear margins. It was the best news ever... Billy was cancer-free.

ALL CLEAR

AUGUST–SEPTEMBER 2024

"Emily Johnson?"

I looked up from my phone and saw a young doctor smiling at me. I gathered my belongings and followed him along a corridor into the ultrasound room.

"Hello, I'm Dr Thomas. If you slip your coat off and pop your belongings on the chair, then hop up on here." He gestured to a surgical bed in the middle of the large room. "Ah, I remember you; I did your ultrasound and needle biopsy last year, didn't I?" he said, returning to his computer to check my notes.

"Yes, that's right."

"Right, let's take a look then."

He ran the ultrasound over my neck, capturing various still images. Within minutes it was over, and he passed me some tissues to clean off the gel. He turned the ultrasound screen towards me. "Let me show you. This is your windpipe, and these are your arteries," he said, pointing to the grey masses on the screen. "And this cavity here is where your thyroid would have been. I can't see anything of any concern here."

I stared momentarily at the black space inside my neck on

the screen. My poor body. I felt so sad for everything it had gone through. I climbed off the bed and gathered up my belongings.

"Goodbye, and all the best," Dr Thomas said, returning to his computer to type in the notes.

"Bye ... and in the nicest possible way, I hope we don't have to meet again," I said, grinning at him and the nurse.

In August 2024, I returned to hospital for a series of injections and comprehensive body scans. They were spread over a six-day period ahead of my final oncology appointment which had been scheduled for the end of October. The first scan was a neck ultrasound. It was on a Sunday afternoon. Staff were working seven days a week to try and catch up on list backlogs. Most of the clinics were closed and I was grateful, for walking through the empty corridors provoked unexpected tears. There are remnants of traumatic memories that surface from time to time and catch me of guard, still.

I sat in the same waiting room, in the same seat as I had almost eighteen months before. The same doctor called me into the same treatment room. The low-iodine diet and thyrogen injections, vocal-cord check-up and the body scans were all the same too, as were the side-effects. Everything was the same, except for me. I had changed.

A few weeks later, I received an unexpected email from Katie, the nurse practitioner from the Endocrine Clinic. My recent scans had shown no areas of concern, and I was downgraded to low risk. I no longer needed to be seen by the oncologist. I read the email once, and my heart began to race, then twice just to be sure. I began to shake and then sob with relief. Just like that, it was over.

I called Paul, and my mum and told my sons. I told all my friends, my brother and uncle. I wanted to shout it from the rooftops: *I am cancer free!* The immense relief and joy I felt is immeasurable and difficult to articulate into words. Perhaps that was what winning the lottery felt like? Only better: I'd won back my life.

That weekend, I went to *Sunshine* and rang my own bell, loudly dinging my singing bowl in 'healing corner,' a place that had been such a huge part of my recovery. It seemed fitting to share my joy with the flowers and trees, the birds and all my favourite things and as the sound reverberated around the wilderness, the inevitable tears appeared.

A few weeks later, I returned to hospital for the thirty-third time and my final appointment with Katie. My scans and recent blood tests indicated there were no signs of any thyroid cancer. It was finally officially over, and that appointment marked the end of an eighteen-month cancer journey.

As I sat in the hospital waiting to be called in for the last time, something drew my attention away from my phone. It was the familiar sound of a bird. Outside the hospital, sat high on the tree branch was a lone robin, singing the most beautiful, song ... a celebratory chorus just for me.

SUNSHINE

OCTOBER 2024

Autumn has come around once again. The wildflower seeds I scattered in spring around the caravan have played their part in decorating the ground throughout summer with bursts of colour amongst the nettles. The woodland is littered with dots of yellow, of pink and blue flowers beginning to fade.

A gentle wind dances through the canopy of trees, loosening some leaves and sending them circling down around me. I catch one, giggling. The wind chime responds to the breeze with a subtle song, and I smile at the sound.

Before long, the woodland will take a rest again. All the leaves will fall, allowing the weak winter sunshine a chance to peek through the bare branches. It won't matter to me if it's cold. I will still sit here, wrapped in my blanket, Billy with me, savouring this place together. Even if it rains, I will sit for a while and lift my face to the clouds, for every drop that lands on my cheeks will remind me I am alive.

We're sitting in front of the caravan now. Billy's sleeping on a blanket beside me. I look down at him, snoring contently.

We made it, puppy. We're cancer survivors.

There's a collection of sunflowers lying across my lap. They finished flowering some time ago and I hung them up in the awning to dry. I've just gathered their seeds – there are hundreds of them. I will plant them down the bank next spring, and in pots around the caravan. I will grow my own sunshine.

Something below on the steep bank catches my eye, a flash of orange, of black and white. A butterfly. The season is ending now. I must treasure this sighting.

It flutters straight towards me, climbing the bank as if on a mission undeterred by my presence. It arrives and dances above me, and I spin my head around in a circle, laughing like a child as I follow its movement. I watch as it settles on the front of *Sunshine* and bathes in the last of the sunlight filtering through the branches of the oak tree above. I lean in a little closer, cautiously, so as not to startle it.

She opens her wings fully, a beautiful Painted Lady, welcoming the last of the season's warmth. Then I see it. Her right wing is broken. A small part of her is missing, but she is still able to fly.

"I love you," I whisper, as she brings her wings together, once, then twice, waving goodbye.

AFTERWORD

When I was diagnosed with cancer, one of my first thoughts was I was going to die prematurely. It didn't matter that it was a type of cancer that had excellent survival rates when caught early, it was still cancer, and that word is loaded with fear and death in most people's minds. And just like my father, and the rest of my loved ones, I was no exception.

During the weeks following my diagnosis, I spent considerable time in a state of high alert. Every new headache or chest pain made me anxious. After the surgeries, there were many unusual symptoms of my body adjusting to functioning without a thyroid. I had frequent leg cramps, headaches, pins and needles and heart palpitations. I convinced myself more than once they were signs that the cancer had spread despite the reassurances from my treating doctors. It was hardly surprising given my father's experience.

I became a little obsessed with everything I ate, drank, and put on my skin that might potentially harm my health. It was exhausting and short of living in a bubble, almost impossible to maintain. I changed what I could, eating less processed food, wearing natural make-up, skincare and deodorant but I remained living in a town centre surrounded by pollution. Some things weren't that easy to change.

Something else was preoccupying my mind. I needed to know *why* I had cancer. I'd never smoked, or drunk a great deal of alcohol, and had kept active all my life. I believed finding the cause, would make it easier to accept somehow and began searching for answers that were impossible to find.

From the age of thirteen, I hated the girl I saw in the mirror. Hatred is a powerful emotion. It's also a destructive, toxic one. I carried that poison inside me, for almost forty years. I was overcome with grief over my dad's sudden death as well as the guilt I felt from our unhealed relationship. Old abandonment wounds turned me into a serial people-pleaser, in an attempt to prevent people from leaving me. I prioritised everyone else's wellbeing over mine and continued to gather painful experiences pushing those emotionally charged feelings down, burying them behind a forced smile. It was exhausting.

As I approached my fifties, I was overwhelmed with an eating disorder and lived for several years in survival mode under unimaginable amounts of family stress. My body was stuck in fight-flight mode and running on dangerous levels of cortisol for sustained periods. I used all these memories dangerously and weaponised them against myself at the beginning of my diagnosis. Blaming myself first seemed the most obvious reason at the time. I know old emotions can't be surgically removed from the body, but that's how it felt just before my first surgery. It was as if a ball crafted from years of self-hatred, grief, and stress, and all the things I *should* have said, were cut out from my throat that day and I was free of that painful part of me.

My diagnosis blindsided me. My body was warning me, but I wasn't listening and missed the signs. I didn't have the usual tell-tale symptoms such as changes to my voice, or difficulties swallowing or breathing. However, for two years before my diagnosis, my body was showing me something was wrong. I had several illnesses that lingered for weeks: Covid, the flu, nondescript viruses and eventually burnout that floored me for almost two months. I had rashes on my arms and legs, painful toes, and cracked heels. My immune system, which has an interactive relationship with the thyroid, was struggling, yet I put all the periods of sickness and exhaustion down to my age and stressful lifestyle. I also missed a very obvious sign – a swollen neck. Looking back at photos over the last few years, I see it now, but at the time I avoided mirrors and photos, and I *never* looked at my neck.

I discovered only recently that there is a strong family history of cancer on my father's side. Dads only brother had prostate cancer and thankfully survived his. Both my dad's parents died of cancer, his father, prostate and his mother, leukaemia. Her father before her also died of cancer. It's affected four generations that I'm aware of, though there may be more going back further. I hope that genetic trait ends with me.

I will never know how long the tumours were there. It no longer matters. After Billy's diagnosis, I realised something important: cancer happens. It is caused by several different factors including environmental, genetic and lifestyle, and often we don't know the reasons why.

Billy is a happy-go-lucky dog who's enjoyed a good diet, plenty of exercise and always been cared for and very much loved, but he still got cancer. He didn't cause it to himself. It just happened, and his diagnosis helped put an end to my search for the reasons behind my own. I stopped blaming myself. I stopped blaming my body too. It wasn't fighting against me. It never has been. It was tirelessly working to heal itself. Even the seroma that developed after the first surgery – that was just my body trying to fill the empty space my thyroid surgery left behind.

I wasn't prepared for all the emotions I felt throughout the various stages of this journey. Shock, fear, guilt, uncertainty, joy, gratitude – I experienced them all in various degrees and they frequently changed. But they were all a perfectly normal part of receiving a cancer diagnosis – something I have often been reminded by many of the nursing staff, support workers and charity volunteers.

I wasn't prepared for the emotions of people who love me either. Navigating their feelings was difficult and I felt a sense of responsibility at least in part, for their reactions. I wanted to control their responses and minimise their pain. It was well-intentioned and from a place of love, but it wasn't my role to control or contain others' emotions and it took me a while to recognise that.

It was difficult at times to be told I was strong and brave. I didn't feel brave, or strong some days. I was frightened and sick of being strong. Some days I just wanted to say, this is really hard, and I'm scared.

People don't know what to say to you. I know that. I'm guilty of it too. It is always meant with good intentions, but I didn't want to be told to 'be positive'. What if I didn't feel it? Or 'Don't worry, it will all be okay.' Because what if it wasn't? Or that I was lucky I didn't have to fight cancer like others have to. I knew that too, I felt guilty at times for *not* having terminal cancer, but there is no sliding scale of pain and fear to measure yourself against. I had my own bumpy cancer journey.

In the past, thyroid cancer was known as the 'good cancer'. It had excellent treatment and survival rates when found and treated early. But it is still cancer, and some people still die from it. In 2022, the NICE clinical guidelines, which provide recommendations on the appropriate NHS treatment and care of people with specific diseases in England and Wales, recommended that staff no longer refer to thyroid cancer as a 'good cancer' which ensures all patients are given the same standard of care and support and the impact of the diagnosis is not minimised. In other parts of the world, though, it is still referred to as the 'good cancer' at times.

This disease has taken a great deal away from me, not least my dad many years ago. I also lost a vital gland from my endocrine system and that loss has impacted every function within my body. It will impact the rest of my life and may take time to get the balance of replacement hormones at optimal levels to feel well again.

I lost my voice, albeit temporarily. I also lost time through absence from work and any kind of normal life, all overtaken by medical procedures and treatment. I lost a part of the essence of who I thought I was. And for a while, I lost my direction and questioned the meaning of my life.

Despite the things I lost, my cancer diagnosis has given back in many ways. It gave me a scar. One I will continue to wear with pride as a reminder of the transformative journey I've been on. Cancer allowed me to question how I was living my life, or *not* living it, to be more precise. Up until then, I still wasn't prioritising myself or valuing my health. I realised there are no rewards for selflessness at the risk of one's own health. I have learnt I can be caring and supportive to everyone around me, as long as I show myself the same love and support too.

It taught me to stop procrastinating and get out and do it, whatever *it* is, and stop putting things off until an elusive 'better time'. There is no better time. The only time we have is *now*.

Happiness used to be something I strived for 'out there', that golden destination in a future place I'd not yet reached. Now it is here, today, in this very moment. Every day I wear my best perfume, or my nicest dress and the new shoes I've been saving. I light my candles now and savour the fragrance as they're burning. Nothing is kept for a special occasion anymore. Every day I'm alive is my special occasion.

I'm making the most out of life, doing things I never believed I could. I returned to school to study a diploma, went cold-water swimming, walked over hot coals for a cancer charity and gave my first public speech amongst other things. I'm squeezing joy out of every single day despite the challenges.

Cancer gifted me back my unadulterated joy in the simplest things. Like the taste of fresh coffee or the sweet sound of a robin's song. Hugs from my friends. The feel of my dog's fur and the touch of a loved one's hand. I take nothing for granted now, no matter how simple or trivial it seems to others. If a beautiful sunset or intricate flower moves me to tears, I let them fall without shame. My sensitivity *is* me, and I will never hide it away again.

Cancer gave me an opportunity to reconnect with my spirituality and led me back to a daily meditation practice through which I found inner peace and remembered who I truly am. At the time of writing this book, I am studying to become a mindfulness and meditation teacher and once qualified, I will help others discover this life-affirming practice.

Cancer reminded me of the value of love. It's a word I easily say about inanimate objects. I *love* cake. It's a word I used to throw around without depth or meaning. It's also a word I've struggled to say at times. I come from a generation and family who don't openly say it. We all feel it, but we never verbalise that love for one another. It's always felt a little awkward, embarrassing almost. Cancer gave me the courage to express it.

In October 2024, I had coffee with my mum. It was the first time I'd seen her since my treatment as she was unable to fly due to her poor health. I sat and told her how I'd struggled with my feelings throughout life. Before my cancer diagnosis, I was still a wounded child stuck in my adult body searching for examples to affirm my unlovability.

Mum held my hand as I cried revealing those old parts of me I'd kept hidden. I told her how much I loved her for the first time since childhood. She hugged me tightly and told me she loved me too, and I know it won't be the last time we tell each other. I tell people I love them now. It's the most valuable gift of all. We all need to hear it; we all need to feel love.

Through cancer, I have finally made the connection between the outside of my body and my most miraculous inner body. I have never connected the two, nor respected either, until now. That gave me the greatest gift of all – the leap from self-acceptance into unadulterated self-love to a degree I haven't experienced since early childhood. I ditched my anti-aging creams. It's a privilege to be here and wearing these wrinkles. I can now proudly say I love this marvellous body of mine, every single fleshy inch, organ, sinew and fold. My journey back to inner love feels complete.

I pay close attention to my body now and what it tells me, periodically checking it for changes or unusual lumps. At the time of writing this book one in two people will develop some form of cancer during their lifetime in the UK. Thankfully there have been enormous advancements in cancer screening, diagnosis, and treatment since my father's death in 2004. However, the risks of reoccurrence and development of other cancers further down the line remain with me. My blood will be monitored for signs of reoccurrence every six months for the next two years, then annually for the rest of my life.

I have stopped reading about what could happen in the future. It doesn't serve my mental health to dwell in the what-ifs and maybes. It made me fearful, and that fear was stealing my joy. Instead, I wake up grateful each morning. I tell myself it's going to be a wonderful day, no matter what challenges I am facing. I look deeply into my eyes in the mirror and tell that soul she's amazing and capable and in perfect health. I tell her I love her, and I mean it now.

And finally, my cancer journey left me with one very profound and lasting gift. I was in the safest place possible during the critical bleed, in the hands of a surgical team, but in those moments, I thought I was dying. *Something* held me and dissolved the terror I was experiencing. I will never know what happened in theatre that day, and I have stopped searching for answers. I don't need science to rationalise it. I know what I felt, and nothing can ever alter or minimise that for me.

After my experience, I now believe my dad wasn't really alone when he died, and that the fear he may have felt was momentary, and was replaced with the same, most incredible peaceful love as he passed away. We've finally healed the void between us, and it absolved all those years of guilt I carried. Dad's energy is still around me and I feel him through the unexpected little signs he sends me from time to time.

As much as it has been a difficult journey and something I wouldn't wish upon anyone, upon reflection, I'm not sure I would change any of it. Through a serendipitous twist of fate, my cancer was found early, and I won a golden ticket to life. I've never felt more alive. It's such a shame it took me to think I was dying, to begin living.

I went through a life-altering experience, but it's transformed me. I'm no longer scared of dying, I'm just not ready for it yet. I have some living to catch up on first! My life has been forever changed by cancer, and I intend for the rest of it, no matter how long that may be, to be more fulfilling because of it.

This is my cancer story. What it cannot show you, are the inner, most personal feelings of those closest to me. I have asked a few to share their thoughts in their own words on how my cancer journey impacted them.

Lexi

"When Emily told me she had cancer, my heart ached for her and the long journey she had ahead of her. It was hard to watch her because she finds it so difficult to accept help, I felt I couldn't do anything.

"I found it hard to stand back and watch her struggle at times. Sometimes she seemed inwardly apologetic with other people for not having what she saw as 'real cancer' or for looking well. I think perhaps she felt guilty or unworthy somehow. I think she needed to hear that cancer is cancer, that there is no better or worse type and that I was always there to listen, no matter what.

"When she came to stay with me after her radiation treatment because she had no other choice, I finally felt that I could do something for her. Seeing her relax into me looking after her, felt like a gift for me too. I hope that in allowing me the gift of having her stay with me, she will see that she doesn't have to do it alone in life, even in a battle that is so personally hers to fight."

Diane

"When Emily first told me, I was in disbelief. She had already been through so much in her life, so how could this be fair? She is the most selfless person I know. I just couldn't understand why bad things happen to good people. But I had also just lost one of my closest friends just months earlier and I couldn't bear the thought of losing her too. We have been friends for thirty-six

years. I just couldn't imagine life without her. Her positive attitude and outlook gave me strength and reassurance to believe that she was going to be okay.

"Watching someone you love go through cancer treatment is so hard. I wanted to do something to make it go away or take it away from her. I think what she needed most from me was a degree of normality. She wanted to hear about what was going on in my life, to share my joys and help me with my sorrows. She didn't want to always talk about cancer. Catching up on my life gave her an escape from thinking about her illness even if only for a brief time each day. Throughout her journey, she has been so strong and determined. Her zest for life is amazing and stronger than ever, I think."

Lisa

"Working together on her first book during lockdown, Emily and I quickly became online friends. We shared a love of India and spirituality, and 'got' each other. Emily was more supportive of me during that time than my real-life friends were, especially as I was publishing my own books at the time.

"I was, and still am, struck by Emily's incredible generosity of spirit and how amazingly well she'd coped with such a challenging life up to that point. I couldn't believe how unfair it was when she told me she had cancer. I was in India at the time and couldn't comprehend how much one person was expected to cope with. I felt angry at the universe for throwing everything at her.

"I am aware how much of a brave face Emily puts on at times of crisis, but because I edit her books, I now know how much is going on behind the smiles. But we've now taken our friendship into the real world and I'm still blown away by how she has managed to turn even this crisis into a positive. She is still determined to help others with everything she has learned. This book is

part of that determination and I'm very proud of her, both as an editor, and as a friend."

Mum

"When your grown-up child tells you she has cancer, the first thing you want to do as her mother is take it from her. I would have given anything to change those words when she eventually told me. When she was a wee girl, if she hurt herself, I'd put a sticking plaster on her and soothe her, but no words of comfort could change this. I had no choice but to accept the unimaginable. I prayed it would be treated successfully, and she would live her life, although I knew she would live a different one.

"Being diagnosed with cancer must be so hard, but Emily was always so optimistic and brave, at least she seemed that way on the surface. Her optimism helped me cope with it, especially from afar. I'm so glad that no one told me about her emergency surgery or stay in Critical Care until she was through it and safe. It would have killed me knowing my wee girl was going through that and I couldn't be there.

"Cancer is a difficult battle for the patient, that I've no doubt, but it has had an impact on the whole family, in different ways."

Paul

"Whilst Emily was undergoing the tests and first surgery I never really thought about cancer. I took my cue from her language and behaviour around me. But I can vividly remember the day she called me and told me it was cancer. If I'm being honest, my first thought was 'I'm going to lose her'. Cancer – that word to me, anyway – meant death. I thought about her sons. Although Emily's cancer was found early and her prognosis was good, she means the world to those two boys. Thinking

of them and how they might have been feeling broke my heart for them, and her.

"It was very difficult as there are few people left in this world who I truly love, and she is still one of them, despite our separation. Even though she was telling me the stages she had to go through in her treatment, the outcome was still unknown and at times I found the uncertainty overwhelming. Seeing her in Critical Care and afterwards in obvious pain, was very distressing. Seeing her suffering ... in those moments I found it difficult. It was hard to face. I watched both of my parents who I loved dearly, die young and at times, particularly when she was first diagnosed and during the emergency surgery, I momentarily thought she might die. That was terrifying but I had to internalise that in front of her. I was struggling with my own mental and physical health but there was no question of me not supporting her, though I wish she would have let me do more to help her.

"In the months afterwards, sometimes she would get very upset revisiting the traumatic events of her last surgery and I just didn't have the right words to comfort her. I simply didn't know what to say and that was hard for me.

"Through this experience, I appreciate her even more for still being in my life. Her optimism is infectious. I realise now that she wasn't always honest with her feelings around me and others because she wanted to protect everyone, but I do think the way she handled it with grace, helped both her sons, mum, and me cope. She has a completely different outlook on life now. I can see a different level of appreciation for her life, and she gets joy from the simplest things that most of us fail to notice in day-to-day life. It's almost childlike and it's so lovely to be around.

"She has returned to what I feel is her true self and reconnected with her spirituality. She saw her diagnosis almost as a blessing. I think that's admirable... I'm not sure I would have handled it in the same way."

Thomas

"When Mum first told me she had cancer it didn't sink in, like, I heard the words, but didn't process the enormity of them. It wasn't really until the next day when she went out and was gone for a few hours, that's when it hit me. The flat was quiet all day and I suddenly thought, 'This is what it would be like without my mum around.' That's when I realised my mum had cancer, and she could die. It was like a delayed reaction.

"I felt so many emotions, a thousand different thoughts and I felt overwhelmed by them. I thought cancer was a death sentence. I turned all that inwards. That's when I shaved my head. I don't know what I was thinking, it was like an outlet for all the feelings.

"In many ways, it was easier when she came out of the hospital. I could see her and hug her and knew she was safe. I'm glad she didn't tell me about the bleed and Critical Care at the time. I would have panicked.

"My mum is one of the strongest people I know, but seeing her in pain was difficult and watching her cry was really hard. I didn't know how to help her; I felt useless if I'm honest. I tried to treat her and the situation normally, like maybe that was denial, but I thought if I treated her differently maybe that would reinforce the struggle she was going through.

"She coped so well, and her optimistic attitude kept me hopeful. She has definitely become more full of life since her diagnosis and doesn't waste any opportunities. I can see her making the most of each day. She seems more willing and open to taking a chance on things she would have hesitated over in the past.

"I hold my mum in the highest regard already, I always have, even before this. She is the most supportive loving person and I'm so glad she's got through all this."

Jack

"When Mum first told me she had cancer, I went into complete shock. The first thought was she was going to die. Her initial attitude towards her cancer was hard to cope with. She seemed to be overly optimistic. I really respected the fact she was cheerful but, in my eyes, it was something very serious and I didn't understand how she could be so accepting after what her dad went through. I wasn't sure if it was a front, and she wasn't telling me the truth.

"When she first came home after Critical Care, I used to check on her all the time whilst she was sleeping. She never knew, but I would go in and make sure she was still breathing. It was really upsetting watching her in pain and suffering. I felt helpless and I didn't know how to help her. When she lost her voice that was really difficult for me. We talk every day, sometimes for hours, and I missed our conversations, and I was worried we wouldn't get those back.

"From the moment she told me she had cancer, I thought she was going to die prematurely, and those thoughts haven't left me, not really. I feel like I have spent all this time, nearly eighteen months, waiting to hear if she had the all-clear. I couldn't let it go until I knew it was gone. Mum's diagnosis made me think about the fragility of life and how limited our time really is here. It brought us even closer together and I'm grateful for that."

Shortly after I gave my speech at the gala, Bob the Robin disappeared. I have not seen him, or Mrs Bob since, however he left me a parting gift. One of his chicks from his second clutch has taken his place and visits me at *Sunshine* regularly, appearing at the same window waiting for worms. It sits on the same branch, quietly singing. Bob Junior is finding his voice.

Bob was more than just a bird to me; he was a messenger. A tiny, feathered angel that appeared in my life when I felt particularly vulnerable, and he stayed with me until I was ready to fly. My touching encounter with Bob left me with the profound gift of a wild bird's friendship, and although it was fleeting, it is a connection filled with precious memories I will always treasure.

As for Paul and me ... well, I've taught him the joy of catching falling leaves and finding stillness in the simple things. The love we have for one another doesn't need a label. We are best friends, living our lives separately, but slowly navigating the idea of an 'us' after five years of separation. It's taken a great deal of personal healing on both sides, and a cancer diagnosis, to truly value the love we still have for one another. I don't know what the future holds, but that no longer matters to me. Now is all I have, and my now is filled with love.

After all, nothing else matters, only love.

ACKNOWLEDGMENTS

Throughout my cancer journey, from the initial discovery of the tumour to the end of my treatment, I have received outstanding care from the staff of the NHS. They worked tirelessly to make my journey that much easier for me and to them, I owe my sincerest thanks.

To all the wonderful staff of Poole General Hospital, in Critical Care, Theatre and Recovery, Head and Neck, Outpatients, Sandbanks Ward and all the various ward staff who looked after me with so much care and kindness – thank you.

With heartfelt thanks to my consultant surgeon – I felt completely safe in your hands and will always be grateful for your care, compassion, and expertise.

To all the nursing and clerical staff of the Endocrine Clinic and Ladybird Unit, especially Carly – thank you for being there and for your compassionate care and support.

To my consultant oncologist, and all the team from Oncology who looked after me – thank you for your kindness, care, and patience.

To all the staff of the Nuclear Medicine team for looking after me, keeping me company and listening. You made a daunting experience much easier – thank you.

To Doctor Alder – without your 20/20 eyesight, this might have been a different story! Thank you for your ongoing kindness and compassionate support.

I also owe a great deal of thanks to the charity support

services and online support groups that kept me emotionally afloat.

Cancer Macmillan Charity – thank you for being at the end of the phone and listening. Your emotional support was exceptional and I'm incredibly grateful.

Lewis Manning Hospice Care – thank you for your kind, compassionate support for cancer patients in Dorset and to Nicola for giving me the safe space to unpick my experience through therapy.

Dorset Cancer Care Foundation – to Penny, Debbie, Meryl, all the founders, patrons, fundraisers, and everyone at the charity who supported me both financially and emotionally. Thank you for giving me the stage and letting me fly! Leslie-May – special thanks to you for your friendship, love, and support. Cheers to good health and many more coffee-and-cake dates!

Everyday Thyroid Cancer, Life After TT, Low Iodine Diet for RAI Facebook Support Groups Admin, especially Rita – thank you for running these groups and providing invaluable information and support for us all.

To all the people living with thyroid cancer or thyroid disease, you are not alone. I hope this book helps in some small way to raise awareness of both thyroid cancer and thyroid diseases and the impact they can have on a person's life.

To all my colleagues at LUSH – thank you for supporting me in all the ways you do. It means the world to me xx

To Lisa – my editor and dear friend. Thank you for your friendship and support and for helping me turn these thoughts into a book. Here's to more café catch-ups and exploring the entire M&S menu! xx

To Clare B – Thank you for capturing my book cover vision so beautifully again xx

Uncle G – thank you for always being there for me and

supporting my authoring journey. You are my little Robin. I can't wait to hand you a copy of this in person. Love you xx

To my dearest friends near and far – Stacey, Di, Lisa, Ang and Stella, you supported me throughout this wild ride – I couldn't have done this without you. I love you xx

Paul – For once I have no more words, just love and gratitude xx

Mum – I'll always be your wee girl. Love you, Mum xx

To my sons – thank you for believing in me. I love you. Keep shining your light and finding your way in life. I'm so proud of you. Mum Xx

A REQUEST FROM THE AUTHOR

If you enjoyed *Sunshine*, please consider leaving a review on Amazon, or your chosen platform. It will help this book reach other people who need it, so that they know they're not alone.

Emily J. Johnson

emilyjjohnson.author@gmail.com

ALSO BY EMILY J JOHNSON

For anyone who may have stood in front of a mirror at some point in their lives and not loved the person looking back, I've written this for you.

At the age of thirteen, I began my first diet. But that diet quickly turned into an obsession, leading me into a dangerous eating disorder called anorexia nervosa. I remained trapped in a toxic relationship with food and my body for over three decades.

By the age of 45, I had developed binge-eating disorder. I kept it buried beneath immense shame and self-loathing for nearly five years ... until therapy changed everything.

ABOUT THE AUTHOR

Having spent fifteen years living in Western Australia, Emily returned to the UK in 2010 and lives on the south coast of England. Her first book *Pushing Through The Cracks,* was one of four finalists for The Selfies Book Awards of 2022 and nominated for The Wishing Shelf Book Awards 2022.

Her second book, *BELLY*, shares her raw and honest account of struggling with eating disorders and how she finally made peace with food, her body and herself.

Following a cancer diagnosis in 2023, Emily returned to writing during her recovery, publishing her third book *SUNSHINE,* sharing her cancer journey.

Once fully recovered, Emily re-trained as a mindfulness & meditation practitioner and will embark on her teaching practice in 2025, supporting cancer patients along with other members of her community in learning these beneficial practices.

Printed in Great Britain
by Amazon

61364912R00170